BUGATTI SUPERCARS

A CENTURY OF GENIUS

START

Lance Cole

BUGATTI SUPERCARS

A CENTURY OF GENIUS

THE CROWOOD PRESS

BUGATTI

CONTENTS

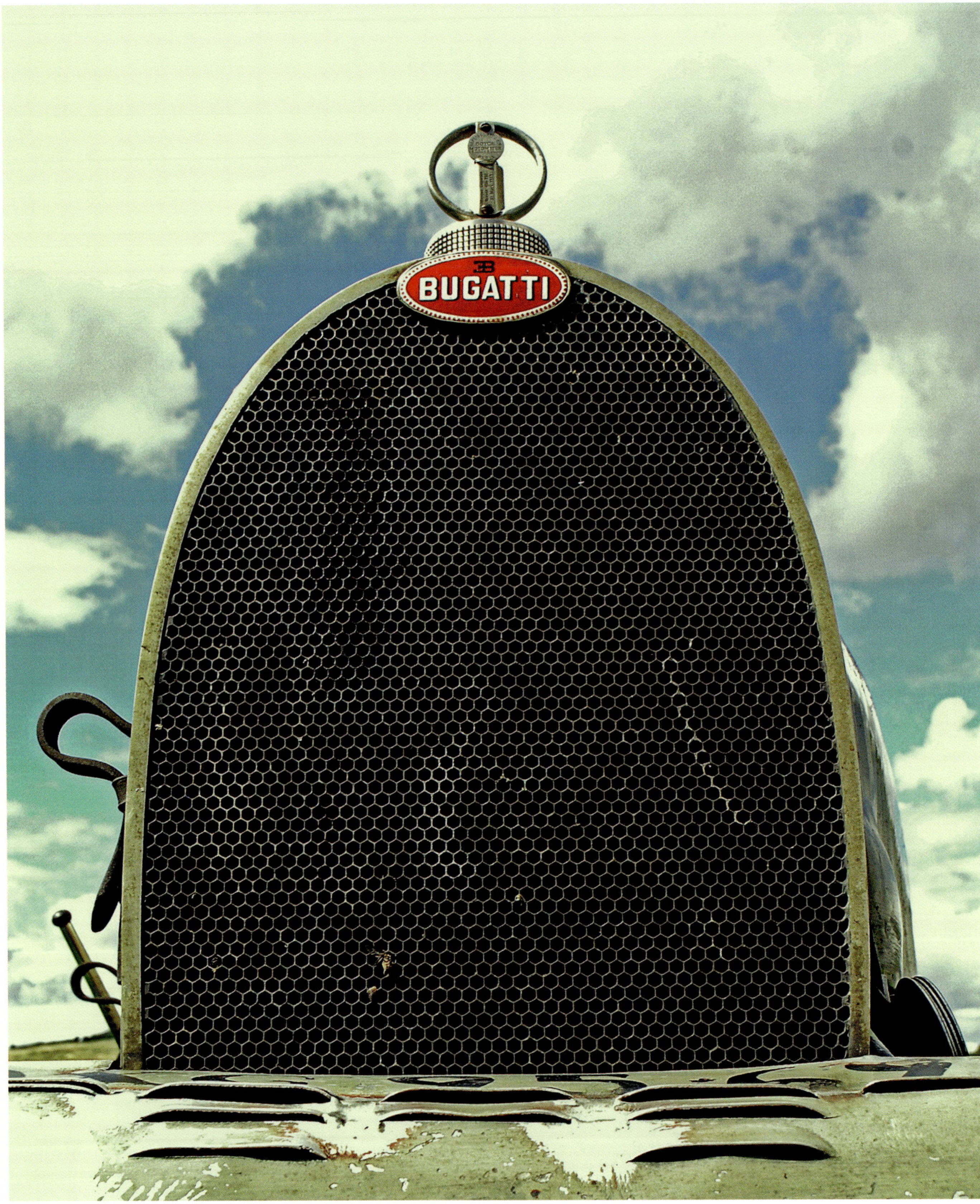

Defining design: Type 35 radiator and design language captured in tribute seen on the front of Chris Hudson's unusually hued Bugatti Type 35B.

Ettore's livery on a late-model Chiron long-tail captured during the Bugatti Grand Tour of America 2023.

This torpedo-bodied 1927 Type 30, chassis #4003, is owned by Peter Zinck, President of the Bugatti Club Denmark and is regularly driven by King Frederik of Denmark who is a Bugatti fan.

INTRODUCTION

THE BUGATTI ETHOS: BRILLIANCE BEYOND COMPARISON

Many years ago there was a wonderful magazine called *Supercar Classics*, which contained within its title the proof that the term 'supercar' had a history. A supercar did not have to be brand new: it could be an older classic that was a supercar, a precursor to more contemporary supercars. Only a few of the marques of these past supercars have produced a modern car of supercar or 'hypercar' status. One such is Bugatti, but this came about via a reincarnation of the Bugatti name and brand, which leaves the door open to argument over what is a Bugatti, let alone what is a supercar or hypercar, and whether a revived brand can truly be said to live in the ethos of its original DNA.

The answer to that is wait and see, but we do have some new evidence to consider.

Few will argue about whether the latest Ferraris, such as the Roma, share any real DNA with their ancestors. Similarly Porsche's new wide-body, short-nosed 911 is seen as a true son of the original, despite their differences. Some say that the new Ferrari four-door SUV cannot be a 'real' Ferrari, but can it? What of a Rolls-Royce, which is now a behemoth of a collection of foreign parts styled to evoke something? Apparently, perceived wisdom claims that it is 'still' a Rolls-Royce – whatever that is. In this context we might ask what is the point of the Bentley Bentayga, other than branding? We can assume Bugatti will not build an SUV 4 × 4 for the sake of it, but then again Porsche did, so who knows. But the Bugatti Veyron, Chiron, Divo, Centodieci and Mistral do give us hope that the 'new' Bugatti *is* more about engineering than about branding. And they would not be here without a car named EB110 and man named Romano Artioli.

Set in the contexts of nuance and history, the latest Bugatti cars surely have at least as much right to be called by that name as does a new Aston Martin or Maserati that bears their respective badges.

The next question is who defines what is 'real'? All Bugattis are 'supercars', yet some question the perceived wisdom by which an old pre-1939 original-era Bugatti can be placed alongside today's new Bugatti cars and their branding. But perceived wisdom is a contradiction in terms, relying as it does upon applying current perceptions and fashionable opinions to known 'certainties', which history has a habit of usurping.

Surely, so long as no exercise in badge engineering has taken place and no marketing con trick has been perpetuated, a supercar of a legendary brand can indeed be a supercar with authentic reference to its ancestor's DNA.

The original Bugatti Type 57 and its 'Atlantic' derivative cannot be ignored as the leading example of an original supercar – anywhere. But does it follow that a Chiron or a Centodieci might be similarly blessed? It takes a bold man or woman to dismiss any Bugatti built after 1939 as being something else and not a Bugatti, but that opinion is not unknown.

This book is not designed for those purists who recoil in horror at the thought of a new Bugatti, or shrink at the thought of an original Bugatti chassis being mated to a non-matching numbered original Bugatti engine and clothed in a new toolroom-recreated bodyshell by a Bugatti expert as an exact copy of the long-lost original. Such purists are very welcome to their niche, and I understand their rationale, but furthering the Bugatti legend may require something less Old Testament in thinking.

Furthermore, there are plenty of original Bugattis with matching numbers that have been, shall we say, 'restored' to a condition beyond their originality, yet they are often hailed at the most exclusive concourse gatherings as being the 'real thing'. I, for one, would dissent from such a description of plastic-primed, acrylic-painted, vinyl-lined, over-dipped chromed pastiche masquerading as the 'better than new' old Bugatti, for it would be a car that has had its soul and psychometry wiped clean.

Ettore Bugatti was not subject to the constraints of 'perceived wisdom' and its self-aggrandising and self-limiting philosophy. He did not just think beyond such constraints or fashions, he thought far beyond accepted knowledge: he innovated and had to be bold, brave and maybe a bit self-centred to achieve his escape from the conventional thinking of the moment. Some say he was a snob who pandered to his wealthy clientele, yet he did not follow fashion, he *created* it, timelessly.

Ettore also further developed the state of the art in engineering and design. As such he was not always the revolutionary sometimes portrayed, a disruptive figure in car design. On occasion he more accurately refined the known practices and mechanisms of the day to an extent never previously encountered. These traits have led to some confusion about his philosophy and practice: was Ettore an innovative revolutionary genius or a clever adapter and improver of the known? I suggest he was both, but the point is that no one matched him in terms of industrial design philosophy. You cannot 'compare' a Bugatti to anything: if you could, it was not a Bugatti. That was Ettore's point.

Ettore himself stated: 'Nothing is too beautiful. Nothing is too expensive.' Therein lay the ethos of the man and his marque. It was also among the factors that led to its downfall.

If you open a pre-1939 Bugatti's bonnet you will find hand-polished, hand-mottled, scraped and brushed aluminium applied all over the engine bay and added to a covering veneer over the engine block and head. Ettore insisted upon this level of the exquisite and the expensive for all his creations.

A book celebrating all things Bugatti and its truly super cars across *all* the ages of Bugatti, then and now, has long been absent. Why not challenge fixed minds and show how Bugatti, its supercars of the past and of today are so very real and so intrinsically linked to one another through their application of Ettore's ethos. Surely only someone whose heart is blocked by antique Bugatti plaque could refuse to consider how today's Bugattis reflect all that went before and do so in a similarly bespoke manner.

Charles Trevelyan, the much respected former Chairman of the Bugatti Owners' Club, trustee of The Bugatti Trust and a serial old-Bugatti owner (as well as owning the world's lowest mileage Ferrari Dino from new), reacted with an open mind when told of this book's blend of old Bugattis with new Bugattis: 'Why not, there's no future in being stuck in 1939 or 1953. We have to embrace a wider, younger audience and persuade them to discover the magic of Bugatti.'

We ought perhaps to recall that, such was the relationship between Bugatti and the British, that in 1939 at the Bugatti Owners' Club dinner in London, Jean Bugatti stood up and announced that he and his father were gifting a Type 51 racing car to the club for the use of those members who could not afford such a car.

Today's new Bugattis represent far more than clever marketing or a brand name. They respect and evoke so much of the earlier, original Bugatti ethos. The time is right to chart both eras of Bugatti together, yet respecting their differences. Anyone who suggests that today's Bugatti is 'exploiting' the brand and its heritage is wrong; such people

Inside the Bolide's new-age cockpit.

just do not understand what is being attempted. If you stop off en route from the originals at the remarkable EB110, and the earlier attempts at reviving Bugatti, you could easily say that there were several eras of Bugatti. It would take someone whose mind is preserved in the automotive aspic of 1953 or 1939 to object to 'their' Bugatti of yesteryear being parked alongside a Bugatti of today, as will be found in this book.

Across the years of my enthusiasm for Bugatti design I have encountered the varying tribes of Bugatti fans, club members and believers – or, as some call them, 'Bugattistes'. Above all, however, there are the cars and the people who preserve and celebrate them and the legend of their founder.

A few Bugatti experts are adamant that today's Bugattis should not be linked to the 'proper' Bugattis of yesteryear. It is a view to which they are entitled, but it is a position that limits access to awareness of Bugatti for newer generations. Of course, a new Bugatti is not an original Bugatti, but does this have to become a self-limiting philosophy?

If we can avoid corporate speak and 'brand-pillars' talk, is it not the truth that today's new Bugattis *do* follow, in their own way, the ethos and spirit of the grand designs that went before.

Geoffrey St John, a renowned supporter of British enthusiasm for Bugattis, often said, notably at Prescott and at The Bugatti Trust, 'Bugattis are a disease. I like their stubborn individualism. There are no comparisons.'

Remember, it was Ettore Bugatti who said that if anything could be compared with a Bugatti, it was not a Bugatti. Perhaps we should therefore not compare today's Bugattis with yesterday's Bugattis, and instead understand better the process now taking place.

The mission of The Bugatti Trust is not just to preserve Bugatti. It is to further the Bugatti legend by touching today's young enthusiasts and engaging with them through a series of educational projects and schemes, not least in engineering and design establishments. The Bugatti Trust, which counted the late HRH The Duke of Edinburgh amongst its patrons, is one of the most vital educational and archival institutions I know, and I urge you to support it and its tutelage of a new generation. Such young people are not 'stuck' in 1939, 1953 or 1979.

Youth cannot be ignored, for they will be the future and the past – as we all become. If a youth wants to fixate upon a *new* Bugatti then why not, and if youth can be taught from where the new Bugattis get their DNA, then so much the better. We need young engineers and designers, and we need them to understand what happened before digital authoritarianism took over car design and car driving. Where better to start and continue than at Bugatti amid its design greatness.

Remember this, in the 1970s, 1980s and 1990s youngsters had posters on their bedroom walls depicting the Porsche 911 Turbo, random Ferraris (if such a thing exists), the Maserati Bora or Merak, or the Lamborghini Countach – or latterly the Diablo. Today's youngsters have posters, home screens and screen savers depicting the latest Bugattis – the Veyron, Chiron, Centodieci, Devio and Mistral. Why would anyone ignore or deny such enthusiasm?

The late Barrie Price, one of the founder members of The Bugatti Trust, former Bugatti Owners' Club leader and owner of several Bugattis (including the Type 57 registration AUK 717), first caught the Bugatti disease when he paid £3,000 for a Type 57SC Atlantic, which he sold a decade later for £85,000. Hindsight being a wonderful thing, this car, now in the Ralph Lauren Collection, has more recently reached the stratospheric heights of a six- or seven-figure value. Price also owned the very rare Type 68 chassis and built a Type 59 'continuation' out of original Bugatti parts and new parts that he made. He even designed and built a totally convincing time-warp body for an original Bugatti Type 57 saloon that had lost its original body. Barrie, the man who saved the Lea Francis legacy, always insisted that youth must be recruited into recognition of Bugatti and its story.

Shortly before his death, Barrie kindly encouraged the author, stating: 'I support anything that promotes learning about Bugatti in whatever context, ancient or modern. Ettore was unique and hugely important. Do not be put off from re-telling his story in your own way.'

Across the 30 years of its existence the original Bugatti concern manufactured something over 7,000 cars and nearly 2,000 remain – plus or minus the 'missing' ones.

We also must celebrate the stunning and vitally sculptural work of the Type 35 owner/restorer and renowned car designer Achim Anscheidt, whose chief-of-design effect upon the current Bugattis and the forthcoming Bugatti Rimac cars cannot be underestimated. Along with designer Frank Heyl's input, today's Bugattis could have had no better design curator than Anscheidt. The contribution of the other Bugatti designers who will be named here has also been vital.

Die-hard old-school Bugattistes who are not sure about Bugatti today should look no further than what has been done with more recent Bugattis, from which they may understand Anscheidt's view that inspiration from the past is not the only consideration. What you understand it to be and then how you turn the past into the future is the key to realising the design projects.

Classic Bugattis line up at Ettore's bend at Prescott, home of the Bugatti Owners' Club.

Let's celebrate Bugatti, always recalling that the current Bugatti movement is something both very special and rare in the world of classic cars and also a more modern enthusiasm. The marque may be thought of as exotic and very special, yet its appeal appears to be surprisingly within reach, both to schoolboys and to older men and women across many social and cultural divides.

All Bugattis, whether from the 1920s and 1930s or the more recent cars, are different yet possess an equally defining ethos. Bugatti enthusiasts share a bond created by the polymath genius of Ettore and his son Jean Bugatti. Their designs have been a lasting inspiration over one hundred years, unique cars that capture the soul through their exquisite engineering and what some might call, perhaps with arguable hyperbole, 'divine design'.

If ever the currently somewhat oversubscribed term 'design language' was appropriate then it was and is for Bugatti ancient *and* modern. They may demonstrate different design languages, of course, but they all display pure *design*.

Despite this, the Bugatti world is not an exclusive club limited to the super-rich. Bugatti is far more open to enthusiasts than some might imagine. The British home to Bugatti at Prescott Hill Climb is an open house to enthusiasts from all over the world. Americans, Antipodeans, Europeans, all have their Bugatti clubs, publications and lovely gatherings; the Bugatti scene is diverse and multicultural, despite some thinking of it as 'posh'.

This book is a conversation about Bugatti and its supercars, drawing on sources that are both 'establishment' and yet also 'radical' or new. You do not have to love the 2022 Chiron Super Sport or the truly amazing Centodieci as much as a 1930s Type 35, nor vice versa, but the point is that the new Bugatti owes its existence in design terms to the earlier Bugatti. It follows that today's Bugattis keep the legend going in the modern context – and are far beyond any accusation of trading on a name and its legend. The brand has not usurped the car: the new Bugattis are far deeper than that, their unique design language and engineering philosophy being as vital as it was in yesterday's cars.

Of course, even this book's title is contentious for, as stated earlier, are not all Bugattis 'supercars'? In the present era of polarised debate, when opinion is posted as fact and nuance has been erased, but with social media and the mainstream media often supine before fashion and celebrity, old Bugattis are often believed to be anachronisms and new Bugattis are seen as celebrity footballers' ego trips and eco-enemy gas-guzzlers. But if you look *beyond* such labels, in Bugatti lies the true art of the automobile and of driving.

This text is intended to reframe the debate rather than define it, since 'definitive' is a hostage to opinion, let alone fortune, in a world of experts more knowledgeable than many of us aspirant hopefuls.

All I can tell you is that the sheer point-and-squirt delight of driving the little Brescia made me realise it was and remains a 'super' car, something far more than the sum of its century-old 'vintage' parts or its humble and petite form may engender in your expectations. The Brescia steered with feel and delight, turned-in with barely credible accuracy, and seemed to defy its engine capacity with torque and pace. The smile and the memory lasted days after driving the Brescia. Just don't mention the brakes.

The Type 35 Supercharged was something else, yet still had the feel of a thoroughbred racehorse or a fighter aircraft. You could power, shoot and scythe along the road and through bends with such accuracy and delight. The car almost seemed to know what the driver was thinking; the soundtrack was dizzying, the steering telepathic.

Rare beast: Jean-Pierre Wimille's Type 59/50B seen on the starting line on its historic return to Prescott after eight decades of absence.

A Chiron prepares to launch from the Prescott starting line.

The ride in a 'spaceship' Chiron was a bit more encapsulated, but no less exciting. The wall of torque, the lack of scrabbling or fight from the drivetrain, the intergalactic feel, it was all stunning and really was in every sense 'immense' or even 'epic'!

What of the 1930s incarnation of the Bugatti, the Type 57, its 'Atalante' model, and then the 'Atlantic' – are these not true supercars?

The Type 55 Super Sport Roadster or the very rare Type 55FHC (Fixed Head Coupé) are surely pure genius. What of the ex-Geoffrey St John Type 55 roadster with its Figoni & Falaschi couture bodywork? How could anyone in their right mind argue against it?

The heights of Bugatti philosophy include the Type 59/50B 4.7-litre monoposto single-seater, represented by Jean-Pierre Wimille's car, which returned to Prescott in 2019 for the first time since its original appearance eight decades earlier (see Chapter 7). Also in these pages you will see Jim Hull's Type 59S Competition 'Elektron' car as rebuilt, not as a 'copy', but as a toolroom tribute containing much original Bugatti content on its original chassis, yet with an accurate new body to replace the one apparently destroyed by the Bugattis in the late 1930s.

How fortunate I was to have been invited to sample and photograph these rare cars on the occasion of their very rare visits to the home of the Bugatti Owners' Club and to The Bugatti Trust, respectively, both organisations of which had a hand in honouring these cars and many others seen in this book.

Leaping forward into a new century, the thoughtful EB110 reeks of Bugatti purism, truly capturing the very essence of Bugatti and showing what reinvention can mean. It was more than a branding exercise to make money, as we can now see more clearly.

The Veyron defines an era of the modern supercar, although in my opinion the Chiron tops it because it has the added ingredient of style, as opposed to the Veyron's sledgehammer approach to being a bolide. Then we have the Chiron Sport, the 2022 Devio, the Chiron Super Sport 300, the Centodieci, the Divo, La Voiture Noire, the Bolide and the Mistral.

Wouldn't most people want one of the ten examples of the Centodieci built as the EB110 reincarnate, with its true hypercar underpinnings?

Does the superb Centodieci really 'bring together all of the components of the Bugatti brand into one extraordinary package', in the words of Christophe Pichon, the President of today's Bugatti, or is that just marketing hyperbole? Not really, for the car is truly a Bugatti, an amazing exercise in engineering, industrial design, art and driving.

As for the Bugatti Bolide concept car, was it a step too far or an ethos encapsulated? The verdict is yours not mine.

Elliptical elegance, compound curves, wonderful castings, hollow axles, lowered *surbaisse* chassis, streamlined sculptures, milled dashboards, wonderful wheels, straight-8s and superchargers, advanced metallurgy – never mind mascots, badges and so much more – Bugatti just keeps on giving (and that is just the cars).

Everyone should judge for themselves as to what is a Bugatti supercar. I can only say that I think the Type 57 Atlantic, the *gouette d'eau* or teardrop Bugatti, is the true definition of what makes a supercar and more, designed at a time before modernism and then digital authoritarianism took over the minds of designers, engineers and drivers alike.

This amazing story would never have got off the ground without 'Le Patron' – originally Ettore Bugatti and then his son Jean – nor a cast of supporters, drivers and Bugatti believers, nor would it be sustained today without the

This Type 40, with the rare 'Spanish' emblem on the grille and the unusual body, was originally supplied to Madrid and today is raced regularly by Adam Ward.

owners, the Bugatti Owners' Club, *Bugantics*, the web-based *Bugatti Pages*, the wonderful *Bugatti Revue* and, of course, the utterly essential Bugatti Trust, which itself is a resource of Bugatti brilliance beyond compare. The Petersen Automotive Museum and the Mullin Automotive Museum, both in California, the American Bugatti Club's *Pur Sang* magazine and the Bugatti movement generally must be cited for their true dedication to all things Bugatti, both auto and aero, in the classic iteration.

Some think that Bugatti was all about glitter and expensive engineering. Admittedly the engineering was expensive, but the truth is that Ettore Bugatti reused, recycled and repurposed many parts, chassis, engines, panels and Bugatti bits to build new cars out of nearly new, or previously loved Bugatti cars. Ettore scrapped very little and refurbished much. Your 'new' 1930s Bugatti might have been a car with a history – or at least had its chassis or body prestressed by some prior experience the year before or so.

Behind Ettore's artistic mind and the vast panoply of his designs, creations and devices – his constructions – there lay a hoarder and, perhaps we can even say with a touch of sacrilege, a bit of a tinkerer in metal and wood. He could turn materials into art, a skill he shared with his brother Rembrandt Bugatti. Ettore's son Jean was similarly blessed. In Ettore and Jean may be seen the rare amalgamation of an artistic brain with an engineering brain, two differing aspects of thinking that rarely join in harmony in the motor industry, but they did in the Bugattis and their output.

Who knows what genealogical diversion created such minds and the synapses to fire all the right notes in the correct order. What a repertoire, what a psychology.

What of Bugatti 'replicas' or 'copies'? Well, it depends on the replica or the copy. The Bugatti replica movement comes in various guises. The expensive modern Pur Sang-branded Bugattis might better be called a 'recreation' and are about as close as you can get to the original idea and ethos. They stem from Argentina and a more recent Californian popularity and should not be ignored, provided we realise that they are what they are, however lovely. Pur Sang also make replacement Bugatti parts that modern owners of 'real' old Bugattis should not ignore if an original is not to be found.

It should be remembered, however, that 'Pur Sang' stems from the etymology of an equine term used by Ettore Bugatti for his early pure or thoroughbred cars. In the early 1960s Hugh Conway Snr wrote a book entitled *Bugatti: 'Le pur-sang des automobiles'*, the title of which refers to Ettore's

The Miller-influenced twin-cam-engined Type 51 with Bugatti restorer Tim Dutton (Ivan Dutton Ltd) at the wheel at Ettore's bend, Prescott.

As the Types 30 evolved into the Types 40, a grand touring design was introduced. This blue beauty defines that process.

The Centodieci, today's 'ultimate' Bugatti, might be different but it captures the spirit and ethos of Bugatti.

Design delight. Jean Bugatti's Type 57 Ventoux body design has more road presence than a Rolls-Royce.

thoroughbred bloodline original manifestations of his design philosophy.

A Bugatti Owners' Club-sanctioned 'new build' old Type 35 built from real Bugatti bits is hardly to be sniffed at. Neither is an exquisite Tula toolroom Bugatti built using many original bits or chassis parts. Jarrot Engines, Ivan Dutton, Gentry Restorations, William I'Anson Ltd, Tula Precision Ltd, Ashton Keynes Vintage Restorations, Crosthwaite & Gardiner, and Bugatelier are just some of the restorers, builders and purveyors of Bugattis and their parts who should be saluted.

I do not criticise the 'toolroom' type Bugatti 'copies' equipped with original Bugatti-built parts that meet the established rules. There are plenty of 'original' Bugattis out there that have been re-bodied with accurate, replacement toolroom copy bodies, and there are many truly original Bugatti parts fitted into cars that are at least three-fifths original parts and are therefore sanctioned as being de facto Bugattis. Can one really object to the Rod Jolley-built Type 57 Atlantic re-bodied open 'Spider'? I suppose some can, but it remains a stunning body on a true 1934 Bugatti Type 57 chassis that once wore a Galibier body.

What of the Madame Itier Bugatti, which was originally re-bodied in the 1930s as so many 'original' Bugattis were by their owners, using 'official' coachbuilders (*carrossiers*, *carrozzerie* or *Karosserie*)? The Itier car is still a real Bugatti even if it has a history.

Sadly, the original Bugatti car company's production was brought to a halt by the events of the late 1930s until a new era, a new reincarnation and new owners of the Bugatti brand. Bugatti Automobili under Roman Artioli did an amazing job in 1992 with the EB110 series. Volkswagen AG, through its subsidiary Porsche, was the next custodian of the marque. Now with Bugatti Rimac, a collaboration between Porsche and the world-leading Croatian engineering and electric powerplant company Rimac Automobili, it has surely reached a new era.

But are we still left with two Bugatti camps – old and new? It takes courage to identify with both, let alone put them in the same book. Each to their own. Here is an attempt to analyse, explain and engage the forces and themes of Bugatti in a way that brings together something old, something new. The Bugatti story is involving and very special. I hope that this will help to join up the dots. We must now either engage a magneto before leaning out of the open cockpit and selecting an external lever, or press a button on a digitalised dashboard and choose warp drive. The choice is yours, but all the cars were and are Bugattis – pure and not so simple.

Lance Cole
Via Prescott, Rose Bay, Katoomba, Arcturus,
Malestroit, Downderry and Walbury Hill

The stunning 1930s Profilée Jean Bugatti design seen alongside the newer Chiron of the same Profilée incarnation.

BUGATTI TIMELINE

1856 Birth of Carlo Bugatti, who becomes internationally famous as a designer and artist: Carlo exhibits at the 1900 Exposition Universelle in Paris.

1881 Carlo's son Ettore Bugatti born in Milan.

1899 Ettore serves as an unpaid apprentice at Prinetti & Stucchi, Milan, and builds his first speculative vehicle/car designs and a 'Type 1'.

1901 Working with the Gulinelli brothers, Ettore creates his Type 2 prototype. The design is licensed to De Dietrich: fewer than 100 produced.

1909 After working with Mathis, De Dietrich and Deutz, Ettore builds Type 10: moves to Molsheim.

1912 Peugeot purchase a licence of a Bugatti design for their new small car, the Bébé. Bugatti himself produces a total of 445 8-valve engined Bugatti cars up to 1914 and the start of World War I. The Type 10 and then the Type 13 become his hallmarks.

1920 Bugatti manufactures the Type 13 and 16-valve cars, achieving an output of more than 2,000 cars.

1922 A version of the Type 12 is named the Brescia after it wins there. Bugatti also competes at Indianapolis. The Type 29 and Type 30 series are followed by the Type 40. Type 32 Tank MkI model experiments in the 1920s.

1924 Launch of the Type 35: more than 600 Type 35s and Type 37s built. Cars of these types successful in 2,000 races/competitions.

1926 Type 41 Royale prototype followed by six derivatives with varying body designs.

1927 Type 44 launched and over 1,000 built up to 1930. Grand Touring Types 46, 49 and 50 produced. Racing models, including Type 51, prove successful as new decade dawns.

1930 80 Bugatti railway power cars/sets produced for the Chemins de fer de l'Etat using variations of the 12.7-litre Bugatti engine. A Type 50 wins Le Mans.

1934–9 Development of the Type 57 including the Type 57 Atalante, Aérolithe, Atlantic and Type 57G Tank.

1939 Jean-Pierre Wimille has success with the Type 59/50B racer. Jean Bugatti is killed in testing accident.

1947 Ettore Bugatti dies. Company enters various stages of legal status and disputes. Attempts are made to reincarnate the brand with new car ideas, but Type 61 and Type 73 do not achieve series production. A planned new factory in Paris is not built.

1952 Bugatti's last motor show stand at the Paris Salon. Bugatti gains ongoing military industrial contracts for non-car production. Roland Bugatti attempts revival.

1956 Type 251 racing car project, limited to two prototypes, is terminated. The Type 252 sports car concept is stillborn.

1963 A curious change is made to the design of the Bugatti marque badge just before Hispano-Suiza (aviation) takes over the remains of the Bugatti engineering company. The Schlumpf brothers buy up Bugatti cars in large numbers for their unique collection.

1978– The Molsheim factory operated by Hispano-Suiza loses its final identity as the last Bugatti badges are removed following the SNECMA company takeover the previous year. All Ettore's children are dead. The Bugatti car brand is long gone, but the company name survives within the Messier-Hispano-Bugatti brand, specialising in aircraft landing gear, now Safran Landing Systems.

1987 Bugatti International founded in Luxembourg by Jean-Marc Borel. A new company, Bugatti Automobili SpA, is registered. The new Bugatti EB110 is announced and developed into a production supercar at a new factory at Campogalliano, which opens in 1990. A revised EB110S design is announced in 1991.

1994 A single EB110 competes at Le Mans.

1995 Bugatti Automobili SpA declared insolvent.

1997 Small-scale production by Dauer Racing of Germany of a handful of revised EB110s as owner of the EB110 licence.

1998 Bugatti brand acquired by Volkswagen. Bugatti S.A.S. formed. A one-off Bugatti EB118 concept car designed by Giorgetto Giugiaro for motor show audiences.

1999 The relaunched Bugatti brand shows off its EB 18/4 concept car at motor shows worldwide.

2000 Concept car derivative announced as the Veyron 16.4 design study: a 16-cylinder, 8-litre mid-engined car named after Pierre Veyron, the pre-war Bugatti racer.

2005 Bugatti Veyron launched. The last Veyron, a Grand Sport Vitesse La Finale, was sold in 2015.

2016 Bugatti Chiron launched 16 March at Geneva Motor Show. Numerous Chiron model variations up to 2023 include the Supersport, Pur Sport, '110 ans Bugatti', Edition Noire, Les Légendes du Ciel and L'Ébé.

2021 Bugatti under revised ownership via Porsche, with Croatian engineering and electric powerplant company Rimac as majority shareholder.

2021–3 New Centodieci, Divo, *La Voiture Noire* and Bolide models.

2024 Limited edition of 99 Bugatti W16 Mistral Roadsters sells out for 2024 delivery. This is the last Bugatti model to use the 8-litre quad-turbo W16 engine, as first used in the Veyron.

Bugatti's exquisite design was applied to everything: note the earlier style of EB logo on this steering wheel boss.

CHAPTER 1

ETTORE: POLYMATH CREATIVE

It was Ettore's fault, for he began the great design and engineering odyssey that led to Bugatti as we know it. Trains, planes and automobiles were at the core of it, but there was so much more.

Some observers think that Ettore was a revolutionary engineer who created and built entirely innovative, previously unseen new devices and vehicles. Yet that is not entirely accurate. Yes, Ettore did invent, patent and produce advanced and special new ideas, but not all of them were innovations beyond previous practices. In some contexts Ettore's works were the state of the art, further refined yet still based in earlier and known ideas, concepts that he took one or more steps further in an evolutionary process that was not necessarily revolutionary every time he put pencil to paper.

But we should not underestimate Ettore's futurism and innovative and disruptive thinking as a creator of new ideas and themes. He was clearly a strong character and some have suggested he was dictatorial yet also benevolent in that command. For certain, however, you could not pursue, patent and produce such creations if you were hiding under the proverbial bushel. Ettore was the boss, and *had* to be.

We should recall that at the birth of the century of the motor car, great engineers were all seeking answers to the same question. Ettore Bugatti, though, may have brought more to the history of car design than anyone of his era, arguably even more than Porsche, Lancia and other illustrious names of the 1920s and 1930s.

Ettore Arco Isidoro Bugatti (1881–1947) designed and invented an array of 'things', starting with cars, before trains and aircraft grabbed Ettore's attention and his money-making requirements. The arts of engineering and design, however, lay at the heart of Ettore's philosophy, life and output. Furniture, consumer products, engines, boats, aircraft, machine tools, aerodynamic and hydrodynamic devices, equine mechanisms, all this and more poured from Ettore's amazing brain.

From planes, trains and automobiles to boats, hulls, a pasta machine, engines, brake systems, a razor-blade sharpener, machine tools, wings, steam condensers, vices, floor polishers, fishing reels, caravans and cameras, and more, Ettore never stopped thinking. He even invented a medical device for surgeons to use during major internal operations. In 1914 Bugatti designed a multi-valve engine and an early rapid-firing semi-automatic weapon, but it was not taken up. Instead he concentrated on his engine designs in an attempt to help the French war effort and was based in the industrial Parisian suburb of Levallois-Perret, surrounded by French car and aircraft manufacturers.

Such a device was far removed from designs for a Bugatti bicycle, a pasta-maker or a beautiful and hydrodynamically advanced twin-masted yacht with its own patented mainsail-reef-roller system. Bugatti was a true polymath. He dreamed up special propellers, a new marine prop-shaft bearing and, notably, a patented high-speed motor torpedo boat with an innovative stepped and channelled hull, all drawn up by Bugatti in his marine moments, which also resulted in the high-speed 'Ninette' type hydroplane speedboats, again with radical hulls and engines. After 1945 Ettore designed a motor torpedo gunboat powered by eight supercharged 50B engines set within a hull made of the new alloy Duralinox: only one prototype was built.[1]

A BUGATTI-ISM?

Best known for his cars, and to a lesser extent his railcars, the truth can be seen that Ettore was a multi-disciplinary designer, inventor and creative whose ideas touched far more than cars. It tends to be the most dedicated Bugatti fanatics who know about his life and work beyond the automotive world. Ettore brought his touch to a vast array of subjects and products from cars to trains, to boats, aircraft and a vast *catalogue raisonné* of machines, devices and useful products.

He effectively created a collection of design themes, motifs, techniques, textures and applications as an artistic and industrial design movement that was without doubt an 'ism' – a 'Bugatti-ism'. It was not just Ettore. His father Carlo had been a furniture and jewellery designer who created a unique style and design language that reflected several oriental cultures amid its own motifs. It was Carlo who established the Bugatti family links with Paris, studying there in the late 1870s and moving there in 1904.

Carlo's second son Rembrandt Bugatti might have become one of the greatest artists and sculptors of his age, but he died too young. Ettore's own son Jean became a significant designer before his own untimely death. The gene pool and its output were truly amazing in the true sense of that overused word.

This Bugatti design output was set amid the better-known names and movements of 1920s and 1930s European art and engineering. I wish to suggest that Bugatti-ism was of far more significance than 'just' his car design, and that Ettore and Jean's output should be framed as going beyond their cars. The Bugattis, grandfather, father and son, defined a major early to mid-twentieth century movement beyond the cars for which the name has become famous.

The concept of the artisan as artist-engineer or artist-inventor was long an accepted norm, notably in Italy and perhaps through the inspiration of Leonardo da Vinci. By the 1940s, however, engineering and design – we dare not call it styling – had been separated, creating two camps that were often in conflict. This was never more obvious than in aviation and automotive spheres after 1945. It has taken years for these two groups to begin to work together again. Ettore, however, like his father Carlo, was an artisan artist-engineer-designer and Bugatti cars have always combined art and engineering in what today we term industrial design, a field that also includes that dreaded word 'styling'.

There is nothing wrong with style or styling, it is just that a manufactured false perception of the term, its meaning and context, was created in the recent past.

Ettore Bugatti created, designed, invented and built many amazing things in a tradition that had very specific roots in northern Italy and central Europe in an age of science and romanticism that introduced great advances across several centuries by inventors, designers, composers, architects and painters. In music we might cite Beethoven, Brahms, Shostakovich, Stravinsky, Bowie or Jarrett. In art and architecture there is Picasso, Kandinsky, Le Corbusier, Lloyd Wright and Utzon. In engineering we might single out Lanchester, Porsche, Citroën, Voisin or Lippisch. The name Bugatti is just as important and vital as these names in terms of artistic and engineering disruption of thought.

Ettore Bugatti seen in the cab of his railcar design, which placed the driver in a fairing on the roof, an idea that was repeated decades later in railway stock design.

The family Bugatti was thrown into this heady mix of social science and history, especially through Ettore's forensic approach and obsession with detail and quality. The Bugattis' move from Italy to France had an interesting precedent in Leonardo da Vinci's own arrival by 1517 at the court of King François I, bringing his drawings and plans of vehicles, aerial craft, inventions and paintings. At the Château d'Amboise he was appointed 'premier peinture, architecte et mécanicien du roi'.

The French clearly knew a design genius when they saw one and Ettore was to be embraced by French design and the French government in the twentieth century. In Paris he was surrounded by like-minded men, many of whom were part of the French intellectual establishment and its principal mechanism of effect, the *École Nationale Supérieure de l'Aéronautique et de Constructions Mécaniques*, known simply as the 'Sup'Aéro'.

Aircraft and railway stock (trains, locomotives and power cars or sets, to use the correct terms) were his passions besides cars; he liked all things equine too. In the 1930s Ettore was focused on railways in Paris, while his son Jean came to shape the Bugatti Company's automotive function at Molsheim. Much greatness would stem from their efforts.

AERO-ENGINES

It was around 1914–15 that the prototypes of Bugatti's aero-engines emerged. That they were not a commercial success and rarely flew in series-production aircraft should not qualify them as failures in engineering terms, since geopolitical circumstances, notably the outbreak of war, intervened.

Spurred on by his friend, the pioneer aviator Roland Garros, Ettore began thinking about aircraft design in 1913.

His process would result in a 5.0-litre engine for Garros's own Bugatti, which was a stepping stone to a derivative 12-litre straight-8 aero-engine design of 1915. Licences for this engine were sold by Bugatti to Diatto of Italy, Delaunay-Belleville of France and to America. Whether or not Daimler-Benz or BMW ever got their eyes on it remains a moot point.

Ettore's thoughts in 1914–17 on aero-engines that might be used by aircraft held much potential. His first 500hp aero-engine, the U16 built in 1917, was a development of his earlier straight-8 250hp aero-engine and its 1915 design origins.

Bugatti's aero-engines were mechanically efficient and notably lighter than competitors' engines, even those made by Rolls-Royce. But were the advanced Bugatti aero-engines too clever for their own good? They have been treated harshly by some historians, but that is a perceived wisdom only.

Bugatti's first aircraft engine designs (straight-8 and -16) were to be developed and soon licensed by Breguet. He went on to create further engine designs. Principal among these, with Jean's input, was the Type 34 aero-engine. A new design dating from 1923 comprised two monobloc engines conjoined to deliver a monstrous 31.4-litre rating and designated the Type 67. It did not enter series production, yet it became the basis of a Bugatti car engine and also featured in the Bugatti railcar designs.

In the 1930s Bugatti would attempt to create an engine and airframe targeted at the world air speed records. This included the intended modification of his 4.7-litre car engine, designated Type 50B, into a suitable aircraft powerplant.

First built for 1917, the Bugatti U-16 Type engine was a 24.3-litre giant, with a double bank, twin 8-cylinder water-cooled arrangement that produced 410hp (306kW). It was not a V- or Vee configuration but instead an innovative U-shaped design in which both banks of cylinders projected out of the top of the engine block, instead of being at an angle of 60 or 90 degrees, for example. The U-void would have made it possible to fit a Vickers gun to provide forward fire for the intended fighter aircraft application. With its multi-valve cylinders and a dry-sump oiling system, the engine really displayed advanced thinking. The engine was also bigger than the W16 configuration seen in the more recent, 21st-century Veyron and the Chiron.

This became one of the first licence-built Bugatti engines manufactured beyond France. After a US government fact-finding tour to France, Bugatti engineer and representative Ernest Friderich travelled to New York with the new big U-16 engine (of three-valve head design). After consultations with Charles B. King of the Duesenberg Company, Duesenberg agreed to build a licensed Bugatti U-16 engine. The company also made material changes and upgrades to the engine notably in terms of the ignition equipment, valves, water pump and propeller reduction gear. These changes were admittedly introduced by King and Duesenberg, but it is probable that Ettore Bugatti would have evolved the engine and its design technicalities if he had pursued further testing and development.

The modified U-16 engine became known as the King-Bugatti. As the USA had entered the war in 1917, it was anticipated that up to 10,000 revised King-Bugatti engines would be made for fitting in aircraft. In reality, fatigue problems in the metal of the Bugatti-specification cast-iron cylinder walls required further development and caused delay. By the end of the war in November 1918 only about 40 such engines had been constructed.

The basis of the Bugatti U-16 in France would emerge via the *Société Anonyme des Ateliers d'Aviation* Louis Breguet (the Breguet Company) with which Bugatti had forged links and sold production licences to. By mid-1921 Ettore had moved on, leaving Breguet as his licensee to get on with it. Sadly, Breguet's Bugatti-powered aircraft production was limited, although aircraft of this type were constructed, advertised and flown in the 1920s. The French company Morane-Saulnier also fitted a U-16 to its first prototype of the AN two-seat fighter in 1918.

After an initial Breguet-Bugatti straight-8 engine concept, by 1919 Breguet had exhibited its own version of the U-16 engine and announced plans to use it in Breguet's larger post-war airframes. Like Duesenberg, Breguet also had to work around cylinder-wall metal fatigue issues, reducing the bore and revising the cylinders. This became the revised Bugatti-Breguet engine and led to the Breguet U-16 Type U.24, which produced a reputed 600hp at a low 2,800rpm. Breguet even joined two of the U.24 engines in-line (but each being de-clutchable from the other in the event of an engine problem) to create the Breguet Quadrimoteur Type A of 1,000hp, making it the world's most powerful engine. This was succeeded by the Quadrimoteur Type B with four banks of eight-cylinders respectively, giving 2860cc and 1,015bhp amid a massive torque rating.

Breguet developed its B.19 bomber into the B.20 single-engined, 20-seat airliner, aptly named the Léviathan, which was powered by two Bugatti engines conjoined into one T32 Quadrimoteur Type A engine and driving a single four-bladed propeller in the nose of the airliner. The engine(s) were mounted in tandem in a cast cradle, driving a single shaft to the propeller from the two conjoined engines via an output shaft via the gearbox that combined the two engines. The airframe first flew in June 1922. Then Breguet decided to remove the nose-mounted engines and create the B.22, which had a pair of Breguet-Bugatti U-16s mounted upon each inner wing. This freed up the nose for a larger passenger cabin and saw the creation of a large wing-mounted twin-engined airliner for late 1922. The airframe was developed into 1923 but was not a success and was destroyed during a forced landing and subsequent fire during a 1923 air race.[2]

100P

Ettore went on in 1938–9 to create an entire Bugatti aircraft. The ultra-streamlined Bugatti 100 monocoque aircraft featured a wing design that incorporated elliptical thinking, forward wing sweep, an advanced patented 'reverse-flow' cooling system with drag reduction, automatic undercarriage and even a semi-automatic flap/spoiler control system, fitted with speed and power configuration sensors that predated today's mechanisms. In its final 100P version the airframe had a small, low-drag tail empennage and tail plane that met with some unjustified criticism, as flight testing eventually proved (just like the Supermarine Spitfire's small fin and tailplane).

Built in wood, this began as a Bugatti design sketch created and drawn by Ettore. Louis de Monge (Vicomte Pierre Louis de Monge de Franeau), who had embraced advanced design and improved aerodynamic concepts in the mid-1930s, further developed the idea and brought it to the production design stage. Bugatti's original sketch is not greatly dissimilar to the final 100P design. We can say that de Monge 'designed' the machine, not least using his knowledge of aerodynamics, but Ettore's sketches were so close to the final result that we must cite Ettore in his own airframe's creation. It was Ettore who originally dreamed up the prototype airframe design (Type 66)

The Bugatti 100P aircraft monoplane design featured advanced aerodynamics in an ellipsoid wing with twin-axis planform and a reverse-flow cooling air supply.

with two almost in-line engines and the transmission and gearbox system configured in front of the forward one. Such ideas would seep into the final Bugatti 100P airframe.

Designed as an air racer for the 1938 season and powered by the Bugatti Type 50B-derived car engine, in a twin-engined configuration the aircraft could easily have been a fighter airframe that turned tightly and scythed through the sky. In fact Ettore called it a fighter aircraft (*avion de chasse*) in his early sketches and envisaged a military version from the air racer origins.

Louis de Monge had built an early experimental example of an all-wing airframe in 1924 and powered it with two wing-mounted Bugatti Brescia engines, the propellor drives of which were oppositely 'handed' to counteract the normal torque-direction effect. The first flight was in 1925 and de Monge became a Bugatti enthusiast.

Bugatti's amazing aircraft was then updated with more power from a lighter engine built using magnesium. In fact it soon had two engines to boost performance and further design refinements. It was this machine that was defined as a prototype. The Bugatti aircraft design featured a through-fuselage drive or 'prop' shaft that passed under the pilot to the nose, in a similar configuration to that used in the American wartime Bell P-39 Airacobra. The North American P-51 Mustang used a clever low drag-thrust component exhaust cooling system, but it might be going a bit far to suggest it was taken from or inspired by the Bugatti system: in England during the late 1930s, both Spitfire aerodynamicist Beverley Shenstone, the Royal Aircraft Establishment's F.W. Meredith and the Bristol Aircraft Company's young engineer Malcolm Sayer, who would later design Jaguar car bodies, notably the E-Type, were working on reverse or advanced-flow/engine airframe cooling system designs.

The Bugatti aircraft, despite being wooden, was 'super' in every respect because it reduced both main types of drag: lift-induced and form- or shape-induced parasitic drag. We might see it in a singular aviation context as a monocoque, twin-axis, ellipsoid-winged Supermarine Spitfire crossed with a wooden de Havilland Mosquito, with a touch of the Dewoitine D.520 added, but created through the vision of Bugatti and de Monge, and incorporating various French, Italian and German design ideas.

A plan to fit the 'on-paper' Bugatti engine Type 67 21.7-litre V16 aero-engine of early 1939 provenance to the 100P's airframe was mooted but would have required increases to the span, length, fin and rudder height/area, and many expensive structural modifications.

Despite all its advances and patents and stunning form and function, the original Bugatti aircraft never flew – the German advance into Paris in mid-1940 put paid to that. A replica version made three brief flights in 2015–16, but on the third it dived into a field, killing the pilot.

TRAINS

Just as advanced were Bugatti's slant-nosed aerodynamic high-speed railcar designs of the 1930s, which did away with a locomotive and created the power cars with which we are familiar today. Bugatti did not invent the power car concept – Michelin and Panhard both built rubber-tyred railcars in France in the 1920s – but he did design and build the most advanced iteration of the idea before German designers claimed ascendance in that field. From the early 1930s Bugatti created truly advanced aerodynamic petrol-powered railcars (with proposals to later use diesel engines) for express and local French rail lines, respectively, run by the state-controlled *Administration des Chemins de Fer de l'Etat* (ETAT), which from 1938 was incorporated into the *Société Nationale des Chemins de Fer Français* (SNCF).

Through ETAT, and later the SNCF, Bugatti's railcars reached their design zenith. The initial railcars, known as autorails, were built in 1933 by Bugatti's own car and grand prix racing workshop team who had been taken off the car building line at Molsheim. The advanced aerodynamic design of the railcars clearly aped the body design of the Bugatti 'Tank' 1923 racing cars.[3]

Bugatti's railcars took a world record for their speeds achieved. Average speeds of more than 144km/h (90mph) were recorded on the Paris-Deauville run and a top speed of 196km/h (122mph) was achieved in 1933 on the Paris-Strasbourg route.

The front view of a Bugatti railcar shows off the advanced aerodynamic design: somehow Ettore managed to find the optimum frontal angle that was later used in many high-speed trains.

Such speeds were principally the result of the expertise of the engine design and the aerodynamic design. The railcars did in fact regularly edge towards 200km/h, but poor fuel economy would eventually count against these petrol-fuelled machines. Bugatti offered two engine outputs: the WR800ch model used four Bugatti 12.8-litre Royale car engines repurposed for railway traction use and giving a total engine capacity of 51.2 litres; and the WLG400ch (Le Ger type) used less motive power, employing a modular construction that allowed differing carriage lengths to be used within the power car set. Bugatti's car-engined railcars were used in France, notably on rural routes, as late as 1958. A total of three distinct Bugatti railcar types were created.

Bugatti used hydraulic fluid-flywheel transmissions for these machines, more than twenty years before German railway engineers made such transmissions popular in their locomotives and technology, which was then licensed to British and American locomotive builders. Similarly, Bugatti's fully sprung bogies were way ahead of their time.

Ettore later came up with an advanced steam engine that used a thoughtful new mechanism to create steam power and transfer it to traction at the wheels.

Of more relevance to the history of Bugatti, however, the original Bugatti railcar projects were combustion-engine powered and not steam driven. It is not clear whether the choice of a version of the Bugatti Royale car engine was simply a plan to use up spare Royale engines, even if, as always, Ettore was repurposing his resources. Nearly 90 Bugatti railcars were built in total, yet only one remains today. Bugatti's railcars were vitally important to helping French railways survive and enter a new age of design. Designed with varying power outputs and as double and triple-engined units, the Bugatti railcars with various speeds and passenger capacities were ideal for the vagaries of the French railway network across express, semi-fast and rural routes.

Such designs can only be seen as precursors to the high-speed trains of recent decades: the *Train à Grande Vitesse* (TGV), the InterCity 125 or High Speed Train (HST), and various German and Japanese express multiple railcar-types. Even in the mid-1930s, however, the Bugatti railcars, which went by the delightful name of 'Automotrices Bugatti', were highly influential across European rolling stock design.[4]

It seems, indeed, that the later TGV exterior designer, Bugattiste and Type 57 restoration consultant, the car designer and industrial stylist Paul Bracq, took inspiration from Ettore's works when shaping the TGV.

What of 'tilting' trains, which are generally thought to be a current Italian design 'proved' by British Rail designers in the 1970s as the Advanced Passenger Train (APT)? Naturally

Chassis 471, the 5-litre car that was Ettore's personal transport, seen with Piers Trevelyan at the wheel at Prescott. The car was chain-driven in a design not dissimilar to the earlier Deutz of Bugatti origination.

enough, however, it was our man Ettore who defined and patented the concept many decades before.

Catch a train today in Europe, Australia or the USA and you will discover the reversible or fold-over seat installed in modern trains, allowing you to face the other way. This was a concept invented and patented by Ettore in 1932 and he even alluded to such a seat design for use in cars: a folding rear seat, no less.

A 1,000hp steam-powered locomotive might have been seen as a step back from 1933's petrol-powered railcar, but nevertheless Bugatti designed such a long-distance train in the mid-1930s. It was innovative in that it was not a traditionally configured locomotive with a steam boiler powering external cylinder mechanisms in a leading traction locomotive, but crucially the steam-creation was to come from heavy-oil diesel combustion, not a coal fire.

In effect the Bugatti steam 'locomotive' was an integrated high-speed railcar and trailer set with the powertrain driving from a transversely mounted Bugatti-designed, variable-supply poppet-valve steam engine, via ultra-short drive shafts, to sets of direct-driven (un-geared) multi-axle bogies. This created 'powered' bogies with matching wheel sizes and therefore different to a conventional locomotive configuration. This also differed from the geared drive system favoured by German designers.

A Bugatti-patented flexible spherical connector joint allowed the high-power steam unit to drive the actual mechanism at the wheels. The exhausts were also flexibly mounted. The powered bogies even had some form of self-steer mechanism to allow for bends in the track taken at high speed. The train carried its own water supply for the condenser-equipped steam supply and therefore did not need to stop to take on water like a conventional steam locomotive. Bugatti-designed round or ball-ended cam-followers in the engine were liable, some experts have claimed, to suffer from fatigue under repeated extreme service loadings. Nevertheless, it was all amazing stuff and the Bugatti works created 35 patents just for the mechanical systems of its 'steam-train'.

Noël Domboy, the lead Bugatti draughtsman/engineer/manager, was specifically hired to translate Ettore's design thoughts into actual engineering drawings, not least for the Type 57 car and the 1,000hp steam-powered express train, which was to receive the backing of the ETAT rail group. A 2,000hp, 64-cyclinder version was to be supported by the *Compagnie du Chemin de Fer Paris*-Lyon-Méditerranée (PLM), which had also purchased Bugatti railcars.

Curiously, there were technical changes (including a controversial change to the wheel size, which had major redesign and cost implications), delays and vast expenses in this massive project. Then came the full, State-enforced amalgamation of the state-controlled and independent French railway companies to form the SNCF. The outbreak of war killed off the realisation of Bugatti's stunning steam-powered high-speed train. It was a rare failure for Ettore; Jean's death that year cannot have helped.

ENGINES

Refining or revolutionising engine design and mechanical practice was the core of Ettore's thinking and method. It is

The Type 35 straight-8 with supercharger shows off the essence of Bugatti design.

the refinements and innovations he brought to engine design that are so vital in his story. Ettore gave his engines their own 'Type' number – different from the Type number of his cars: a Type 13/Brescia, for example, might have a Type 27 engine, and thus be cited with two different 'Types' in its nomenclature. This rationale extended across the later cars and their engines, right through to the last pre-war engine, which was a Type 50/B but was seen in a handful of Type 59-derived racing cars, hence the Type 59/50B description of the famous Wimille race car.

From highly efficient small capacity engines to the 12.8-litre and near 14-litre massive engines of later years, Bugatti put thought, time and money into his engines and their components. The refinements in the engines of the mid-1920s, from the Type 35, frame Ettore's expensive engine-as-art philosophy.

Intriguingly, Ettore Bugatti also created engines that ran on plant-derived alcohol blend fuel. It would be the 1970s before the Brazilian motor industry made a success of mass-producing petrol engines adapted to run on sugar cane 'fuel' and it would be several more decades before bio-fuel became fashionable.

Early on in the Bugatti story the crucial *Bébé*, the second version of Peugeot's first series-production car, which was first launched in 1905 as the T69, arrived as a true mass-production Peugeot known as the Type BPI (Bugatti Peugeot I) in 1912–13. It was not just engineered by Ettore Bugatti but designed by him, and featured bodywork or an early form of styling that was very similar to a design of Bugatti's own earlier patent.

As early as 1903 Bugatti built a 'Paris-Madrid' competition car with a 12.8-litre engine and a curious rearmost driving position, inspired by an earlier racing car of his design. Those who made the rules thought it unacceptable, so Ettore simply moved the driver's command post further forwards. These early days of the De Dietrich-Bugatti were the true learning curve of Bugatti engine design. The advances and innovations inside the Bugatti engine philosophy cannot be underestimated, especially given the era they were created, 1900–10.

A 1.4-litre Bugatti driven by Ettore's in-house engineer Ernest Friderich won its Class at the 1911 Le Mans Grand Prix. Friderich would later become the Bugatti dealer in Nice.

De-rated variants of the Bugatti straight-8 and the bigger (aero-engine derived) U16 series engines (two banks of the straight-8 with a common crankcase but with respective crankshafts) were to be seen in the later cars, notably the Bugatti Royale, and were also destined for rail and airframe use. When the Royale engine was used in the Bugatti railcar, it had no gearbox and deployed a fluid transmission flywheel. Experiments using the Cotal electro-mechanism gearbox were also later tried.

Bugatti's engine designs are stunning pieces of exquisite engineering, whether they are large or small in capacity. Bugatti experts, however, might argue that the efficiencies and torque curve of the Model Type 57 3.3-litre straight-8, with its aluminium alloy pistons and numerous structural refinements, was the automotive pinnacle. If the torque

The Dusenberg-built King-Bugatti U-16 sectioned engine.

figure exceeds the hp/bhp rating then you know the engine is well designed, but exceeding it by so large a margin (160lb ft of torque from 140hp rated output) was outstanding.

If you thought multi-valve or even 16-valve engines were a sports or 'GTI' thing of the 1980s from clever modern car manufacturers, just remember that it was in 1914 that Ettore Bugatti thought of his first *multi-soupape* (multi-valve) head and by 1920 that engine was fitted to the Type 13, a 16-valve super-breathing induction reality that was winning races as the world's first multi-valve engined car range.

David Scott Moncrieff, the respected veteran and vintage car observer, stated in his 1955 book *Veteran and Edwardian Cars* that Bugatti's 5.0-litre engine was one of the 'most outstanding efforts of motor engineering', and that this car was so far ahead of its time, so futuristic, that it was 'virtually impossible to believe that it was designed in 1911'. Such was the respect Bugatti's works imbued.

From machined parts to roller bearings, from varying vee-angle configurations, from two, three or four valves per cylinder, to curved (banana) shaped tappets in a four-valve head, or double-cranked aero-engines, refined crankshafts and clever camshafts, Ettore thought of it all. To say that his smaller engines were complex, notably the 1940s Type 72 cyclemotor 'economy' engine for the post-war period of austerity that he knew was coming, would be an understatement. In Paris, along with his railway fixation, Ettore churned out ideas for innovative engines with clever engineering and lots of valves, pinions, mechanisms such as a roller-bearing connecting rod (beyond his earlier roller bearing cranks) and expensively machined parts, as if it were easy.

Expensive metals, alloys, bronze, copper, real 'white metal' technology and more all went into creating these engines' blocks and components. Bugatti created his own designs' and engineering hallmarks, but that was not to say he could not learn from others, such as, shall we say, 'adapting' some of the refinements of the American Miller-type engine cylinder mechanism.

As late as 1946 Ettore's exploration into a new engine cycle via a liquid-cooled (but revised to air-cooled) 4-cylinder but 'twin' configured engine (with twin crankshaft), with a rotating cylinder head mechanism as an actuating 'valve' assembly between the paired cylinders, was patented by his son Rolando 'Roland' Bugatti (1922 –1977).

The tools to make and machine his designs, notably the engines, were even the subject of design origination or design improvement by Bugatti – and patented of course.

Apart from Ferdinand Porsche's early experiments into 'electric' powerplant designs for road vehicles and the work of a few other such thinkers, Bugatti was the leading engineer experimenting with electro-hybrid motorised transport in the early years of the twentieth century. Ettore patented an electro-type axle-driven 'motor' in 1920 with a power pack *in situ* at the rear axle. By 1931 he had learned enough to launch a Type 56 with a single, 1hp electric engine mounted within the rear axle and geared drive unit. A hybrid 'mixte' petrol-electric dynamo-charged motor was the subject of a Bugatti patent by early 1932, in effect a self-recharging engine.

Intriguingly, in 1927 Bugatti had dabbled in electric drive by producing a small number of scaled-down Type 35 'models' as cars for children tagged 'Type 52'. They were not powered by pedals but by a 12-volt electrically driven rear wheel (single) propulsion 'motor' via an accumulator mounted under the bonnet. It is said that more than 200 of these cars, including a slightly increased scale-dimensioned version, were produced between about 1927 and 1931.

Children who 'drove' scale cars of this type in their early years at home included Giovanni Agnelli, who grew up to head FIAT, Sir Malcolm Campbell's young son Donald Campbell, and Tom Karen, who later became a famous car designer and industrial designer. Karen's wealthy father Pavel Kohn owned a full-scale Bugatti and his mother Margarethe Ferraris-Kohnová flew aerobatic sport aircraft in the 1930s before the family escaped from the Nazis and ended up in England.

One of Ettore Bugatti's cleverest further designs, in the field of suspension, was the one-piece forged axle with a hollow centre section or tunnel. The tunnel along the axle was bored out and square slots for mounting the springs were then set in. When the axle was heated it could be forged to any shape required, in particular an angled 'bend'.

Bugatti is said to have had over 1,000 patents to his name covering a diverse array of inventions, but this may include derivatives and revisions. Perhaps a slightly smaller number

Jean Bugatti, the design and driving 'hero' of the story of Bugatti's later years.

The Type 50 *Profilée* was one of Jean's most integrated designs. Note the windscreen pillar rake.

of actual patented *single* devices might be more accurate. Even though Ettore Bugatti's IQ must have been well beyond normal, it is hard to understand how he had the time to come up with his designs, let alone the energy to see so many of them patented and actually made or taken to series production.

Commentators call Ettore Bugatti a genius, but maybe we should call him a polymath, simply because his expertise and his thinking went beyond just one genre or discipline. His list of designs is one thing, but the man was an inventor, not 'just' a designer. He never stopped thinking.

Ettore was not alone in his creativity. His brother Rembrandt Bugatti (1884–1916) was a sculptor and draughtsman whose tragic suicide was a great loss to early twentieth-century art. He devoted much time to animals, which he studied in Antwerp Zoo. His work is exhibited in such major museums as the Victoria and Albert Museum in London and at The Bugatti Trust Museum itself. It is fitting that Rembrandt's reputation remains high and much credit must go to Edward Horswell of the Sladmore Gallery in London for building his profile through the book *Rembrandt Bugatti: Life in Sculpture*.

Ettore's first 'vehicle', the Prinetti & Stucchi tricycle.

JEAN BUGATTI: MAESTRO OF DESIGN

Ettore's son Jean, or more formally Gianoberto Maria Carlo Augusto Bugatti (1909–1939), was well on the way to becoming one of the defining car engineer-designers of his era when his life was also tragically cut short – in a Bugatti on a French rural road. Who knows what course the Bugatti company would have taken if Jean had not died so young.

Jean was born on 15 January 1909 and spent his later childhood at the Bugatti factory, where the family lived on site. Jean followed in his father's footsteps and learned and absorbed much. Engines fascinated him, notably the twin-cam principle and the Bugatti deployment of Miller engine design thinking.

Up until the mid-1920s Bugatti relied mainly on supplying coachbuilders (the famed *carrossiers* or *carrozzerie*) to body its cars, either through direct contract or via customer choice and commission. In 1927 he expanded his own Molsheim facilities to body his cars at source before delivery to customers, starting with the Type 43. Perhaps Bugatti's closest relationship with a supplying coachbuilder was that with Gangloff of Colmar, while his least known may have been with Veth & Zoon in Arnhem, the Netherlands. Ghia of Turin also clothed Bugattis.

By the early 1930s Jean had begun to take the lead at the Molsheim factory (Ettore was by now in Paris working on his railway projects). The two defining outputs of Jean's influence have to be the Type 57 cars and the coachwork design and styling that he created. Built when he was just 23, Jean's entry card into global car styling was the stunningly scaled Esders Type 41 Royale Roadster, a car that seems to be perfect from every angle and unfailingly presented the observer with a sense of occasion as it passed by.

From that car there followed the Type 55, the Type 57 and ultimately the Type 57 Atlantic coupé, a car so different that it remains a true design icon to this day. This was a car of scale, style, stance and sheer intent that transcended the fashions of the day. There is no doubt that Jean's most vital impact came with the Type 57 range, curtailed by his untimely death on 11 August 1939 while testing a Type 57C Le Mans Tank on a public road.

THE DNA OF GREAT DESIGN

The Bugatti family had roots going back many centuries in the vicinity of Milan in northern Italy. Ettore's grandfather Giovanni Luigi Bugatti (1823–1880) started by making agricultural and trade implements and became a decorative stone-carver, specialising in interior architectural features such as fireplaces for Milanese villas. He also cast ornaments in various metals. For many years he worked on plans for a machine to achieve perpetual motion, squandering his resources without any known success.

Giovanni Luigi and his wife Amalia Salvioni had a daughter, Luigia Pierina (known as 'Bice'), who lived with the painter Giovanni Segantini but was unable to marry him due to his stateless legal status, and a son, Carlo Arco (1856–1940). Carlo's early interests in architecture and interior design marked the next step in the Bugatti artistic DNA and evolving design 'language', which was not a set identity but a series of elemental themes using different materials that would later find expression in wheeled and winged devices.

Carlo studied at the *Accademia di Belle Arti di Brera* in Milan and may have attended the *Ecole des Beaux-Arts* in Paris. He would later market his drawn designs and three-dimensional output essentially via a design and build bureau that went by the title of C. Bugatti & C., *Fabbrica Mobili Artistici Fantasia* – or loosely translated, 'Carlo Bugatti's artistic and fantastic jewellery company'.

This produced wonderful and truly 'fantastic' jewellery and inlaid wooden bureaux and cabinets as 'exotic furniture'. The styles he created were new, derived not from the dark and static European Gothic or classical sources that dominated contemporary design, but reflecting instead the more vivid influences of Islamic and Japanese art, and even Romanesque architecture. Carlo's furniture seemed to combine elements of Islamic, Indian and Japanese artistic cultures through its shapes, forms, materials, colours and application techniques, often inlaid with ebony, ivory and mother of pearl.[5]

Carlo also designed the first Bugatti mechanical device, a bicycle, which had an unusual trapezoidal frame design.

The 'Snail Room' installation he exhibited at the *Esposizione Internazionale d'Arte Decorativa* in Turin in 1902 won him the Diploma of Honour, but declining local interest in his products persuaded him to take the momentous step of moving to Paris in 1904. By 1910 he had begun an association with an emerging French carmaker, Clément-Bayard. Carlo also produced jewellery and ornaments that must have influenced the watch designs that later became part of Bugatti's output, such as a wristwatch in the shape of a Bugatti radiator that was manufactured by Mido.

SCALE AND SCULPTURE

The curved forms, ellipsoid shapes, arches and spans set within elegant scaling are essential parts of Bugatti's design language, both the old and the new. These can be seen in Ettore's and Jean's car designs, even in the recent Chiron, and can clearly be traced back to the curved sculptural forms created by Carlo Bugatti using steamed and joined wood. Carlo, it seems, deserves greater credit for founding the Bugatti variant of the Arts and Crafts movement. This was far more distinct than Art Nouveau or any later 'school'. Add in Carlo's application of a northern Italian taste for textiles, vellum and finished surface treatments and you have the beginnings of a defined Bugatti technique that would become an industrial design hallmark that exists to this day.[6]

The design story framed by Ettore and his legend actually begins with his father Carlo, drawing on creativity and new ideas that remain both innovative and unique. The intrinsic, inherent talent for scale and shape that characterised Ettore's and Jean's output can be seen in Carlo's earlier furniture and in Rembrandt's captivating sculptures.

Ettore grew up to be clever and confident, later becoming somewhat sure of his certainties – but the reader must understand that these lay far beyond any blinkered vision of artistic, engineering or design fashion, constrained by practice or perceived rules. Indeed, Ettore was not officially an engineer. He fired off free thinking and never let anyone take him down. All he needed was luck, backers and opportunity, and those elements soon delivered themselves.

Artistic without doubt, the young Ettore's first significant engineering effect came in the form of modifications he made to a powered tricycle manufactured by the Milan firm of Prinetti & Stucchi, which opened the door to an apprenticeship there from 1898.

Ettore raced 'his' tricycle and at the age of seventeen won a major long-distance race in 1899, in the process beating another competitor bearing the surname Agnelli, which would later be not insignificant in the world of motoring. Some cite the three-wheeler as Ettore's Type 1, but debate on actual Type numbers remains fluid.

Yet the Bugatti die was cast, introducing an experimental and inventive period that took him from the early three-wheelers to four-wheelers and 'one-off' self-designed light cars.

Ettore also worked at this time with Gianoberto Gulinelli and his brother Olao Gulinelli from Ferrara. With the help of other backers Ettore created his 'Type 2', a 4-cylinder, water-cooled, chain-driven single-seater (*monoposto*) four-wheeler weighing less than 650kg. Ettore exhibited it at a major sporting show in Milan and also won a race there. He was awarded a medal of recognition by the Automobile Club de France and this secured his place on the stage of early motoring. A licence for production of this Type 2 design was later agreed with De Dietrich.

We should not forget that in the first decade of the twentieth century neither Britain nor America led the world in automobile or airframe design. France was in the lead, with Italy and Germany close behind. Ettore Bugatti was in the right place at the right time. The Wright brothers even brought their new aeroplanes to Paris when there was resistance to their ideas at home. Gabriel and Charles Voisin also took huge leaps in aeronautical innovations before Gabriel turned to automotive design after the death of his brother.

The first flights in Britain were undertaken using French Voisin aircraft, and the first heavier-than-air crossing of the English Channel was in a French Blériot XI. In the early 1900s the British establishment initially ignored their own prescient engineering experts, such as Frederick Lanchester

Ettore took his ideas forward from 1911 with the defining Type 13. This is an early car with the pre-ovaloid radiator design. Ernest Friderich won his class at Le Mans in 1911 in such a car.

and J.W. Dunne, only later to embrace their genius in order to catch up with the Europeans. The same was to happen in the 1930s to R.J. Mitchell and his revolutionary Supermarine Spitfire aircraft design.

Back in 1901, as the century had just turned and the new age of aeronautics and the automobile took pace, Ettore created his speculative early car designs and his stream of thoughts and ideas accelerated.

So began Ettore Bugatti's early career designing cars. His true four-wheeler design had a lightweight racing-style chassis with a 4-cylinder engine. It was this car that opened doors for him with De Dietrich, Mathis and Deutz.

Baron Eugène De Deietrich backed the young Bugatti and suddenly Ettore had the resources, the buildings and the tools to start building what he saw in his mind's eye. The outcome would be the De Dietrich-Bugatti cars with engine ratings that increased from 16hp to 60hp. The 60hp car was intended for racing and had a radical low-line chassis.

Ettore, Italian by birth, now found himself living in Alsace, the disputed eastern border lands between France and Germany that would alternate over the centuries between French, Habsburg, Prussian and then German rule. Since 1871 most of Alsace had been under German rule, but it was returned to France by the Treaty of Versailles in 1919.

After his early residence with De Dietrich at Niederbronn, Bugatti would gravitate to Molsheim, where within a few years he would establish the Bugatti factory base.

In 1904, however, De Dietrich dispensed with Ettore Bugatti's services following an apparently fractious relationship; this spurred Ettore on to new heights, risks and increased self-confidence.

Having taken onboard the Bugatti design ethos and techniques, the 'système Bugatti', the Lorraine-Dietrich company continued with its French-built range of cars in a confused outcome after the De Dietrich family withdrew, ending the German-based De Dietrich efforts at car making.

Enter a new partner – car dealer extraordinaire Emile Mathis from nearby Strasbourg. Mathis had handled De Dietrich, Turcat-Méray, Panhard, FIAT, Minerva and the rare Rochet-Schneider marques. But Mathis wanted to create his own cars and Ettore must have appeared as the means to enact that dream. Bugatti moved to Strasbourg to work on a new Mathis under a complicated licensing and facilities contract.

The outcome was the vehicle known as the 'Hermes' (also as the Hermes-Simplex or Hermes-Bugatti), which featured a chain-driven driveline. The car's Bugatti-designed engine had a reversed camshaft fitted with a pull-rod system in the bottom of the engine, instead of a push-rod mechanism atop the engine. It is thought that about fifteen of these Mathis Hermes types were built.

Ettore, however, saw a limited future with Mathis's limited production facilities and low-volume sales of cheaply engineered cars and the pair parted company before 1906 was out. Ettore Bugatti took himself off to a 'shed' workshop where he employed Ernest Friderich as an assistant engineering mechanic and started to modify an old Mathis chassis using a new Bugatti overhead camshaft engine. In the course of 1907, still set on exquisite engineering ideas, Ettore engineered and built his first single-overhead camshaft type engine. He also furthered his ideas of two-valves per cylinder.

The German company *Gasmotoren-Fabrik Deutz* knew of Bugatti's work and grabbed the design licence for the engine, paying him a fee and allowing him the freedom to carry on creating by actually employing him on a contract at its own factory. Bugatti, however, chose to keep his own private workshop back in Strasbourg. It seems that, while working on contract for and at Deutz, he thought he had the right to pursue his private interests and external contract work operating out of his old shed.

When matters came to a head Deutz briefly employed Bugatti, then only 26, directly under stricter terms. Under this agreement, Bugatti's designs or types, notably the Type 8, became Deutz Types, including the Type 21 with an advanced Ettore-designed engine. Missing Type numbers are not as obvious as they seem and are framed by the various machinations of what Bugatti and Deutz agreed to regarding the ever-evolving 'Types'.

In 1908 Ettore privately designed (at home) a small, lightweight and nimble sporting car to his own specification and ethos. It was a 'pure' or thoroughbred design and Ettore termed it the 'petit pur-sang', a small thoroughbred in the French idiom. Within two years Ettore had founded his own company and begun limited early production runs, at the same time as his father Carlo was making connections in Paris with the Clément-Bayard marque. The relationship between Ettore and Deutz would soon dissolve.

BUGATTI STANDS OUT

From such beginnings and endings came a stream of new Bugatti car designs and chassis and engine combinations. These ultimately led to the creation of the defining Bugatti Type 13, a developed concept of the little 'petit pur-sang'. The Type 13 is the true starting point of Bugatti car production.

In 1909 Ettore Bugatti had secured backing from a Prince of the Hohenlohe of German lineage, and this was when the move to Molsheim also enabled the first established Bugatti factory to be built and where the family would also live. Within a year Bugatti had produced ten of his vehicles; within three years he had 200 employees and had produced 175 vehicles.

Crucially, by 1911 Bugatti had persevered with his passion for ultra-efficient small cars and engines and created a Type 19 design that the Peugeot family would seize upon in 1912 to become their mass-production small car, known as the Peugeot *Bébé* (or Baby) in its second iteration. Peugeot had been building bicycles since about 1880 and low-volume production runs of car designs (including under the Lion-Peugeot name) since 1890. It produced the Type 69 or *Bébé* MkI in the hundreds from 1905, but series mass production in the thousands began with the Bugatti-designed *Bébé*, launched in October 1912.

Copying an earlier chassis and body that Ettore had drawn up, reputedly for the German marque Wanderer, in the region of 3,065 Peugeot Type BPI cars were built with a fee being paid to Bugatti for each. Effectively this was the best-selling Bugatti design in history; it was also the first mass-market Peugeot.

Again this type-licensing arrangement gave Ettore more income and more freedom to develop his ideas. You might say that this Peugeot was Bugatti's first fully realised, mass-production car design – albeit one bearing another name. According to Peugeot at the time, the car was cheaper to run than a horse.

Effectively it was a *voiturette* in the style of those lovely little light cars that were a degree or so more than a cycle-car, such as the Bedelia, and are now so redolent of an eccentric period in early French car design: bathtubs on wheels that drive with joy and today make us smile. The bodywork was also more Bugatti than Peugeot. In fact the body shape seemed to convey the 'tulip' type, a low-nosed and flared form not entirely dissimilar to that of an early Ferdinand Porsche body design. However, the *Bébé* was not a sports car and did not possess the chassis and suspension set-up that would soon make Bugatti famous. The *Bébé* was by general agreement a bit wobbly, but it steered and went well and was shaft-driven, not chain-driven, a notable step up from the cycle-car era.[7]

Bugatti had been influenced by the smaller, 1.2-litre Isotta Fraschini cars, designed by Giustino Cattaneo, that competed in many races, notably the 1908 Coupe des Voiturettes at Dieppe. Bugatti drew up his own car design in 1909–10 and called this, the first true, all-Bugatti-built car design, the Type 10. Weight, and its reduction, was to become a Bugatti obsession in car design long before later design greats focused on such factor.

In 1911 Bugatti built a one-off single-seat racer using his Type 10/Type 13 underpinnings, but with an extended wheelbase. It was the first time he had used a streamlined fairing at the front of the car and a sharper tail profile to try to direct airflow off the rear end. The car had twin bonnets and two 8-cylinder 2.8-litre engines. It might be considered as an early stepping stone to a more performance-oriented Bugatti with some attention to bodywork design.[8]

When war broke out in 1914 Bugatti left Germany and went to Italy, which was then still neutral, and then to France, where in a Paris hotel he designed aircraft engines, notably an innovative straight-8 whose configuration was adopted by the Duesenberg Corporation in America. Did Voisin or Rolls-Royce learn anything from Bugatti's design and treatment of his engines' components?

The production of cars bearing the Bugatti badge was interrupted by the war and Ettore moved to neutral Switzerland, yet he ended up in Paris assisting with wartime aircraft engine design. As peace arrived, Ettore returned to Molsheim and the disputed land of Alsace, which by the terms of the Treaty of Versailles was returned to France. Bugatti got his Molsheim factory back.

After the forced hiatus of World War I, Bugatti hit the big time from 1919. He began by reviving and improving his pre-war cars, starting with the Type 13 and then the Types 22 and 23. By July of that year factory production of his cars was under way. By the 1920s Bugatti's 8-valve engine

The early grille/radiator design motif, as also had been seen on the Deutz types.

cars had given way to 16-valve models and a host of design improvements were being introduced. Bugatti went racing early on as he knew it improved and 'proved' his engineering and created sales through public relations, a higher profile and popular acclaim.

MOLSHEIM MASTERPIECES: THE DETAILS OF DESIGN

It could not have been more inconvenient for Ettore that, just as he created the race-winning Type 13 and established the roots of the true Bugatti cars, war clouds were brewing across central Europe.

The Type 10 prototype had become the Type 13 production car, boasting many features that refined existing design practice or introduced new innovations. It had a one-piece block with integral head, overhead valves, a bevel-driven overhead camshaft, unique curved tappets, an aluminium crankcase, bronze bearings, a four-speed gearbox (not three-speed), and a low sports-tourer body with a long bonnet and two upholstered seats mounted towards the rear.

Of note the camshaft was lubricated by wicks in an oil-bath and the crankshaft was a three-bearing type with main and big ends treated with bronze.

This prototype was followed by actual, financed, 'Bugatti' car production in a new factory at Molsheim. The first cars to be made were sold as the Type 13, of which approximately 500 were built between 1910 and 1914. Initially these small cars did not possess a defining Bugatti radiator design motif: that would appear later. But they were quick, nimble and agile, and had a multi-valve 1327cc overhead camshaft engine that had torque and was eager to rev. A tuned engine such as this was very rare at the time. The gearbox had an unusual high-speed layshaft-type design in that its gear cogs were at the rear of the gearbox and the gear shaft rotated at a higher speed than the engine itself. In effect this provided a preselection speed that reduced the effect and the time needed to speed up or slow down in the gear selection action. This gave very smooth gear changes.

A reverse-pattern quarter-elliptic rear suspension design would soon be added to the Type 13. This remained a Bugatti design hallmark into the Type 35 many years beyond. The steering was direct, the wheelbase short, and the whole car was tailored to be a driver's car, which made it one of the first to be so. The Type 13 of 1913 onwards was fitted with Bugatti's own reversed-leaf spring design (semi-elliptic type), which would be found on all his subsequent cars. Ettore soon enlarged the engine to 2.0 litres and added an oil pump at the front of the cam-box; twin magnetos came later.

What the early Type 13 lacked was style. But Bugatti worked on the body design, devising a distinctive ovoid egg-shaped radiator and cowl fronting an ovoid body that ran back into a cockpit. His subsequent hallmark radiator design may have been inspired by the shape of a horseshoe, but some claim that in reality it evoked the shape of a leather yoke of the type fitted around the neck and shoulders of a horse to pull a cart or wagon.

Improved lubrication was also installed in the car. By 1914 engine lubrication by an externally operated pump was fitted. The fuel tank or bolster tank remained externally

The Bugatti Chateau at Molsheim in recent times. A rare later Type 101 with Guilloré coachwork can be seen in the foreground.

mounted and strapped down. While never a beauty, Type 13 soon evolved. Every aspect of the car was thought through. The gearbox casing, for example, was cast with the Bugatti name and brand logo as an artistic expression, even if the body 'styling' was minimal, apart from the ovoid radiator motif design.

Bugatti's Type 13 set the standard for a new Type or road and race car beyond its light car or *voiturette* origins. The Type 13 was a small go-kart type of car that had point-and-shoot characteristics.

Wooden wheels soon gave way to Rudge-type metal wheels. Five chain-driven 5.0-litre cars (with at least one at 5.2 litre) were built by Bugatti about 1912. Although using his generic new design ingredients, the chassis was arguably a derivative of an earlier layout that Bugatti had created at Deutz. Some evidence exists that three of these cars were constructed at Molsheim as late as 1914.

Ettore built a 5-litre, 4-cylinder version of his early engine and this was the core of the Type 18 of 1912–14. Chain-driven and producing about 90hp, with a very distinctive long and pointed tail that had a crudely streamlined effect, Ettore used one as his personal car and drove it to Le Mans in 1912. Its narrowed, frontal cowl, intended to aid streamlining, did not do much for the radiator cooling and it also deprived Ettore of the ability to mount his large leather travel bag across the front of the car on a luggage rack.

A pre-1914, 5.0-litre known as 'Black Bess', or car number 474, may be the most famous of these early Bugatti cars. Painted in black, the chain-driven type debuted the three-valve per cylinder head design. This car was delivered new to no less than the famed French pilot and racer Roland Garros (hence the Garros sobriquet to this Type). The car raced at Brooklands in the 1920s and remains in use today. Like other early Bugattis, the brakes were less than brilliant: Ettore is recorded as having stated, 'I design my cars to go, not to stop!'[9] How typical of the man.

EARLY 'AERO'?

The early years of the science of aerodynamics were not ignored by the Bugattis. Long before Citroën claimed the plaudits. Jean Bugatti and his in-house designer Joseph Walter seem to have created a blend of art and aerodynamic effect that stood the test of time, fashion and knowledge. Much of it was of course intuitive to Jean through his genes.

Admittedly Voisin, Cayla, Lefebvre, Lanchester, Jaray, Ledwinka, Rumpler, Porsche, von Koenig–Fachsenfeld, Kamm and others were investigating the pure science of road vehicle aerodynamics and airflow in the 1920s and early 1930s, but Bugatti turned out cars with 'aero' (as we now call it) in production cars early on yet without access to wind tunnels. Only the spectre of unwanted lift off the rear of the fastbacked Bugatti cars manifested as an issue, and never fundamentally detracted from the road cars.

The 'Bugatti Baby' by the Little Car Company wonderfully evokes Ettore's earlier Bugattis with electric power.

As for style, allied to streamlining, can we really argue against a Jean Bugatti-, a Figoni- or Schlatter-styled Bugatti that touches every design motif, every hallmark, and the very essence of not just the era, but a futurism that was not yet born?

But there was more to Ettore than engines and style. On 12 May 1937, for example, he applied for a British patent for a large, multi-wheeled, four-wheel-drive off-road or all-terrain (and possible amphibious) vehicle powered by the Bugatti 5.0-litre engine of Bugatti Type 46 provenance and featuring a multi-ratio gearbox. This put Ettore just ahead of the Willys-Overland Jeep and well ahead of the Land Rover as all-terrain vehicle concepts. It was also ahead of amphibious vehicles and large military all-terrain transport types. Ettore was granted a US recognised patent for the idea in 1940. This stunning design clearly had military use stamped all over it, but was never built. We can only speculate as to what happened and who was involved in 'borrowing' the Bugatti design.[10]

Ettore and then Jean Bugatti brought something unique to car design and engineering. It could be argued that they operated within an exquisite industrial design bubble and were unique. Ettore it seems had a bit of attitude. Purchasers of his cars were expected to have the financial resources to not just purchase a Bugatti, but keep it maintained and live up to its creator's expectations.

Design delight in the Type 13 radiator grille. Factory racing versions often had the brightwork blackened.

CHAPTER 2

BRESCIA: PRECURSOR OF THE SUPERCAR LINEAGE

However quick it was, the early 1910 ultra-lightweight, 8-valve Type 13 was a bit short of ultimate high-speed power for endurance racing or driving of a type that emerged as the Type 13 series evolved from the end of the first decade of the 1900s. But its acceleration through the gears and its ability to gallop along at 65mph (105km/h) in third gear, and 75mph (120km/h) in top, made these cars real driving tools that competing manufactrers took years to catch up with.

The 'Brescia' that was soon developed from the Type 13 was an early racing car, yet it spawned a series of road cars or, should we say, road-use derivatives. A 16-valve Type 22 was created as early as 1914, but it was the early 1920s that saw the Brescia derivatives populate the 'Types' numbers.

Frail looking yet actually quite rugged in its channel-frame construction, the Type 13 appeared as both a 'dog cart' type and a 'sports' iteration. The Brescia version soon evolved with a longer chassis and more room, making it more adaptable beyond slithering around French roads and early circuits.

The Brescia could lope along at 60mph (97km/h) while doing just 2,600rpm, not highly revved at all. Larger engines would soon come. Initially fuel supply was by a hand-pressurised flow from a pump operated by a passenger or riding mechanic. 'Proper' (mechanically driven) fuel pumps would soon arrive. The fuel system, just like the oil system, needed care and priming before starting the engine, and the oil needed warming before extended acceleration. Sticking to such rules, and the original rev-limit of around 4,000rpm, ensured the little engine remained in good health.

With a cockpit that was mostly 'open', an exposed 'bolster' fuel tank strapped to the back and some rather lovely coils of tubing, the rudimentary body and chassis combination hardly revealed this little car's actual ability. Longer chassis, better bodies and a touch more comfort would soon arrive.

Bugatti manufactured 435 of the Type 13 series cars between 1910 and 1920 based on the original underpinnings that weighed less than 500kg. Continuous evolution and enlargement created the later Brescia family Type 13, 20 and 23 variants, of which 2,005 were built. The original engine capacities were 1327cc, 1368cc, 1453cc and 1496cc. Never did an original 30hp and an initial top speed of just over 75mph (120km/h) go so far for so long: The Type 13 as developed offered the first 4-valve head in a production car engine and, as we have seen, Ettore had built a 5.0-litre car as early as 1912.

By 1919 a 3.0-litre engine had been designed as the next step on from the 1.4- and 1.5-litre 4-valve units. The 3.0-litre international racing classification for engines, however, was soon reduced to 2.0 litres, so he abandoned the 3.0-litre to develop a straight-8 2.0-litre. Key to the engine's reliability was a better lubrication design with oil jets and special lubrication channels fitted within the engine.

After World War I ended in 1918 Bugatti had returned to car production, re-engining and enlarging the Type 13 into a series of cars with more appeal. Licences to build the Type 13 were sold to Diatto of Italy, Rabag in Germany and Crossley in England (*see* below).

The Type 13 won many races and took all four top places at the 1921 Voiturette Grand Prix, also more correctly known as the *Gran Premio delle Vetturette*, held at the Montichiari circuit at Brescia, Italy (hence the later version of the Type 13 becoming known as the 'Brescia' Bugatti). Lap speeds of 116km/h (72mph) were set by the Type 13s. It was this event and Bugatti's victory that changed things for the company and for racing car design.

The Type 13 would go to Le Mans in 1923 as the Brescia 16S, driven by Max de Pourtalès and co-driver Sosthène de La Rochefoucauld. The pair finished in the top ten overall, a strong showing for the small yet nimble car with 16 valves.

By this time Bugatti had perfected the use of the 16-valve head, something the car industry did not apply more widely in mass-production cars for another seven decades. Bugatti sold 40 of the race-type 'full' Brescia specification short-chassis cars, tuned-up and tweaked for extra performance.

Brescia types from 1924 to 1926 would see improvements in the lubrication mechanism and changes to the camshaft. The pistons were of note due to their length and multiple-ring design. The crankshaft lubrication design was typical Ettore, sucking oil through external copper tubing from one side of the engine to the other by a gear pump that then sent the oil to the inlet side of the pressure filter. From there a gallery-feed pipe on the left (exhaust) side of the engine on the lower crankcase then squirt-spilled the oil into the circular wens of the crankshaft. Special channels or troughs allowed the oil to work its way into the engine's main bearings or 'big ends'. The higher-level camshaft was lubricated by way of a special bypass-type mechanism off the oil pump.[1]

Key to expanding the Type 13 into the Brescia range was the differing chassis lengths and wheelbases available. Given that most owners would buy the chassis and then send it to a coachbuilder house for a bespoke body design to be added, there were many options for a personalised Brescia type.

Longer-wheelbase versions of the Type 13 were created as the Types 13, 16 and 17. The Type 22 and 23 series were further developments of the configuration under the *Modifié* banner. The Type 13 derivative had a wheelbase of 2m (6ft 6in), while the Brescia Types 22 and 23 *Modifié* series sported wheelbases of 2.4m (7ft 8in) and 2.55m (8ft 4in), respectively. All these types, however, shared a common track width of 1.15m (3ft 9in).

Extra chassis-to-body bracing could be installed and differences in the front crossmember were noteworthy between the cars: some had a bowed tubular crossmember bracing the chassis between the front suspension shock absorbers, whereas others had a split-ended tube that fitted into the chassis channel sections at the front. Cast iron rear brake drums were lined with Ferodo-type brake 'shoes' as the type evolved. The external handbrake lever was also to be moved inboard for non-racing *Modifié* cars.

Of interest, the Brescia's delightfully sharp and communicative steering would stem from Bugatti adopting a worm and worm steering mechanism to replace the earlier and less direct worm and roller. Easier to spot was that the steering box, originally mounted on the chassis, was moved in the later *Modifié* cars to the stiffer crankcase housing.

The later larger, full-bodied Types 22 and 23 emerged in various forms, including as a further tangent in the Brescia *Modifié* series. A longer wheelbase, four seats and larger 2.0-litre 8-cylinder engines were introduced across the Types and evolved into the Type 20 series, known as Tourers, and ultimately as the 8-cylinder Type 30 of the 1920s.

The *Modifié* type and classification require a brief description. The Brescia 1496cc fixed-cylinder head, with 4 valves per cylinder operated from a single overhead camshaft with 'banana'-shaped tappets, was a starting point for the *Modifié*. Of note, the single-magneto specification was also a standard for the engine. Racing versions of the engine, however, had twin magnetos mounted high up in the dashboard/ scuttle. With other changes, notably a twin-spark system, these were known in factory parlance as the 'full-*Modifié*' specification.

Early Type 13 series cars up to the Brescia had the pear-shaped or horse-collar shape radiator, but from 1923 the radiator and its distinctive surround was reshaped into a more ovaloid form. The racing variants had an outboard gear-change lever linked via a curious tube and rotation mechanism to the gate. Later *Modifié* cars had an inboard gear lever.[2]

The developed, faster Brescia types created a new chapter for the 1920s. In 1923 a Brescia Sports model with twin-magneto ignition and various design tweaks further enhanced the model line. The Brescia 'original' used the special bearing design on the engine with ball bearings on

A Type 13 Brescia with an interesting air scoop modification applied. Julian Eckersley's 1921 car resting at Prescott.

The Eckersley Brescia seen charging up through the Esses on Prescott's classic hill climb.

The Type 13's 'dog cart' design is evident in this study, which captures the essence of a *voiturette*. Note the exposed rear fuel tank.

The ovaloid grille and barrel-shaped 'tumblehome' are classic ingredients of this great small supercar.

journals two and three with circular webs. A taper joint was deployed to conjoin the two halves of the crankshaft. Other variants of engine across the Type 13–22 and 23 series had plain bearings, but modifications were common.

The mid-1920s saw the Brescia *Modifié* series with a larger 68 × 100mm bore and stroke and 11.5hp rating. Adding a part-roller bearing crankshaft (the front bearing was plain but the other two were of roller-type) created a new sales angle for the small but nimble Bugatti. The company was learning and creating a full production range at what we now call 'scale'. These *Modifié* cars were more comfortable and more road-user or daily-driver compatible than the rather raw original Type 13 Brescias.

With the exception of Ettore's earlier 5.0-litre chain-driven cars of 1912–14, which featured two 4-cylinder engines conjoined in-line, the subsequent larger-engined cars were shaft-driven, which was unusual for the time, never mind for a light car.

In the 1920s the Bugatti Works racing team seemed to think it a good idea to convert the Brescia parts-bin for the subsequent Type 28–30 series into a single-seat racer by installing the new Bugatti 8-cylinder engine. Mechanical issues emerged, however, and an expensive trip to the USA to compete in the Indianapolis race turned into a PR disaster for Bugatti when the cars failed and only one of the five Bugatti team cars finished.

It would be 1926 before Bugatti offered cars with front brakes, as we understand the word to mean mechanically, as a £25 option instead of a driveline 'brake' band mechanism in the transmission. This front brake system was a direct 'reverse-engineering' lift from the new Type 35 and soon became standard equipment.

By that year the Brescia range had evolved from an early minimalistic light-car *voiturette* or *vetturetta*, a 'dog cart' styled light car, into something more substantial and more 'styled': a more viable 'touring' road car with up to four seats (there was even a three-seat cloverleaf example) and some degree of cabin comfort and weatherproofing. Even the earlier, exposed fuel bolster tank (sometimes left in its copper metal state rather than painted over) would fade from the car's design.

Many of this evolving model range that followed on from the Type 13 and the Brescia were sold in Great Britain, which became Bugatti's biggest export market at that time.

BLUE BUGATTIS AND THE FIRST BRITISH BUGATTIS

Many of the Type 13s and Brescia variants were painted in blue, maroon, green or shades thereof. Occasionally a red Brescia was seen: British Brescia owner and racer B.S. Marshall had his finished in black with gold stripes – copying the Ettore Bugatti personal in-house livery design. Sadly Marshall did not opt for a polished copper bolster tank; in the second half of the 1930s King Leopold III of Belgium would own a black and gold-striped, nose-cowled Type 59. Not until the 'JPS' sponsored black with gold lines livery of the 1970s Lotus racing team was such a treatment to be seen on a racing car again.

Marshall won the Boulogne Grand Prix in both 1924 and 1925 in his Brescia as well as numerous other events, notably at Brooklands. The Brescia became deservedly famous across many classes and circuits. Here lay the further foundations of brand Bugatti.

As early as 1919 the car import firm Charles Jarrott & Letts exhibited a Bugatti in Great Britain when they hosted a 10hp, 1306cc, 16-valve Bugatti on their stand at the London Motor Show at Olympia. The price of the rolling chassis with engine was £750 (a body would cost you extra). The 'Crossley-Bugatti' was exhibited at the Motor Show in 1921.[3]

Early licences to build Bugatti's cars in Britain were issued to industrialist Sir Kenneth Crossley's Crossley Motors (also known as the Crossley Engineering Company) in Manchester, England – cited from 1921 but with principal Bugatti manufacture from 1923 to 1925. A series production of 500 had been planned, but curiously just 24 were built, or built up from supplied components. It seems that this was an early form of the motor industry's concept of semi knocked down (SKD) or completely knocked down (CKD) production.

Of interest the Crossley family, at one stage Crossley Dunlop Ltd, had as early as 1869 acquired the near-global rights (except Germany) to the Otto & Langen gas-powered atmospheric internal combustion engine; they then purchased the rights to the Otto four-stroke engine. Soon would follow purchase of the rights to Rudolf Diesel's engine. As early as 1905 Crossley Brothers were working on the design and engineering of their first car and Crossley Motors Ltd was born in 1906. Henry Ford visited the Crossley factory in Manchester before he became the leading light of global production-line car building and he took a Crossley engine home to fit to a Model T.

The Type 13 and its Brescia brethren went well, cornered beautifully and had superb steering. This one is at Ettore's Bend at Prescott.

For Crossley, there came car and motorcycle engine manufacture and supply, and then came the famous Crossley light trucks and military vehicles. as proven in World War I. Crossley staff cars for high-ranking officers found much favour; with their smartly styled bodies and beautiful full-width road-wheel covers. Kenneth Crossley in particular was a pioneer in the field of automotive and aviation engineering and was an early private aviator before 1914. During the war Crossley supplied aircraft engines. Kenneth Crossley also initiated the licensing agreement with Willys-Overland that saw American vehicles made in Great Britain after 1919.

It is little surprise that Crossley became interested in Ettore Bugatti's ideas and output. Later on Crossley would effectively further the life of airship designer Sir Dennistoun Burney's outrageous and innovative Streamliner car of 1929, which had a very limited production run, by licensing production from the Burney company to build more than 20 further developed, yet more conventionally styled, examples from 1933 to 1935, branded as the Crossley Streamline.

For Crossley Motors it looked like it was an easy step to a Bugatti licence. Like Bugatti, Crossley embraced shaft drive early on, while others were still using chain-drive mechanisms to the driven axle. As with Bugatti, Crossley also created or supplied stylish bodywork.

Clearly the Crossleys were vital, yet often forgotten, elements in the early decades of the motor car and the expansion of the Bugatti legend in Great Britain. Yet just 24 Crossley Bugattis were sold, instead of the several hundred envisaged, and the reasons for the failure are unclear. Clearly there was no technical or design impediment, so was it due to price or even name?

Crossley Bugattis could also be ordered through the original British Bugatti concessionaires Charles Jarrott & Letts and a variety of coachwork design and supply options could be added. It seems that varieties of Bugatti technology specification were offered, including 'twin-spark' heads and a worm and nut steering mechanism (as opposed to the revised mechanism). Variations in back axle and gearbox design specifications were also cited. Crossley of Manchester actually built nearly 20,000 cars and 26,500 buses, goods and military vehicles in its history from 1903 to the 1950s. A highlight of the story is the production of Bugattis in Great Britain, as licensed by Bugatti itself, and which ultimately saw Bugatti establish itself in Great Britain and later in London.

Bugatti interest in Great Britain reached a new peak in 1922 at the Isle of Man Tourist Trophy races when Pierre de Vizcaya, Jacques Monés-Maury and Marshall entered 16-valve Bugattis cars, but they were equipped with basic bronze-treated big ends that protested at their treatment.

As well as the famed European Bugatti racing drivers, famous British names such as Henry Seagrave, Patrick Densham, Marshall and Mays became well-known exponents of the Brescia series. Raymond Mays created the much-modified pair of cars known as 'Cordon Rouge' and 'Cordon Bleu'. Whilst the non-roller-bearing engined 'Cordon Rouge' (a 1922 car) could rev towards 5,000rpm, the later 'Cordon Bleu' roller-bearing engined type, which had been tweaked by Amherst Villiers (of supercharger renown), proved Ettore's engine design skills by regularly running to more than over 6,500rpm, with nearly 7,000rpm cited for brief, non-circuit use, for example on a hill-climb. These cars lapped Brooklands at 160km/h (100mph).

This version of the dashboard (*tableau d'bord*) is evidence for a different twin-magneto location.

Mr Ward Snr at the wheel, demonstrating how small the Type 13 body is.

As ever, oil supply and the mechanism for it was to be a Bugatti issue – perhaps the only issue in the engine design, if we ignore the sometimes fragile gearboxes.

Of specific interest in the etymology of the Bugatti as a supercar, note should be taken of the Brescias with a torpedo-type body style driven by L. Du Montant, Captain Clive Gallop and B. Blackstock in 1924 at Brooklands as part of the J. O'Day racing team, the first major event in which a Brescia found fame in England. These cars featured the major revisions to the Bugatti bodywork style, which included a narrower, lower, cowled or faired nose over the radiator and bow, and, of vital significance, a curved rear section boat-tail arcing down to an 'edged' stern plate.

Such design elements were first applied to the team of straight-8 Bugatti racing cars in 1922 and then modified for 1924. As such, this design can only be seen as an element of a design process to the Type 35, which employed similar body design elements on a grander and more efficient scale.

Independent coachbuilders (notably French *carrossiers*), even such small outfits as Dorr and L. Maron, Pot et Cie of Levallois-Perret, outside Paris, created boat-tailed 'torpedo' style bodies for Brescias between about 1924 and 1926, but it is debatable quite how much they reflected Bugatti's original ideas as opposed to their own designs.

One of the better-known Bugatti Brescia owners in England was a friend of Ettore Bugatti, the banker Baron Leo d'Erlanger, whose collection included a long-wheelbase Brescia Type 23 *Modifié* and a Type 44 Fiacre. During World War II Leo and his cousin Baron Gerard d'Erlanger made significant contributions to British aviation and the Allied war effort. Leo's Brescia car was re-bodied in the 1960s. During the time of his ownership the car lived in Tunisia, where he spent much of his later years on account of the warm climate.

One of the earliest experiments with aerodynamics involving a Bugatti was in the early 1920s. In 1923, a

Fuel tank and copper pipe detail – keep pumping ...

16-valve Bugatti (Brescia type and possible chassis #1869), delivered in November of that year in London, was very quickly fitted with an experimental, torpedo-tailed 'aero' body designed by a Mr Morch of no less than the Bristol Aeroplane Company, where he was the plant manager and had studied aircraft design and raced at Brooklands. Curiously, this car was exported to Australia by 1924. Clearly it was not a 'factory' body, and it remains an unsolved riddle of a story.

AUSTRALIA

As far away as Australia, local coachbuilder designers were putting bodies on imported Bugatti chassis: Martin & King of Melbourne bodied a 1925 Brescia (chassis #2567) with a pretty upturned boat hull-tailed body, which also featured vital mudguards and wings/deflectors.

Bugattis raced extensively in Australia, notably at Maroubra, Caversham, Gerringong, Phillip Island, and at the

Brescia by night: these little cars are still hard-charging today in competitive events.

TYPE 13 TO BRESCIA AND TYPES 20/23: KEY INGREDIENTS OF THE STANDARD, *MODIFIÉ*, SPORTS AND TOURING VARIANTS

- Forensic Ettore Bugatti design approach with every element considered separately and as part of a whole concept
- Multi-valve engines: 8-valve to 16-valve overhead cam
- High revving strong engines – later models exceeding 5,500rpm in roller-bearing equipped engines
- Varying ignition systems (twin or single magneto), carburettor variations
- Direct steering with minimal rebound or variances
- 'Point and shoot' driving dynamics in sports mode
- Consistent suspension behaviour, noteworthy for reversed quarter elliptics (rear)
- Superb handling and turn-in gives nimble dynamics
- Stiff chassis with integral bracing from engine and gearbox
- Wheelbase variations as per chassis choice
- Bodywork variants to optioned coachbuilders' designs
- Potential of minimal frontal area and lightweight bodywork

In the right hands, a Brescia can be urged on to stunning performance, as seen here.

Rupert Marks at the wheel of his interesting type, with an early and original chassis under the 'short' body.

Scything at speed into Ettore's Bend at Prescott, with a well-known Brescia *pilote* at the wheel.

Julian Eckersley keeping it tight out of the same bend.

Hurstbridge and Rob Roy hill-climb events of the 1930s and 1940s. The majority of the Australian-exported Bugattis came from shipments of running chassis organised by the London agent Colonel W.L. Sorel. The cars were then locally bodied in Australia. This gave rise to some very interesting chapters in the Australian Bugatti story, involving local designs, modifications and on-offs.[4]

From the 1930s through to the 1950s well-heeled Australians, including several of the wool-millionaires of the era, imported racing Bugattis and Bugatti chassis into Australia.

A straight-8 Type 30 won the inaugural Australian Grand Prix at Goulburn in 1927. Further grand prix wins would establish the Bugatti name in Australia and New Zealand, where Bugattis also featured by the 1930s. Purists might want to look away at the mention of an Australian conversion to a Ford V8-engined Bugatti Type 37A, or a later Holden-engined Type 37A.[5]

By 1926 Bugatti had established a main London concession in, of all places, Brixton. Soon the 'Corsica' series of British-bodied and retailed Bugatti cars were also introduced. The Giles brothers were to prove essential not just to Bugatti's British sales, but also to racing Bugattis (*see* Chapter 7).

In the 1930s members of the Bugatti family, notably Ettore and Jean, as well as factory staff and drivers, would spend many weeks living in London or nearby in order to drive and compete, notably at the hill-climb circuits such as Prescott. Francis Curzon, 5th Earl Howe, a racing driver and serial Bugatti owner, hosted the Bugatti family at his ancestral home for several weeks. Curzon became a luminary of much that was Bugatti in Great Britain and later owned a beautiful Type 57S Atalante as chassis #57502, which was bought new in May 1937.

The British were ardent Bugatti fanatics in the 1920s and 1930s. There must also have been reasons why buyers in pre-1939 Australia, given its difficult driving conditions, wanted Bugattis, these likely being their power, torque, strength, ground clearance, twin magnetos, handling and pure ability in outback 'rough-as-guts' conditions.

It's detail like this that makes a Bugatti such a delight.

The story of how the Type 13 of 1910 developed into the Brescia of 1924, however humble in size or power rating, cannot be overlooked as the true beginning of the Bugatti supercar, simply because the type was advanced, defining or, to use a modern cliché, 'game-changing'. It can arguably be viewed in a modern context as an original manifestation of the theory and process that led to the Ariel Atom or the Lotus Elise – or more likely a Lotus Seven or perhaps its Caterham 7 version. Like these more recent cars, this original Bugatti 'added' lightness, handled like a track car or go-kart, and drove as if it was part of you. Adding more power turned it into something truly unique. The car created an ethos and set a design language. The Brescia proved you did not need brawn to be the best; you needed a brain, a Bugatti brain.

The Brescia series cars were adored by the motoring media. *The Light Car*, *Autocar* and many overseas publications raved over the cars' steering, handling, dynamics and the engines. Whether on hill climbs, on a circuit or on public roads, these little cars became the car of the moment, and as such they might be said to have 'made' Ettore's early international reputation and all that came from that. All of them, of course, noted Ettore Bugatti's lack of interest in providing anything more than a rudimentary form of braking.

Not everything Ettore did was touched by genius: for example, he stuck with leaf-spring suspension long after his competitors, such as Alfa Romeo, went for independent suspension. Bugatti used cable-operated brakes long after the more efficient hydraulic mechanism became fashionable. He did not get the aerodynamics of the Tank Type 32 completely correct either. Oil feed into the engine and the reliability of

NX 6600 is a Type 23 chassis #2051, rebuilt to Type 13 specification, that used to be hill-climbed by noted Bugatti expert and assessor David Sewell.

NX 6600's dashboard is a delight: twin magnetos, a wood-rimmed alloy-spoked wheel and old leather, metal and wood.

Charles Trevelyan, at the wheel of the Brescia-evolved 1926 Type 23 'Sport', keeps it authentic nearly 100 years after the car was built. This car has driven in rallies all over Europe.

The author captured this view from the Trevelyan car going up Prescott with Kraig Mycock at the wheel.

The detail under the bonnet of this 1926 Type 23 'Sport' displays all that Bugatti was about in the early 1920s.

Ettore made sure his name was everywhere, even on this transmission casing.

hard-worked and highly stressed drivelines/gearboxes were also 'competition' issues for the marque: Ettore quickly upgraded his engine lubrication systems and solved certain cooling issues.

The early Bugattis of Type 13 and Brescia developments of the Type 20 series and then the Type 32 Tanks were vital stepping stones towards defining the Bugatti engineering ethos and design language. They also framed the outcome that produced the Type 35, probably the first attempt at a car that from its inception was something more than the sum of its own parts, a supercar no less: here began the brilliance of the Bugatti.

This lovely and rare 1920 Type 22/27 'Torpedo' Brescia Sport two-seater, seen on the terrace at Prescott, captures what the Brescia years brought about in terms of development and design 'language'. This car was exhibited at Retromobile 2021 on the Lukas Huni stand.

The inherent elegance of early Bugatti design is captured in this shot of a Type 22 Brescia Skiff as it slips away at sunset.

Evoking a 1920s poster style, the author's Type 35 artwork captures the 'face' of Bugatti.

CHAPTER 3

TYPE 35: THE WORLD'S FIRST SUPERCAR?

Enter the thoroughbred: surely here lies the DNA of the 'supercar' as we know it.

Today the Type 35 (or *Tipo* 35) is not just a rather special old car, for this is the car that framed the 'Grand Prix' type of racer design, a movement that is now a multi-billion dollar industry of global fame. Ettore Bugatti's Type 35 was crucial to this process. It was arguably the world's first purpose-built, forensically designed, pure racing or production 'concept' car – hence its sobriquet of the 'Grand Prix Bugatti'. It was also road-usable in daily driving conditions if you were well-heeled, for this was a road-going car too, available in touring and sports specifications.

Other cars claimed racing DNA, but few could match the sheer level of detail design and exquisite engineering of the nimble Type 35, a car obsessive in its design delights but never at the cost of functionality. This was not a modified road-car turned into a racer. In fact it was a racing car for the road, one you could buy for private and normal road use where it would perform without, usually, too many temper tantrums. Then there was its looks: low, smaller than fashionable and sheer perfection from every angle with not a line that did not 'work'. True it was technologically a visual step backwards or sideways from the all-enclosed 'pontoon' bodywork of the Tank Type 32, but there were good reasons for that; after all the Type 35 had a wider appeal and a broader application than the Tank and its story.

Alfa Romeo, Delage, FIAT, Mercedes-Benz, Audi, Bentley, Aston Martin, these are the names of the great marques that excelled as sporting cars and racing cars in the 1920s, the 1930s and beyond. But it was the Bugatti Type 35 in 1924 that defined a new engineering and motor sport record. As such, this car is a lodestone in the development of the motor car in its first century; many might argue that it remains such an icon and is the inspiration behind so many cars, the new Bugattis included.

The Type 35 offered new levels of chassis design, engine specification, body design/styling, handling and steering. The car steered, drove, handled and went like nothing else. Nearly one hundred years later, the comments of Chris Jacques, owner and racer of a 1926 Type 35 (Chassis #4809) seem appropriate: 'Type 35 is an amazing drive, almost telepathic.'

Ettore Bugatti thought about and seemingly obsessed over every detail of every part of this car. That is why the Type 35 was not just innovative and an advance, but the road-going racing car of its age – and beyond.

An example of Bugatti's profile and the risks of getting history incorrect are illustrated by the story of the 1927 Type 35B that was owned by the famous Fauvist artist André Derain (chassis #4847) for just one year. This car, which has been in both 1500cc and 2300cc engined configurations, was in fact converted to a Type 51 specification after 1934 and since 1951 has lived in Australia. Confusingly, this same car as a supercharged Type 35B and wearing a streamlined nose appendage was raced in the 1934 Grand Prix de Le Mans by Robert Sénéchal for the Serbian owner Count Veličkovič.

Derain was a noted Bugatti connoisseur yet is an unfashionable Bugattiste due to his alleged wartime activities. Of interest, he had his Type 55 chassis #55227 converted to a unique lookalike Type 57 body style, which makes it a very rare non-Type 57 indeed. Noted Bugatti historian Pierre-Yves Laugier has provided vital documentation about Derain and the artist's ownership of four of the later Type 57s after his Type 35 tenure. Derain owned up to fourteen Bugattis.

DESIGNER DETAILS

With its exquisite engine (with the expensive full roller-bearing technique applied in a 'one-piece' setting), careful suspension design (machined, hollowed, joined at the front then forge-closed), cast alloy wheels, fully compensated four-wheel brakes, tailored chassis 'waisted' at the rear,

Supercharged delight on wire wheels resting at the Bugatti Trust. Debate about the small radiator and larger radiator shell designs used across early Type 35, Type 35 T/C, the Type 37 and the blown-Type 37A, is the stuff of Bugattism.

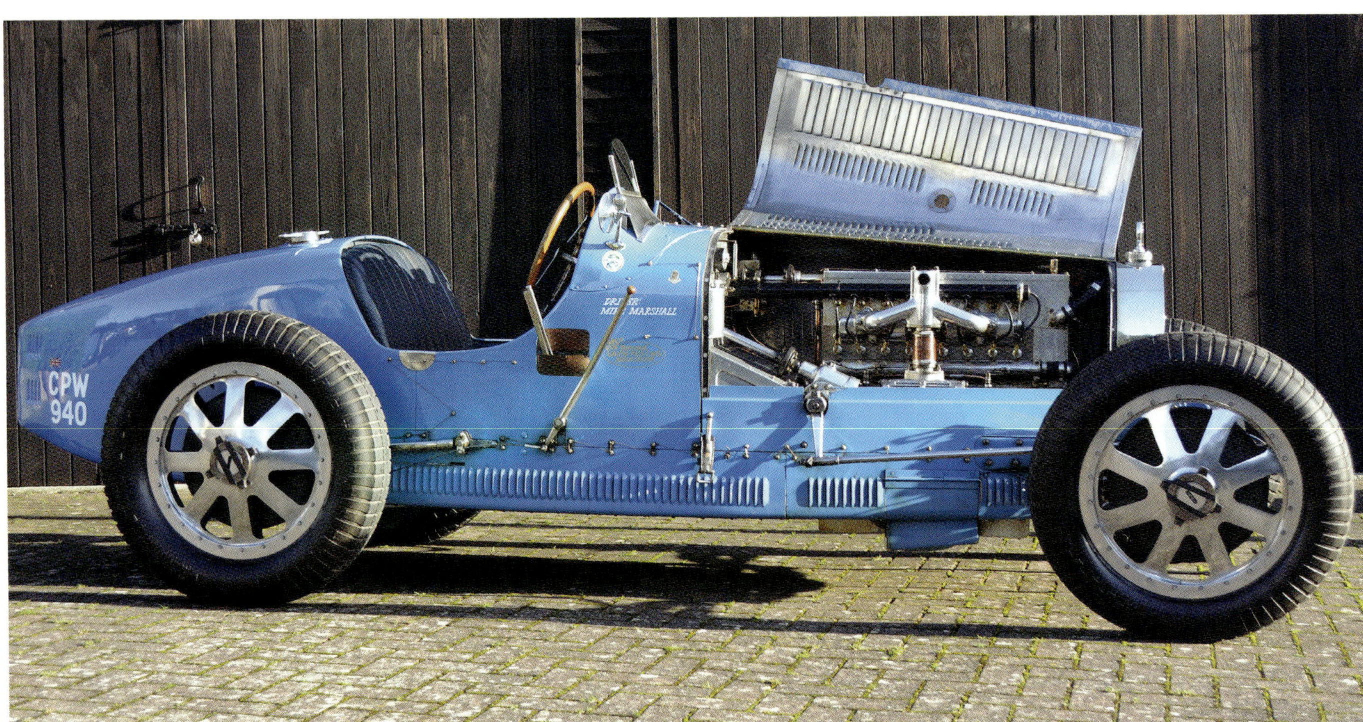

The Type 35B, under the bonnet. Note the high-mounted supercharger and its air-hole.

A few early Type 35s, and the Type 37, had the narrower radiator design. The Type 35 also had a different bow-shape to the Type 37. This one is the 1926 T37 chassis #37147 – the Derek Hitchman-owned car of notably fine history and restoration.

narrow nose (later widened), milled alloy 'veneer' covers to the engine block, underbonnet components and to the fascia, an air pump to pressurise the fuel, leather seats and the option of 'Bugatti Blu' paint, the Type 35 was a jewelled and faceted wonder of a car that still inspires today.

Of significance, the 'new' engine used one-piece, lightweight connecting rods and split the crankshaft itself into sections, then set together ('cottered') into alignment as assembled via multiple rollers. The crankshaft was case-hardened steel alloy of the most expensive chemical quality (less brittle than cheaper materials) and then ground or machined on all the vital wearing or operating 'faces'. The new crankshaft solved the earlier Bugatti engines' oil-lubrication issues. Larger valves were also fitted. Roller-type con rods were also part of the specification of the first Type 35 'race' cars.

As for the distinctive ellipsoid, boat-tailed, small-fronted, aluminium alloy body, it was 'designer' perfect from every angle and made a massive design language statement. There was not much more you could say about it then or now. From every perspective the body was defining. It looked like a cross between a car, a boat and a racing aircraft fuselage, and some said it was somehow equine.

The Type 35 went on the market at £1,136 (100,000 francs), which was enough to buy a very large house in central London at the time.

First launched in 1924 at the Lyon Grand Prix, the Type 35 (let's call it the original or Mk I) drove and steered with standards of precision and response previously unknown even by Brescia drivers. Above all, the Type 35 added power and torque. The strong, yet light, chassis was just flexible enough, which greatly benefited the handling, and the torque delivery ushered in a new era of performance. In 1925 Čeněk Junek won two international hill-climb events in his personal Type 35. Carlo Masetti won the Rome Grand Prix in February 1925 in his Type 35 and the Bugatti works team won the Targa Florio with Bartolomeo Costantini and his riding mechanic Piero Soderini in the Type 35 of Automobiles Ettore Bugatti.

From 1925 onwards Bugatti began the numerous tweaks and alterations to the specifications of the Type 35 as a series of variations. This would lead to a family of separate model derivatives that included steel bodies (not alloy bodies), smaller engines, de-rated items and simpler systems that yet ultimately became the basis of the different, but related by DNA, Type 51 (*see* below).

The Type 35A launched in 1925 offered normal buyers the looks and image of a racing car in a sports tourer daily driver. It cost £675 new, which was £425 less than the full-spec racing edition of the same car. The Type 35A had a three-bearing crankshaft and was less powerful than the original Grand Prix Type 35, and also less powerful than

The chassis detail and differential of the Bugatti Trust display Type 35 shows just how forensically Ettore kept the chassis weight under control. Note the tapered rear rails and transverse tube members. At its thinnest the chassis member depth is just 2cm: at the thickest 15cm. The pliable chassis is one of the secrets of the car's handling.

the subsequent Type 35B, which was supercharged and had a significantly improved performance. Ettore had initially refused the perhaps 'vulgar' engineering concept of the supercharger, but even he changed his mind.

Although the Type 35A had cheaper engine blocks without the expensive *rouleaux* or roller-bearing crank and con rods, and less power, it still went well with a lower rev limit (4,000rpm versus nearly 6,000rpm in the racer). The use of a coil/distributor ignition/system (deleting the expensive magneto) was a factory decision, although a handful of early Type 35As had the magneto system. The car also had a solid front axle, which was deemed acceptable, and so were wire wheels; however, you could put 'racing' magnesium alloys on your A-model. These early cars retained the narrow radiator/grille shape and the beaded edge wheels with high-pressure tyres and smaller brake drums.

Approximately 139 of the cheaper Type 35A were made (the sales records vary in citation from 124 to more than 130); 87 of the original, un-supercharged Type 35 full-specification cars were sold in the same period. The derivative 1.5-litre Type 37 would become a good road car for private use and in its supercharged Type 37A form was nothing short of a sporting driver's delight in its agility and balance allied to geared 'oomph'.

Several 'specials' or one-off modified Type 35s were created for individual customers and for racing specification. One rare car was the Type 35 fitted with fully enclosing front and rear body panels and wings (or fenders) to create a bulbous 1930s touring type style draped over the lithe form of the Type 35 body.

With variations in the specifications, and more recent modifications and restorations, charting the Type 35 can be challenging. Yet true originals do exist.

A stunning Type 35 is chassis #4541, which has recently been sympathetically restored in the correct sense (recommissioned) by Gentry Restorations. This car is one of the very early Type 35A production cars and arguably the most original example in use today – originality and authenticity being the proper standard to many minds. Chassis #4541 may even be the first Type 35A as it has No.1 stamped on its engine, No.1 on the front axle, No.2 on the rear axle, and No.12 on the gearbox: here lies true Bugatti history, yet as useable today as it was in spring 1925. This sort of Type 35A represents supercar 'purity' beyond value or points at a posh concourse event. simply because it is about a real car, not a 'fashion', nor a so-called 'better than new' amalgam of new parts. Put simply, in cars like #4541 we are looking at a rare and defining example of Molsheim authenticity.

Stephen Gentry of Gentry Restorations described chassis #4541 to the author: 'It is so nimble, less powerful but really useable. The lower-revving engine is not a huge disadvantage. The car is original, including the seat covers.'[1]

TYPE 35 VARIANTS, 1924–31

Type 35 'GP' 2.0-litre naturally aspirated

1924–27: 8-cylinder, un-supercharged, 1991cc, 2.0-litre: 3 valves per cylinder. Straight-8 engine with five-bearing crank, roller-bearing camshaft, rods and 'curved' specification tappets offered. Leaf springs front and rear, hollow front axle, solid rear axle. Cable-actuated drum brakes set in cast alloy wheels. Lightweight bodywork. Used a magneto system. Race standard car also sold to buyers. First car built was chassis #4323, registered 1 July 1924.

Type 35A 2.0-litre

1925–30: de-rated road car but still 8-cylinder monobloc of 2.0-litre, 3-valve overhead camshaft, straight-8 with cam of three-bearing type/ball races. 70hp. Leaf springs front and rear, hollow front axle, solid rear axle. Wire wheels. Specified as a much cheaper 'base' version framed for customer road use and cited as the 'Tecla' series Bugatti, also called the defining cheaper iteration of the purer race Type 35 as a 'Course/Circuit Imitation' Type 35A. More than 130 were made 1925–9. Very early Type 35As used the Type 35 engine block with closed-off roller bearing feed lines due to the deletion of the roller-bearing specification. Later Type 35A blocks were made without the oil feed machining, which was no longer required.

The concept of a cheaper Type 35 was also developed into a second variant as the Type 37 with an interesting and typically Bugatti-detailed 4-cylinder engine. To confuse matters further, a supercharged Type 37A (or CP) was then to become available and this was a delightful road car (see below).

From 1928 the cars were fitted with a pressure-feed oil supply rather than splash lubrication.

Type 35T 2.3-litre

1926: 2262cc, 2.3-litre enlarged 8-cylinder engine, unsupercharged. Bore 60mm. Stroke 100mm. The T signifies Targa Florio racing specification. A 'roller-bearing' type.

Type 35C 2.0-litre supercharged

1926–30: 8-cylinder, supercharged. With Roots-type 2.0-litre, 3-valve overhead camshaft, straight-8 engine with roller bearing camshaft. 90hp/67kW. Bore 60mm. Stroke 88mm. Leaf springs front and rear, hollow front axle, solid rear axle.

Cable-actuated drum brakes set in cast alloy wheels. Lightweight bodywork and drilled chassis.

Type 35TC 2.3-litre supercharged and Type 35B

Late 1926: 2262cc. TC was the initial nomenclature for Targa Compressor (supercharger).

This became the definitive supercharged Type 35 series race car. The B series was introduced in 1927. 130hp/96kW. Modified-lobe Roots supercharger driven off the front of the crankshaft. Higher pressure ratio. Type 35B supercharged with long-stroke crankshaft. Top speed 205km/h (130mph). Changes to track 1,245mm (4ft 1in) at front, 1,194mm (3ft 11in) at rear. Delivered more torque yet higher specific fuel consumption.

Type 37 1.5-litre, 4-cylinder

1925–31: Similar chassis to the Type 35 but with single overhead camshaft, 3-valve head, 1496cc, straight-4 engine. Effectively the Brescia replacement, some said, but that ignored the Type 40. Bronzed valve guides secure the alloy head to the main engine casting and screw sockets to retain the overhead camshaft in position: a very rigid engine of tall and narrow dimensions. The Type 37 was cheaper to purchase as a basic specification car with de-rated engine with plain bearings (non-roller). Small inlet valve type later enlarged. Wire wheels. Bore 69mm. Stroke 100mm. 60hp/44kW. Magnetos deleted and coil ignition and lighting system added. Crankcase mounting changes to chassis due to shorter engine. A few T37s were re-bodied in closed-cabin, two-door lightweight coupé form by Million & Guiet.

This supercharged engine demonstrates just how exquisite the Type 37A was under the bonnet as well as in its exterior design.

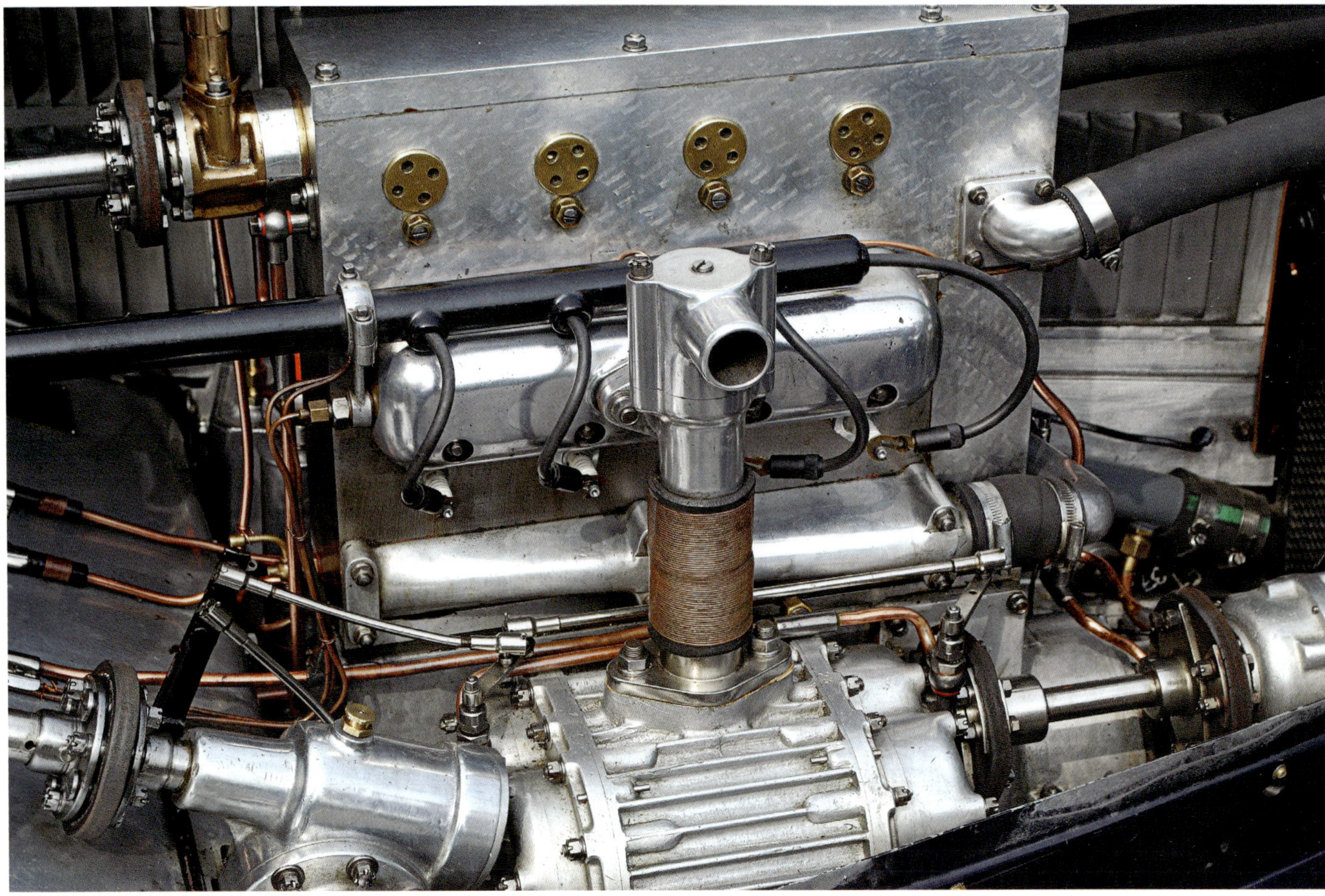

The Type 37A's small bore supercharger and engine in detail. The swirled and polished finish to the engine block and head is an applied external 'veneer' that Ettore used to 'dress' his engines.

Type 37A 1.5-litre, 4-cylinder, supercharged or 'CP'

1926–31: Type 37 of 1496cc, but with added 'compresseur' supercharger (with smaller casing length of 135mm than the Type 35 supercharger of 185mm) giving 90hp/67kW. Dashboard-mounted magneto added for racing edition. The Type 37 retains the original narrow radiator/cowl design. Larger brake drums. Approximately 290 of the Type 37 and Type 37A series were built in total with many used by amateur drivers in competition.

Type 39 1.5-litre

1925–29: 1,493cc. Intended to meet new Grand Prix Formula One engine rules as a de-bored straight-8 of shorter crankshaft. Same general specification as the Type 35 except for crankshaft/plain/roller bearings mix. A 1.1-litre version (reduced bore) was a one-off. Launched in July 1925 at the Montlhéry Touring Grand Prix as a five-car race team with special bodies. The team took the top four places.

Type 39A 1.5-litre, supercharged

As per the Type 39 but with a small supercharger. Produced for the 1926 Formula rules. Some with 1495cc and bore of 52mm with stroke of 88mm, others 60 × 66mm. Won the 1926 French Grand Prix and also driven in 1926 British Grand Prix as an ex-works car by Malcolm Campbell.

Type 39D

Revised engine with special block with modified cam box and different exhaust. Five cars built for racing in 1927.

Polished dashboard, wooden rim, and the smell of alloy and leather – Type 35 magic. Note the external levers.

SPORTING LEGEND

The Type 35 was Bugatti's most successful racing car and its variants enjoyed further victories. Cars of this Type won many a Grand Prix, the 1926 World Championship, five Targa Florio victories; it took places at Le Mans and excelled in hill climbs, rallies and national club events all over Europe (and beyond).

René Dreyfus competed privately in a Type 37A with great success. He sold this to finance the purchase of a Type 35B with Ernest Friderich (now the Bugatti dealer in Nice) and using this private car beat the Bugatti works grand prix team's Type 35Cs at the 1930 Monaco Grand Prix, a race that was packed with Bugatti-driving privateer entrants. Ettore was reportedly extremely annoyed that a private Bugatti had beaten his works team: they were using the less powerful but more reliable Type 35C, but Louis Chiron's works car, in the lead, had a mechanical issue. A private Type 35 2.3-litre was, it seemed, the equal of the factory works 2.0-litre Type 35. Dreyfus also drove a Type 51 in competition at the Grand Prix de Brignoles, as described in his autobiography *My Two Lives*.

A Type 35 even raced in Western Australia at the long-forgotten races at Albany and Caversham, and most notably the desert Grand Prix at Lake Perkollili. Successful Bugatti Type 35, Type 37 and Type 39 racers in pre-war Australia included Arthur Terdich, Carl Junker, Bill Thompson, Hope Bartlett and Harold Drake-Richmond, a wealthy privateer racer and Marconi radio pioneer.

Terdich had a runaway victory at the 1929 Australian Grand Prix at Phillip Island, Victoria, and Junker followed with another such victory. A Bugatti won the Australian race from 1929 to 1933, with several top-three podium places in the race also being taken by Bugattis, firmly establishing the marque 'down under'. It is fair to state that the Bugattis helped establish motor racing in Australia and also Bugatti's presence in New Zealand.[2]

The rich and famous flocked to purchase these cars, both for personal use and to enter them in races. In 1927 the Type 35 and its variants took sixteen international class Grand Prix victories and seven hill-climb/rally victories. In 1928 this had risen to 25 international class victories and seven hill-climb/rally victories.

William Grover-Williams won the inaugural Monaco Grand Prix on 14 April 1929 in his green Type 35B and also won the Grand Prix at Le Mans two months later. Throughout 1929 the Type 35 or its variants won at least one major international class Grand Prix race per month, often several times a month, including Arthur Terdich's win at the Australian Grand Prix at Phillip Island on 18 March 1929 in his Type 37A supercharged 1.5-litre, making a total of eighteen international class victories. Among their eight major

THE DEBUT COMPETITION YEARS, 1924–6

1924

2nd San Sebastian Grand Prix. Bartolomeo Costantini's Type 35 leads but mechanical issues push him to second place. Fastest lap recorded

1925

1st Rome Grand Prix. Driver: Carlo Masetti
1st Targa Florio. Driver: Bartolomeo Costantini.
1st Circuit of Garda. Driver: Count Aymo Maggi
1st Brno-Soběšice Rally. Driver: Čeněk Junek
1st Dubí-Cínovec Rally. Driver: Čeněk Junek

1926

1st Circuito del Pozzo-Verona. Driver: Alessandro Consonni.
1st Rally of Roma-Valle Giulia. Driver: Count Aymo Maggi.
1st Targa Florio. Driver: Bartolomeo Costantini.
1st Tripoli Grand Prix. Driver: François Eysermann
1st Grand Prix of the Automobile Club de France, Miramas. Driver: Jules Goux
1st Grand Prix of Europe. Driver: Jules Goux
1st Grand Prix of Spain. Driver: Bartolomeo Costantini
1st Grand Prix de la Marne, Reims. Driver: François Lescot (pseudonym of Jean Lebaudy)
1st Grand Prix de Comminges, Saint-Gaudens. Driver: Louis Chiron
1st Rally Cup Acerbo-Pescara. Driver: Luigi Spinozi
1st Grand Prix des Voiturettes, Boulogne. Driver: George Eyston
1st Grand Prix of Italy. Driver: Sabipa (Louis Charavel)
1st Grand Prix of Milan. Driver: Bartolomeo Costantini
1st Grand Prix of Marseille, Miramas. Driver: P. Matusserie.
1st Circuit of Garda. Driver: Count Aymo Maggi.
In the same year Čeněk Junek took four first places and his wife Eliška Junková took one first place in hill-climb/rally events in Czechoslovakia.

hill-climb/rally victories in 1929 were no fewer than five by Hans Stuber in his Type 35C.

Sir Malcolm Campbell purchased and modified a Type 35 road car, including cutting an access hatch in the rear bodywork to create a boot/trunk space. The Vizcaya family, who were Bugatti backers, purchased more than one Type 35 and the two Vizcaya sons also raced in several Type 35s.

In 1930 the Type 30 and its variants took fourteen international class victories and seven hill-climb/rally victories. In 1931 the Bugattis took five international classes, including the Australian Grand Prix for the third time, and six hill-climb/rally victories.

After the end of its frontline international Grand Prix career, the Type 35 family of cars carved a major niche in Great Britain via the Bugatti Owners' Club and its Prescott Hill Climb. Brooklands, Shelsley Walsh and numerous British hill-climb tracks and racing circuits also saw the Bugatti cars in action. A. N. Spottiswoode set the fastest time of the day (FTD) at the first Bugatti Owners' Club meeting in 1931, winning a gold medal for a time of 23.6 seconds on the 357-yard course at Chalfont St Giles, before the club was based at Prescott. George Harvey Noble took a Type 25 to the Lewes Speed trial in 1935.

Charles Brackenbury got his Type 35 completely airborne on the banking at Brooklands in 1938 when winning the Whitsun Handicap of 1938. C. Lister Clark took his Type 35C to the first Prescott meeting in 1938 and was third at the autumn event.

In the mid-1930s Ettore and Jean Bugatti and the works team were regular visitors to Britain and to Prescott, where

Mike Preston powers a 1926 Type 35B in road specification through the bends accompanied by a young enthusiast. The Preston family have played a significant role in British Bugattism.

Sir John Venables-Llewelyn Bt, a luminary of things Bugatti in England captured at the wheel of his Type 35, which had a long, low driving position with the steering wheel close to the chest.

the new Bugatti Owners' Club had made a home and a wonderful hill-climb track that is in use to this day; the club celebrated its 90th anniversary in 2019. Ettore even donated a Type 35 car to the club in the 1930s, and Jean-Pierre Wimille appeared at Prescott in 1939 in a Bugatti Type 59/50B (*see* Chapter 7).

Current Type 35 owners and drivers adore their cars, but are not afraid to use them as intended. Mike Marshall, until recently the owner of a Type 35B, said at Prescott: 'It's so fast, so accurate.' The likes of Nick Mason, Duncan Pittaway, Richard Crosthwaite, Edmund Burgess, Julian Majzub and a club of competitive Bugatti drivers love these cars and drive them fast at events across the vintage motor sport calendar. Hamish Moffatt, Neil Corner and many more names populated the record of Type 35 driving in the modern era.

One of the forgotten British Bugatti privateers of the 1930s was a Thomas Steuart Fothringham who raced a Type 35 from 1931 and then sold it to the famous actress and racer Kay Petre. This car was eventually owned by Hugh Conway and still races under its current ownership. Steuart Fothringham also owned an ex-factory 1927 Type 39 (ex-Malcolm Campbell), which was converted to Type 35T specification. Kay Petre borrowed the car and set a lap record in it of 124.14mph

BUGATTI WOMEN

Women took to the Type 35 too. Eliška Junková drove hers in the Targa Florio in April 1927. Hellé Nice, whose dancing career had been ended by a skiing accident, raced one and purchased it in 1930. Jannine Jennky drove a Type 35B to victory in the Coupe de Bourgogne four hours race in 1928. Anne-Cécile Rose-Itier won a series of events in her Type 37 and a Type 51. Aniela d'Elern raced a Type 35 in 1929, and later Kay Petre drove a Type 35 in competition at Brooklands, as did Eileen Ellison. More recently Julia de Baldanza, a celebrated modern-era female racing driver, has described her Type 35B (chassis #4965): 'The car has everything. It is so perfect in every way, and I can see equine influences in it.'[3]

The Bugatti Trust's Curator is Angela Hucke, who comes from a well-known Bugatti family and drove her father Uwe's Bugattis in races, rallies and events all over the world. She has described driving the Type 35 as 'incomparable' and 'wonderful'.[4]

A Type 37 in road touring 'rain' specification. There's a lot of canvas going on there!

This Swiss-registered car looks long, low and powerful as its owners launch it into the rain.

Two of the most vital examples of the Bugatti Type 35 series captured on the terrace at Prescott with their innards exposed. The pale blue car is chassis #4604, a Type 39 Grand Prix 1500cc supercharged (one of ten), sympathetically refurbished to its original state for owner David Hands by Crosthwaite & Gardiner, Tula Precision (Charles Knill-Jones) and Richard Scaldwell. It raced in the 1925 Italian Grand Prix and by 1926 resided in Australia, where it became a well-known race car. The red car is GNE 801, an ex-works Type 35C known as 'Genie', more recently owned by Peter Rae.

The pale blue Type 39 YN 1369 shows off its originality and a rare walnut steering wheel. Beside it is the red supercharged Type 35C (chassis #4423), 'Genie', the sale of which helped fund the setting up of The Bugatti Trust in the late 1980s.

(199.78km/h) at Brooklands. This car was more recently owned and raced by a well-known Bugattiste J. Majzub.

Another British Bugattiste was Richard Ormonde Shuttleworth, who won the Brighton Speed trial in a Type 51 in 1931: he also won various hill climbs and races in Bugattis including his Type 35B and a Type 51; perhaps Shuttleworth's highest profile race was victory at Donnington Park in 1935. Today the renowned Shuttleworth Collection provides a wonderful tribute to his life and passions.

RED NOT BLUE

Great Type 35s still race and are still driven as tourers. One noted car that has significant originality is the red Type 35C registered as GNE 801 and known as 'Genie'. This was the car whose sale provided funds for the establishment of The Bugatti Trust, the world-leading repository of Bugatti artefacts, learning and knowledge transfer that is based at Prescott alongside the Bugatti Owners' Club.

'Genie', wearing the correct period red paint, is original, unmolested and has not been denuded of its patina or its story. Thankfully, it has not been made 'perfect'. This car was a Bugatti works car of 1991cc supercharged and the spare team car, chassis #4423 (originally 4899 but over-stamped by the factory in one of Bugatti's typical adjustments). Genie holds the class hill-climb record at Prescott and is still used on public roads despite being worth millions. It competed in a Grand Prix class race in Italy, but was then sold to Count Carlo Felice Trossi, who entered it in late-1920s hill climbs. In private ownership it then gravitated to Jack Lemon Burton, team director of Scuderia Lemon Burton, who brought it to London in 1938.

He sold the car on to Alan Kershaw Haworth of Rochdale, who added 40,000 trouble-free miles (64,370km) from 1946. GNE 801 was then sold to John Bentley. More recently it has been owned by Peter Rae, who ensured its safe keeping and as near-original condition as essential maintenance allows amid its utterly authentic originality.

FURTHER VARIATIONS ON THE TYPE 35 THEME

Type 51 2.3-litre, 8-cylinder supercharged

The Type 51, which looks a little like a Type 35 on steroids, was the result of Jean Bugatti finally managing to persuade Ettore to 'tweak' various aspects of the original Type 35 grand prix specification car's engineering.

Jean was initially permitted to modify the new Bugatti 5.3-litre engine by fitting a new cylinder block of Miller-type design that had inclined angle overhead valves operated by twin camshafts. This engine was used in the Type 50 and might be said to be derived from the Type 46S (supercharged). A reduced stroke was also applied and the piston diameter increased from 81mm to 86mm.

From such developments came a modified 2.0-litre twin-cam as the Type 51. A new engine block with a gear-train driving the camshafts at the front, yet cleverly grafted onto the crankcase and camshaft vertical drive. This was a 2.0-litre engine, although a 2.3-litre version was also developed. Other detail changes included: differences in the manifold and the magneto positions; the drives had to be changed relative to the camshaft's drive positions; a supercharger 'blower' exit hole was added to the bonnet cowl; and identifying twin filler caps for the fuel tanks, something that had already been incorporated on the last of the Type 35Bs. A revised type of alloy wheel design with fixed rims also helped in identifying a Type 51. Larger brake drums were fitted.

The Type 51 (latterly the Type 51A) had great speed, torque and ability for a few brief years until rivals came to fit much larger engines. It was a very competitive grand prix car capable of at least 200km/h (125mph) on a sustained and consistent basis. On the road its performance was devastating as it ate up the miles. Oil pressure and gearbox maintenance were the usual Bugatti issues that had to be monitored.

This first Type 51 came out in 1931 and were distributed to chosen drivers: Louis Chiron, Achille Varzi and Francis Curzon, 5th Earl Howe, each received one. Varzi's was delivered first and he soon won the 1931 Tunis Grand Prix at Carthage in the car. Varzi had a second Type 51 delivered later in the year, in which he won again at Tunis in 1932. Chiron won the Monaco Grand Prix in his Type 51. This car was subsequently owned by the Swiss collector Charles Renaud, who later established the Fondation Renaud. Fitzroy Somerset, 5th Lord Raglan, owned a dark red Type 51 and competed with it across numerous events, including taking the car to Thailand in 1989. He also competed in the 1983 Grand Prix Historique de Monaco meeting for Bugattis that Uwe Hucke had organised. This has been described by Raglan's co-driver in that event, Sir John Venables-Llewelyn, who took his Type 35, as one of the 'most memorable events ever'.[5]

In 2023 Edmund Burgess set a new record at Prescott in his Type 51 with a time of 51.3 seconds.

The Type 51 was the first Bugatti Grand Prix car to be powered by the Miller-influenced Bugatti engine with specially shaped cylinder head chambers. The revised 8-cylinder engine block had twin overhead camshafts and some internal differences. It was of 'monobloc' type with roller-bearing crank and rods, and two inclined valves per cylinder. Further variations were made to create the Type 51A with the power increased to 150hp.

Type 43 2.3-litre, 8-cylinder supercharged

This was as an extended wheelbase sports-tourer variant of the Type 35B. It had a modified crankcase, but the engine was otherwise similar. The car had revised chassis longerons and a larger cabin with extra seats.

Type 45

Only two examples of this Type 35 variant were built. Its engine employed certain aspects of Bugatti aero-engine design inherent within its road-car application as a monobloc 16-cylinder, twin-supercharged engine with roller crank bearings, yet with plain big-end bearings. Problems in adequately lubricating and cooling the gear-coupling of the two cranks became apparent. Without any competition success, this application was effectively a rare technical failure for Bugatti.[6]

Type 54 4.9-litre supercharged

A further variation of the original Type 35 base design with a larger engine. In 1931 a 4.9-litre engine from the Type 50

A Type 51 on the go with Edmund Burgess letting it rip at Prescott. More raw Bugatti power made the Type 51 a bit of a beast.

Colin Bullock's dark blue Type 51 seen at rest on the terrace at Prescott. Note the twin fillers and mudguards.

A Type 54 with its 4.9-litre supercharged howler of an engine exposed.

Removing the Type 54's bonnet reveals the sheer brilliance of the design and the supercharged straight-8.

was fitted in a Type 45 chassis that incorporated body shaping. This made for a real 'beast' of a Bugatti, whose engine power and delivery at the wheels was probably too much for inexperienced drivers. As a supercharged 4.9-litre the car went like the clappers and could easily slither off a circuit or road. Such was the car's acceleration that the driver and co-pilot's faces would pucker under the g-force and wind speed encountered!

The Type 54 only won one race, the Internationales Avusrennen in Berlin in 1933, although it achieved placings in others, but this might have been pushing the base origins of the car too far. The Type 54 was a Type 35, grown up into a Type 45 frame, then using Type 51 experience to make the 'ultimate' Type 54 design, which manifested as a lower, wider and much more powerful Bugatti racing car. Bugatti's old, redeployed suspension and axle design was far too rigid for the dynamics of delivering such power as torque. As a result it was fast – in a straight line.

Five Type 54s were made. See one in action and you will know why it was a successful failure.

COLOURS

Ettore Bugatti mixed his own colours to his own chemical formulas. His famous house/team colour of blue was not French Racing Blue, nor a turquoise-tinted sky blue. Photographs can be misleading in colour due to the effect of strong sunlight causing both original-era and modern cars to fade. There are also photographic limitations. Restorers and modellers can consult web forums (for example www.bugattibuilder.com) to access information about mixing the correct specific blue hue. A slightly darker shade of bright blue that is sometimes seen is Garter Blue, as used on the Gresley A4 Pacific Class locomotive, which may be connected as Gresley and Bugatti were friends.

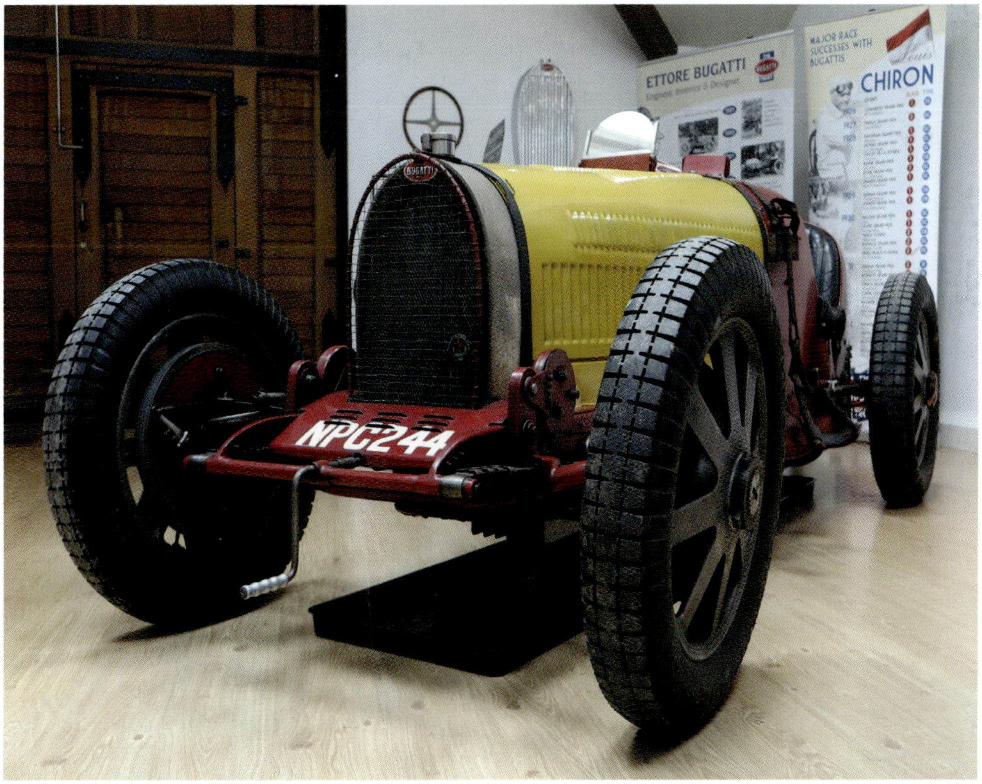

The Louis Chiron 1932 Type 51 chassis #51146, seen at The Bugatti Trust. Driven by Chiron, who was known as the 'Silver Fox', this car won several races, including the 1932 Grand Prix de Dieppe. The car was brought to England by Jack Lemon Burton and owned and raced by him for some years. Post-war owners included K.W. Bear, J. Fry, C.S. Henderson, F. Wall, J. Richards, D. Heimann, Dean Butler and Terry Cardy.

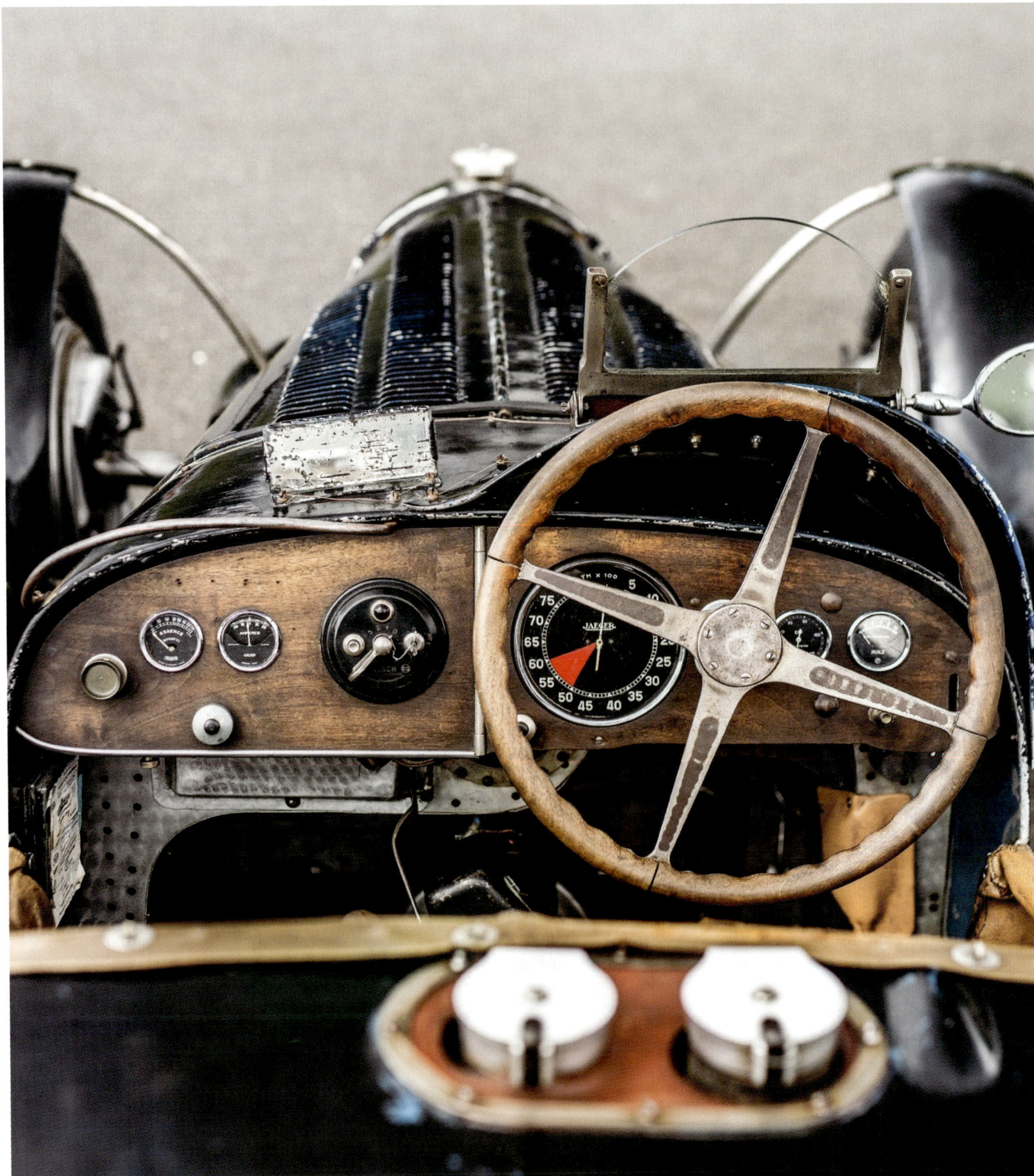

The pure originality of the 'King Leopold' Type 59 3.3-litre needs no introduction for the Bugattiste. This car won the 1934 Belgian Grand Prix with René Dreyfus at the wheel. Other names to have driven it included Robert Benoist, Jean-Pierre Wimille and King Leopold of Belgium. The car is now safely in the custody of the Pearl Collection.

CHAPTER 4

TANKS, TYPES AND TOURS DE FORCE

The British Royal Air Force might be responsible for the fact that the original drawings and build sheet specifications for the later Bugatti 'Tank' models are missing, or that just one example of the Tank was found bruised and battered after the RAF had bombed the Bugatti factory at Bordeaux in World War II. The Allied forces who arrived in late August 1944 are subsequently said to have burned wood at the factory to keep warm. Did they know they were burning Bugatti car components and jigs? Somehow, however, other Bugatti treasures were to survive the war at the Bugatti family chateau at Ermenonville, north-east of Paris, even though the estate was commandeered by the Germans in 1941.

The three examples of the Type 57G Tank that were seen in the mid-1930s display not just Bugatti brilliance, but a view into the future of car design, styling and aerodynamics.

Before this version of the 'Tank', however, there had been a precursor, an earlier 'Tank' known as the Type 32 Tank, effectively a Tank MkI, as opposed to the 1930s Tank Mk2 that was the Type 57G Tank.

TANK OR TRAIN?

The Bugatti Type 32 or Tank MkI, one of the most vital examples of Ettore Bugatti's workaholic brainpower, was created from all the Brescia design developments in the early 1920s. That it shared some brainspace with Ettore's later railcars in terms of its body design just adds to the allure of Bugatti design. Ettore's 'Tank' Type 32-dedicated racing cars and his railway rolling stock both drew on similar revolutionary thought.

Some have argued that the aero-weapon of a racing car dreamed up by Bugatti, known as the Tank in reference to its high bow and slab-sided appearance, was perhaps inspired by the works of Gabriel and Charles Voisin, who had successfully transitioned from early aircraft design and manufacture into designing and building cars. Notable among these was Gabriel Voisin and André Lefèbvre's low-fronted, high-tailed, wedge-shaped (and flat-bottomed) aerodynamic Laboratoire racing car design of 1922, which ran in many races from 1923.

Bugatti's own such aero-racer, the Type 32 was another huge step in the brand's reputation, yet in body design terms it was the aerodynamic *opposite* of the Voisin's shape, so the claim that Ettore 'cribbed' the idea from the Voisin Laboratoire is clearly nonsense. Bugatti had reversed the aerodynamically ideal Voisin low-front/high-tail design, by creating a high-nosed, chamfered lobe body design that ran through to a low, narrowing curved tail and rear end.

Although the Bugatti Tank design had some advantages from the standpoint of frontal airflow penetration, its reducing tail shape actually created lift (whereas the alternative Voisin tail design beneficially reduced lift), and did not provide a stable, consistent airflow separation point. The suggested truth is that Bugatti's design was argued to be better aerodynamically at the front but worse at the vital rear, where lift and drag were evident to a greater degree than in the Voisin design. Perhaps we should not be too hard on Ettore Bugatti as these were the early days of road vehicle and aviation aerodynamics.

The Tank's wheels were covered with metal discs to reduce the airflow disturbance normally associated with

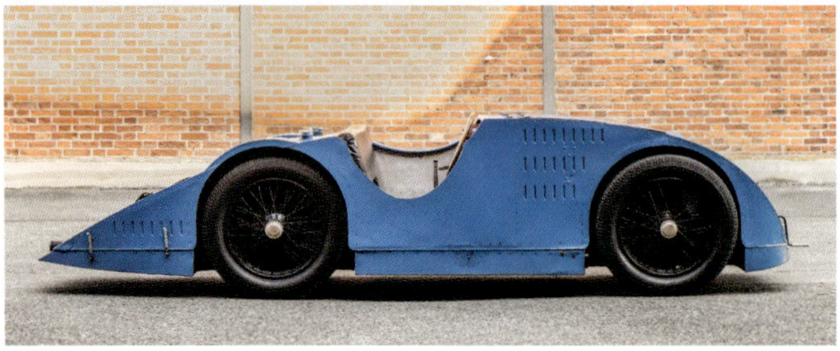

The radical 'teardrop' profile of the Type 32 'Tank' MkI aerodynamic racer marked the beginning of the era of the 'Aerodyne'.

Since there was no inner structure inside the hull of the Tank MkI, the driver sat exposed to the chassis and the engine.

wire or spoked wheels, just as they were on the Voisin Laboratoire.

The Tank used the Bugatti 2-litre straight-8 of just under 100hp and was set low, very close to the ground in order to follow the theory of airflow, as then understood. The handful of cars were constructed at Molsheim and never saw a wind tunnel as no full-size facility of the type was known to Bugatti. Quite correctly he did not trust the 'scale' effect of small-scale wind tunnels on small-scale test shapes. The key point, however, is that the Tanks were the first fully enclosed, all-enveloping 'pontoon' design-style bodies built at Molsheim. No mudguards or wings were used and all four wheels were set within the body 'shell' or its carapace, perhaps making the Tanks look more like a beetle than a tank.

The Tank or Type 32 used low-line underslung axles and the all-round quarter-elliptic suspension spring points were inclined in Bugatti fashion.

Tank on the go: the short wheelbase and lift generated off the rear body made it somewhat 'twitchy'.

ROULEAUX AND RACING

A 'standard' Bugatti engine, if such a thing exists, deployed roller-bearings to the crankshaft and connecting rods (although sometimes to the former but not the latter). Well known for using roller-bearing crankshafts (and connecting rods) in several of his engine designs, the allure of the exquisitely engineered roller-type reached its reputational zenith in the Type 35. Long before then, however, in his early designs Ettore had focused on refining the art of the crankshaft and connecting rod design, specifically of the *rouleaux* type. It would appear that he always intended the Type 30 to be Bugatti's first volume production 8-cylinder touring car, equipped with this type of engine technology.

First seen in 1920 and fitted to the prototype Type 28, this 'rectilinear' straight-8 engine set the style for all subsequent Bugatti engines. It evolved into a 2-litre engine with a single overhead camshaft and three valves per cylinder for use in the production Bugatti Types 29 and 30 after 1922. Here lay the origins of the Type 35's 8-cylinder engine.

Various 'roller' applications were applied to machined parts of the engine across the years of its development, covering three, then four or even five main bearings, all expertly cast, machined and profiled roller parts. The evolution of the roller fetish began with the Type 13/Brescia and the Type 13/27 multi-valve engine (16 valves) variation for racing car engine development – even if some these engines had lubrication that was riskily un-pressurised.

This was prior to the 1924 debut of the Type 35 as a racer at the Grand Prix de l'Automobile Club de France (ACF). The first competition use of an 'experimental' ball-bearing equipped Bugatti engine is thought to have been in a Type 13 at Brescia, as reported in the 17 September 1921 *Autocar* by W.F. Bradley, who was reputedly well connected in Bugatti inner circles. H.G. Conway and others, however, later questioned the changes to the engine cited by Bradley, given the magnitude of their implications. Although modified, the engine used at Brescia by all the Bugatti team entries at that race seems unlikely to have been the full three main 'roller' Type design as later defined. Research by Conway and The Bugatti Trust, citing evidence from Pierre Marco, one of the cars' pilots, suggests that these 'experimental' engine modifications were a stepping stone by having two main crankshaft rollers and one plain main bearing, and that the connecting rods had rollers.

Three main roller bearings would require changes to the engine's dimensions and casting, as were later adopted. But it should be noted that not all Bugatti production or racing engines were to be of the roller or *rouleaux* type.

There were engine failures to follow and some trouble with these expensively created components, but this is how it was that Ettore experimented with mix-and-match roller parts. He designed out the earlier spectre of bearing failure and went on to develop his 'roller' Type engines, improved the lubrication and reached the heights of his engine design and specification. Engines of such design were to be seen in the Types 35, 39, 43 and 51

As for the racing Type 32 Tanks, they used roller bearing conrods (big ends) like the Type 35, but these were of normal split construction.[1]

Of note in the first Type 32 Tank, the gearbox was at the rear due to the lack of engine-bay space, resulting in almost a form of transaxle configuration. The gear shift stick was *centrally* configured, which was rare at the time when most were located to the right side of the cockpit (or externally to the right side). The Tank had both cable brakes (rear) and hydraulic brakes (front), a curious design that for once displayed a moment of enlightenment.

A lightweight body with no internal baffles or bulkheads meant that the Tank had an all-up empty weight of under 750kg (as did the Voisin *Laboratoire*). Four Type 32 Tanks were built (chassis #4057 to #4060) and raced; a further final chassis number #4061 was retained by the Bugatti factory.

Having an ultra-short wheelbase and with ever-increasing high-speed lift off the rear end made the Tanks very twitchy. It took real courage to push them to high speed on a poor road surface that could launch the car and driver/riding mechanic airborne at any moment.

Bugatti first went racing with the Tank in 1922, but its profile was raised when Bugatti financier and driver Pierre de Vizcaya piloted chassis #4057 in the Bol d'Or in May 1923. Drivers Ernest Friderich, Prince de Cystria and Pierre Marco then drove the Tanks at Tours in the 1923 Grand Prix de l'ACF. Two crashed out on the rough surfaces. Since the Tanks were hard to hold steady at high speed, this failure was not entirely due to the road surface, but Friderich finished third.

That Grand Prix was to be the main event at which the Tanks competed, but it was clear that although much had been learned in design terms, fundamental mistakes had been made. The Tanks, however, had an interesting fate. One was sold off and raced by a privateer in 1924. It is recorded that de Vizcaya purchased the prototype Tank (#4057), and chassis #4059 was sold to no less a figure than Čeněk Junek and his soon to be famous wife Eliška Junková, only for the car to be later traded in at Bugatti for an early Type 35. The Junek Tank, however, won a hill climb, its only outing.

Parts from the ex-Friderich Junek Tank reappeared in the 1970s and were restored to form part of a restoration/recreation that added many further original Molsheim parts and some other items that were specially created. This is the car that was further restored by Pietro Ratti in Italy in the 1990s.

The other two Tanks, #4058 and #4060, have unclear fates but we do know that de Vizcaya crashed #4058 in practice for the 1923 Tour de France, so that car may have been written off. The last chassis number Tank #4061 was retained and eventually found its way to the museum at Molsheim.

Bugatti influence touched British engineering beyond cars. The railway locomotive designer Sir Nigel Gresley was friends with Ettore Bugatti and visited him in Paris. It is thought that Gresley's A4 Pacific Class streamliner locomotives of the mid-1930s were influenced by the design of the 1920s Type 32 Tank and the early 1930s Bugatti railcars. This is especially apparent when A4 4468 *Mallard* is seen in Garter Blue paint.

The Tank in action at a major French race about 1923.

TYPE 57G: THE 'MK2' TANK

In 1936 Bugatti launched the Tank Mk2 in the form of three Type 57G Tank cars with aerodynamic bodywork draped over the standard, road-going Type 57 chassis and engine. This was a second bite at the aerodynamic apple. After the short run of 3.3-litre Type 59 racing cars, the Bugatti racing team needed something else for its next step. It also needed to save money, which, as often at Molsheim, was being spent.

Enter the Type 57G (or Type 57 'S' Tank), an unsupercharged racing 'aero-weapon' with a fully enclosed, 'pontoon' body that brought aerodynamics to the fore. The three cars were built to develop the aerodynamics of the bodywork and the mounting of the engine. The three Type 57G Tanks competed in the 1936 French Grand Prix at Montlhéry. One of them, with Jean-Pierre Wimille and Raymond Sommer at the helm, won the race. Subsequent victories and a clutch of Class C racing records surely confirmed the essential correctness of this car's combination of engine and 'aero'. Winning the 1937 Le Mans 24 hour race proved the point for the Type 57G Tank as driven by Wimille and Robert Benoist.

In 1937 a single, developed Type 57G Tank had significant changes to the shape of the body and used the new, more powerful 4.5-litre engine variation known as the Type 50B, which was reputed to produce over 400hp. It was effectively a Bugatti aero-engine in all but its initial application and by 1938 was indeed cited with the Bugatti aircraft project. This revised 1937 Tank carried the nomenclature of Type 57S. It was intended to run in the 1937 French Grand Prix, but Ettore withdrew the cars for external reasons, not least a clash with racing officialdom.

From such chassis and engine developments came the single-seat Type 59/50B development car (see Chapter 7).

In the closing days of the 1930s, one of the Type 57G Tanks would receive bodywork modifications and the addition of a supercharger to make the Type 57G 'C' Tank: a 'compressor' car. This was to become the 1939 Le Mans winner: Ettore had saved money by not entering the 1938 Le Mans race, having won the previous year, and proved his point in 1939.

We might wonder if Bugatti's 1930s aerodynamic railcar body shapes were reverse-engineered from the form and profile of the original 1920s Type 32 Tank, and then forwards engineered into the Type 57G Tank 'Mk2' cars, particularly their frontal design. A visual comparison suggests an easy answer to such conjecture.[2]

DESIGN

Jean Bugatti is generally credited with much of the early 1930s body design work at Molsheim. We should, however, also mention his in-house designer/draughtsman, Joseph Walter, and the contribution of Antonio Pichetto to Bugatti design, not least to the Type 57G Tank. Archive materials at The Bugatti Trust clearly show Pichetto's early design sketches for the Type 57G Tank's all-enveloping body design. Jean Bugatti had been inspired by a racing car design by Pichetto's colleague at FIAT, Giulio Cesare Cappa, and it led to Cappa and Pichetto both dealing with Bugatti at Molsheim. Their input influenced the body design of the Bugatti Type 53, one of the first four-wheel-drive racing car designs ever seen. Only three examples were made. The car was noteworthy for its transmission design featuring couplings, universally jointed hubs, a form of limited slip differential and a special gearbox mechanism. Its bodywork, however, was hardly revolutionary.

Each of the three Type 57G Tanks was subtly different, notably in the front end 'aero' treatment related to cooling the air input. There were also variations in the thickness of the metal for the body skin and in the localised chassis engineering, resulting in differences in weight and nose-profile airflow behaviour.

Tanks were slab-sided and had simple curvatures in their body forms, primarily because the metal used was magnesium or duralumin alloy, which are more brittle than aluminium alloy and therefore presented restrictions when forming and shaping curves and compound forms. Nonetheless, magnesium panels were preferred for the Tanks' body skinning and also underneath in their formers and some frames. The remaining original Tank (the Simeone Foundation car) even used magnesium alloy for its large scuttle panel. Rivets were

The Type 57-based Tank Mk2 was a more rational body design of one-piece or 'pontoon' style. This one is seen on the lawn at Monterey.

the preferred Bugatti method for joining panels, even on the front nose and rear tail sections where magnesium and aluminium panels adjoined.

In 1936 who cared if magnesium might burn, this was a race car not a grand tourer.

If it had not been for the enforced stagnation in car production brought about by World War II, as opposed to the rapid advances made in aviation design, the great leap forwards that these expensive and rare Type 57G Tanks represented might have filtered down more quickly into mainstream car design practices and production cars. As it was, Bugatti's Type 57G Tank lost its chance to be seen for what it was, something truly stunning and actually an early definition of what we later termed the 'supercar'.

The so-called great advances of the jet-age styling era that General Motors and Ford 'invented' for their late 1950s American GT tourers and roadsters seem to echo the Type 57G Tank design and styling. Even the sculptural styling introduced from the late 1940s onwards by Stabilimenti Pinin Farina of Turin, later known as Pininfarina, was in its balance and purity of form redolent of these mid-1930s Tank Bugattis – and their original innovation.

QUESTIONS?

Which chassis formed the basis of later Tank Types? Were they built on a Bugatti 'gondola' frame chassis or on a Type 57, shortened Type 57S frames, or a blend of bits in true Bugatti style?

Evidence from The Bugatti Trust archives shows that the Type 57S that morphed into the Type 57G Tank used a drilled, lightened and modified (or *Modifié*) chassis with unique new aspects to its form. A rear axle passing through the chassis cradle was hardly a surprise on a Bugatti, of course, but it seems that all three of the 1930s Tanks used such a modified chassis configuration that was not just a shortened version of the long chassis as previously used, which was a theory promulgated by several Bugatti commentators over the years.

Three of these wonderfully sculpted aerodynamic Type 57G cars were created. One was the car in which Jean Bugatti died when it crashed on a public road. Another (#57335) is owned by the Simeone Foundation in Philadelphia. Further details of the other car's history will be found in Chapter 5. It was dismantled, yet its recycled or upcycled Type 57G Tank chassis, which had been raced in 1936, can be found in the W.S. 'Bill' Turnbull car as chassis #57503 or 'DUL 351', the Type 57S that became a Corsica-bodied Tourer yet was originally built in 1937. This famous *surbaisse* (lowered) car is now known to have been built on a drilled chassis that was one of the two modified Grand Prix types.[3] This car has massive appeal as a road-going car and not simply a museum exhibit.

The Type 57G Tank was a one-piece bolide like its predecessor of the 1920s, but it was also elegant, sculpted and highly advanced: the 1937 revision as a Type 57S 45 had further body shape developments incorporated, while the 1939

Colin Bullock at the wheel of the 1931 Type 43 chassis #43295, an ex-Bernard Kain car that is being driven as intended.

This Type 30 chassis, #4048, owned by Mike and Sue Raahauge, was one of the first built, invoiced for 24 May 1923 to Carosserie Moderne of Strasbourg. It is a rare and authentic Bugatti.

A Type 49 in racing blue hastens along in a memory of all that a Bugatti supercar should be.

Tank variation took the aerodynamic body design theories a further step.

The 'Tank' story, notably in its final Type 57G design and revisions, is yet another example of Bugatti futurism and genius. That it would later influence other marques' cars should not be forgotten.

A NEW ERA: SPORT, TO GRAND SPORT AND GRAND TOURER

The Tank was a tool for racing, but where was Bugatti going? Was it making racing cars that could also be sold as road cars for road use? If it was, that was indeed a very limited market. Bugatti needed to make money, and it needed to expand its design and driving appeal. A start was made in creating the Type 40 as the baseline 'tourer' car, from which would evolve the grand touring context – or *grand routière* – by way of several clever stages through sports cars and on to grand touring cars. However, we might think that Ettore went a bit over the top with the bipolar character of the sumptuous, all-or-nothing Bugatti Royale.

So it was that Bugatti created cars as stepping stones to larger, more capable, more comfortable, yet still exquisitely driving cars that performed. From these cars came the true supercars of their era. They are generally classified as the 'Tourers' (Type 30, Type 40, Type 44) in their initial iterations, and then as the 'Grand Sport' cars (Type 38, Type 43, Type 55), and finally as the defining 'Grand Touring' cars, such as the Type 41 Royale, the Type 46, the Type 50 and,

TYPE 40 FIACRE CABRIOLET

In 1928 Jean Ettore created a car for his sister Lidia, hence 'the Lidia Bugatti'. It was in fact his first full bodywork design. The Type 40 may have been the new 'entry level' Bugatti, but this one was rather special.

It used a Type 40 chassis with a supercharged 1500cc engine from a Type 37A and with a body based on old-fashioned design motif of a nineteenth-century horse-drawn carriage known as a fiacre. The heavy cabriolet woodwork, the chassis, the folding cabriolet roof, glazing and fully trimmed, leather-lined four-seat interior all meant that the car needed the supercharger to give it back some performance lost to that body weight.

The car remained with Lidia, who married François, Comte de Boigne in 1940, and the Bugatti family for 70 years. Later owned by Mrs Pat Preston and more recently by Julia de Baldanza, the well-known historic racing driver who has taken the car on a number of international rallies and also drove with the earlier Bugatti 'Queen' Eliška Junková. As can be seen in the accompanying images, the car is driven and not preserved in aspic.[4]

The famous 'Lidia' Type 40 built by Jean Bugatti for his sister in 'Fiacre' style.

The styling, however elegant, belonged to an earlier age. Jean Bugatti would soon step into the future.

The car remained with Lidia and the Bugatti family for 70 years. Its current owner, Julia de Baldanza, is seen here at the wheel.

Sidelights as you have never seen them since – forensic Bugatti 'design' on the Type 40 Fiacre.

ultimately, the Type 57. The numerical nomenclature, however, did not always follow chronology or logic.

The straight-8 Type 38 engine, developed from the Type 35A, made an early impression: this morphed into a supercharged Type 39 specification and then later became the Type 43 series design. Beneath that came the cheaper, more accessible Type 40.

THE TYPE 40S AND A RAKISH STYLE

A mark of the success of the Type 40's recipe was that in 1930 a Type 40, privately entered by its owner/driver, Odette Siko, and her co-driver Marguerite Mareuse, achieved a seventh place overall finish at Le Mans. The duo may not have been as famous as Hellé Nice or Eliška Junková, but they made their mark, as did the Type 40, which was easy to drive and brisk enough if stirred along, even though not a grand prix racer. Bugattistes tell the less than flattering story of the Type 40 being a 'cooking apple' Bugatti or worse – 'Ettore's Morris Cowley'. Yet the Type 40 did possess most of the essential ingredients of a Molsheim Bugatti, just being a little slower, which hardly made it a proletarian Bugatti!

Using the well-proven 1.5-litre engine (ex-Type 37), the Type 40 was a collection of parts from the Types 37 and 38, together with other items from the Molsheim parts-bin that seemed to include some Brescia-style shallow-channel chassis side longerons. Production began in the summer of 1926 and nearly 800 were built up to 1932. Main production ceased in 1931, but some modified cars (the Type 40A) were built later. Along the way, various engine and bodywork options were enacted across the Type 40 series, notably a more substantial, reinforced chassis that would become standard specification. The Type 40 was offered with an American-style roadster body. It also became a Grand Sport-bodied factory model with upgraded specification and even a larger engine. The Type 40 used the 'standard' 4-cylinder, 5-bearing crank engine, but the Type 40A had twin plugs per cylinder allied to a twin-spark distributor.[4]

Géo Ham, the famous automotive and aeronautical artist of the 1920s, drove a Type 40 Grand Sport. The Type 40 coupé created for Lidia Bugatti by her brother Jean, featured here, is an interesting moment in Type 40 history.

TYPE 44 AND A FAUX CABRIO IN EXCEPTIONAL PRESERVATION

Bugatti's Type 44 came in various guises, variations and specifications; some Type 44s were low-slung or lean-looking racy cars, others were upright, stolid saloons of very conservative

This incredibly original and unmolested 1928 Type 44 emerged from decades of storage in France in 2022 and now resides in England.

design. The choice was down to the customer and the carrosserie that they chose to clothe their new Bugatti chassis.

Curiously, a few of the models of the Type 40 series were built with the accelerator in the middle-pedal position, a configuration soon outmoded by the pedal layout we accept today as normal. Having to remember that the brake was the accelerator and vice versa must have required concentration.

First launched in 1927 and using the 8-cylinder twin-block single-camshaft, three valves per cylinder engine and various parts from earlier Bugattis, it replaced the Type 38 and offered more scope for factory and *carrossier* interpretation. Of note, the camshaft had plain bearings (not roller).

A revised and strengthened Type 38 chassis and, of course, the usual Bugatti semi-elliptics and quarter elliptics in the front and rear suspension, respectively, created a car with much potential and long-range grand touring ability. The Type 44 had revised shock absorbers and four-wheel cable-function braking with Dewandre Repusseau-type servo activation.

The supercar selected for attention here is a Type 44 with an interesting provenance and preserved in a remarkable, near-original condition that is evident to this day. The author has spent some time with the car and the owner, and seen it in action being driven with verve and style on challenging roads.

Having had a recent mechanical fettling by marque experts, this car drives with torque, pace and fine handling, and demonstrated this during its first-ever visit to Prescott and the home of the Bugatti Owners' Club in 2023.

The car is a 1928 Faux Cabriolet by Carrosserie Maison de Labourdette (of 104 avenue des Champs Elysées, Paris) and is at the time of writing owned by Yushan Ng, the internationally known legal expert who also drives a lovely new Renault Alpine. Mr Ng's recently purchased Bugatti was sold at auction by Artcurial in 2022 and has to be one of the most exceptionally preserved, most authentic and near-original condition Bugattis on the road today. Money cannot put a price on such originality, especially in a world of 'pebble bleached' Bugattis that have been stripped of their history and psychometry.

'It's my first Bugatti,' said Mr Ng to Angela Hucke, Curator of The Bugatti Trust when he proudly took it to Prescott and ran it up the famous hill-climb track in 2023.

The Type 44 Faux Cabriolet by Carrosserie Maison de Labourdette is hustled along by its new owner Yushan Ng after receiving many admiring glances at Prescott.

Frontal detail of one of the world's most original Bugattis, which must be rising in value by the day.

The Labourdette badges are original and still attached.

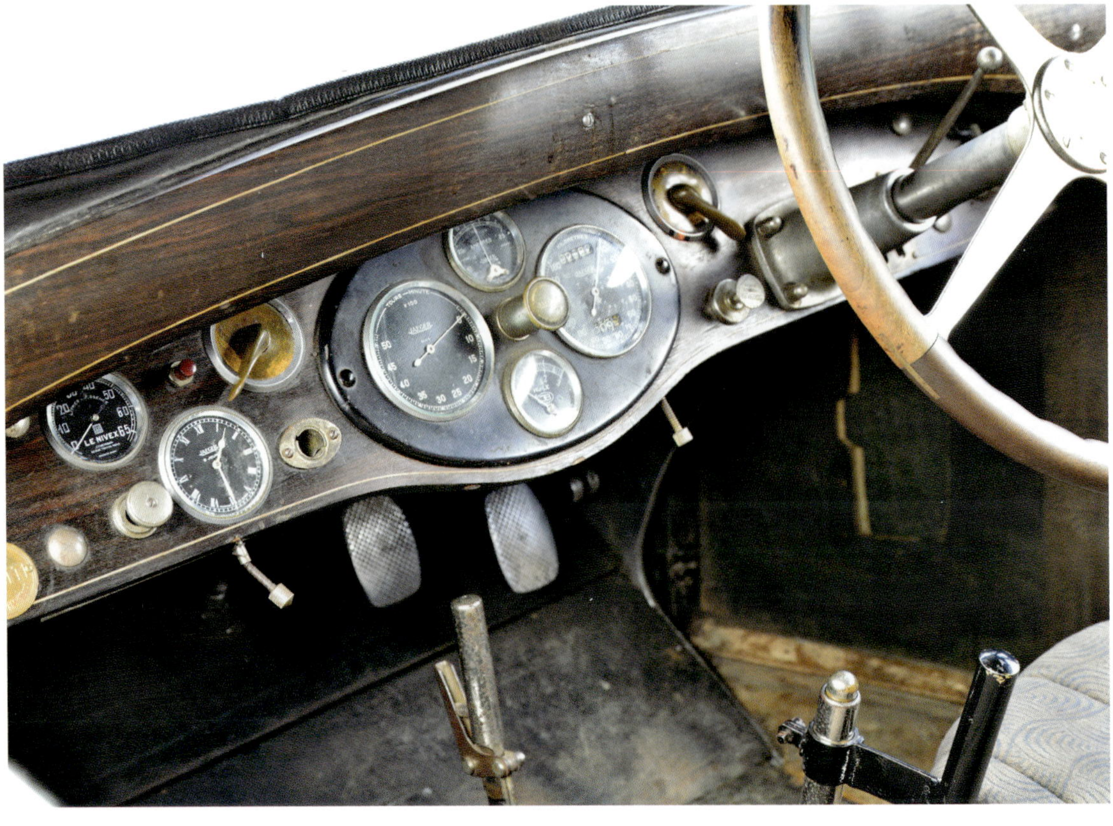

The interior of the 1928 Type 44 is as authentic as its exterior.

'What a first Bugatti to have!' was Angela's reply as she admired the sheer delight of the car's stunning originality and its exceptional preservation, which reeks of Bugatti, patina, psychometry and the love shown by a family who had owned it before. Where else in the world were you going to just happen to bump into an original, un-ruined example of absolute purism? It is possible, but it would take some travelling.

Chassis #44342 with the 3-litre engine (engine No. 76) was built in late 1928 at Molsheim just before the 1929 global financial crash. As such, the car sat around unsold for many months but emerged from factory storage as the 1930s dawned and was fitted with a racy faux-cabriolet two-door body design replete with chromed side arms that were purely decorative. The Labourdette body was fabric covered, except for the wings and front body being in steel: the Labourdette number for the car was 4140.

It seems that in 1934 the car was sold by the father of Louis Trintignant, who had died in a crash in his Bugatti Type 35C during a practice lap for the 1933 Grand Prix de Picardie. The subsequent long-term owner was a M. D. Gros from Cavaillon, whose initials can be seen on the car's doors. After the war the engine developed a fault and the car was put into storage decades ago. After his daughter inherited the car her husband tried unsuccessfully to fix the engine.

In 2010 the collector Bruno Lafourcade secured the car from the Gros family heirs. The internal and mechanical parts were restored by Laurent Rondini at Ventoux Moteurs Ingénierie, while leaving untouched the true patina and utter originality of the body, trims and, above all, the interior. The original factory seat covers were protected, however, with suitably empathetic new slipovers. The dashboard or *tableau d'abord* is replete with all the original instrumentation including the Jaeger rev counter.

Looking somewhat American 'gangster-esque' with its long, low, narrow-glazed look, the car has become known as the 'Buick of Molsheim'. Seeing it in action is very rewarding as the car runs with mechanical perfection, the correct sound, lots of compression and resultant torque, and it seems to steer and ride very accurately. Certainly it negotiated sweeping 'S' bends in the Cotwolds with style and pinpoint ability and easily went to high revs and fourth gear sweetness. The four-wheel drum brakes, however, might require a touch of forethought.

But above all was the sight, sound, smell and sheer authenticity of its body and interior, like being in a time-warp. It might not be blue, nor overtly racy, but this is a long-distance Bugatti GT supercar and the very essence of what a Bugatti of this Type was supposed to be.

TYPE 46

Following on from the Type 44s came the Type 46, most of which were fitted with the single-block 5.4-litre (5359cc) 8-cylinder engine and a three-speed transmission. Produced from 1929 to 1932, the Type 46 used lots of leftovers and modified parts from the Type 41 Royale project, hence the sobriquet *La Petite Royale*. Compared to the Royale, the Type 46's wheelbase was nearly 90cm (3ft) shorter, with smaller overhangs at front and rear.

Early Type 46 engines had the single-spark plugs design, but twin-sparking plugs were later standardised in the head.

Unlike the short-run Royale, of which only six were sold, the Type 46 (with various body designs) sold to 465 customers, if you include the eighteen with the supercharged later Type 46S specification. Early Type 46s had wire wheels, but later cars had something more exquisite in terms of spokes. Available in two-door, four-door, saloon (Berline), coupé and tourer bodywork, the key coachbuilders that offered bodies to the Type 46 included Corsica, Weymann, Van Vooren, Grummer, Ottin, Gangloff and, of course, the Bugatti factory itself.

Rarer Type 46 offerings came from the Belgian D'Ieteren coachbuilders (who would later body Porsches) and very exceptionally from the Dutch Veth & Zoon coachwork supplier, which had held a warrant since 1914 to provide coachwork for the Dutch royal family's cars.

The Type 46 was large and powerful, yet also low and had excellent roadholding abilities. As *Motor* said in 1930, the Type 46 'combines the luxury of a large limousine, the perfect flexibility and top gear performance of a thoroughbred low carriage with the perfect roadholding, the speed and acceleration for the best Type of sports model'.[5]

Arguably the most interesting Type 46 would be the late-model Type 46 *Profilée* fixed-head coupé, designed by Jean Bugatti, which featured an innovative design to the highly swept windscreen and A-pillar. Swept back at a 'fast' angle that was not seen on other production cars, this radical feature gave the car a unique Bugatti design feature that was to be repeated in a second iteration of the design feature as a Type 50 *Profilée*. That car, however, lacked a new Jean Bugatti design idea in the form of an extended swept and curved fast-back rear body shape (with twin rear windows), which was then applied to a Type 50 *Profilée* variation exhibited at the 1932 Paris Salon. Few can doubt that this developed rear body design must be seen as a precursor to Jean's later Type 57 Atlantic design.

The later Type 57 two-door Ventoux with *Profilée* swept windscreen lacked the swept and curved fastback rear body shape.

TYPE 49

Prior to the Type 50, and distinctly separate from the Type 46 of the same era, Bugatti had created the Type 49, which replaced the Type 44 and was to prove popular in England with coachwork by Weymann and James Young. Other coachbuilders, not least the Molsheim factory, produced Type 49s with somewhat transatlantic-inspired body styling. A Gangloff-bodied Type 49 even came with certain design elements clearly borrowed from then current American styling motifs.

The 3.3-litre Type 49 was the last of the single-overhead camshaft-engined Bugattis. With twin-spark plug (per cylinder) mechanism and changes to bore and stroke, the addition of a larger cooling fan, as well as modifications to the gearbox and drivetrain, created a car that was smooth to drive and well-mannered at low speed and at touring velocity. As such the Type 49 was popular and perceived as a supercar within its own context. A total of 470 Type 49s were built up to late 1932, of which 127 were bodied by Gangloff of Colmar.

TYPE 41 ROYALE: THE FIRST HYPERCAR?

The terms 'supercar' and 'hypercar' are flexible definitions often limited to modern or very recent cars in the age of digitisation and a computer-driven complacency, but as we know, such cars have long existed. Yet across the era of the car there have been cars of stunning, advanced and exquisite engineering and design that have set the course along the highway of the great first century of the automobile.

The Bugatti Type 41 or 'Royale' must surely top the list of such over-the-top cars of its era and perhaps beyond, cars in which everything about them is heightened to the level of design fetish. Did this car actually reveal the level of Ettore's aspirations or was it just the madness of exquisite design talent taken as far as could then be achieved? The answer is probably both.

We might argue that more recently the Bugatti Veyron accurately echoed such elements of the supercar into hypercar story. Before that happened there was Bugatti, and there was the Bugatti Royale.

As far back as 1913 Ettore Bugatti had dreamt of designing and building a large, powerful and, above all, impressive car of grand status, to be sold to people of grand wealth. Even back then he was thinking of a big engine with no less than 8 cylinders. In Ettore's own words it should be a 'car beyond any criticism'.[6]

His confidence then was astounding. Bugatti was going to exceed even Rolls-Royce in terms of engineering and style. In fact, the final Bugatti Royale chassis #41141 was offered for sale from the factory at the 1932 London Olympia Motor Show at a cost of over £6,500, twice the price of the most expensive Rolls-Royce of the day and enough to buy several very large country estates.

Within fifteen years of his first thoughts for a range-topping car, Ettore had set down and enacted his plans for what was then his greatest car, with the largest engine in both size and capacity, the model that became the Royale,

Bugatti and the Royale: not a monster, but definitely a leviathan.

which was announced in 1926 and a reality in 1927. The Royale must be seen as the greatest display of Ettore's talent and also his ego. It was beyond normal thinking, and intriguingly looked across the Atlantic Ocean to the dawning of the new era of American automotive confidence and excess for its own philosophy and new concepts.

The engine design of Royale was described in *Autocar* on 11 June 1926 as 'The Golden Bug'. A straight-8 of 14,726cc lay behind the headline. When finalised it was de-rated to just under 14 litres. The engine design derived from a French Government-funded aero-engine of around 15 litres. Although the project was to be stillborn, it led in de-rated capacity form to Bugatti's sensational engine for the equally inspired Type 41 Royale. It would also later power the Bugatti railcars in two variants of configuration.

The car's name was said to be inspired by King Alfonso XIII of Spain, who expressed an interest in purchasing such a car. Ever the showman of extravagance, Ettore tagged the car project 'Royale' perhaps as a way of pandering to the king, while the King of Romania and King Farouk of Egypt also hinted at interest in the car. Some members of the British royal family drove Daimlers, but getting a Bugatti into royal hands must have appealed to Ettore.

Originally intended to be a massive 15-litre device, the Royale that emerged had a slightly smaller capacity of 12,763cc, but nothing about the car's grand design was de-rated: it *truly* was a fantastic or amazing car. In terms of supercar design it would be true to say that the Royale was both elaborate and extravagant. Depending on the body type chosen, the Royale could seat six, seven or even nine adult passengers.

The single block engine on its own weighed 349kg (770lb) and the crankshaft a massive 97kg (220lb). The chassis was hardly lightweight either. Depending on the body fitted, the Royales weighed about 2,750kg (6,062lb). The Royale was a 2.75-tonne goliath, yet the drum brakes were cable operated and had no servo assistance.

The engine employed both cast iron and alloy construction, the cylinders being a special Bugatti-specified aluminium alloy. Bugatti's design for the three-speed transmission system was notable because it was effectively a trans-axle type configuration with the gearbox situated aft of the engine and not integral to it, with the alloy-housed clutch mechanism being aligned midway between the two. A separate crawler-gear function was provided. A 'long' high-speed touring ratio was a de facto overdrive. For the most part the Royale would remain in second gear.

At their deepest, the Royale's chassis members were 25cm (10in) in section. The mountings of the front semi-elliptic suspension members and rear quarter-elliptic suspension were integral to the chassis design and construction and its ability to carry their loadings and dynamics respectively. The front-axle was essentially a scaled-up Bugatti grand prix type design, being solid-forged and bored out from end to end, but then metal-worked and with the insertion of solid forged outer ends to create a hollow centre section but solid-ended axle of great strength.

So large and heavy was the Royale that the Rapson-type four-ply tyres were specially designed and created to cope with the weight and tread and the sidewall loads imposed. A highlight was the new single-cast Bugatti-design alloy wheels, which featured a finned circumference design and integral brake drum mountings. Even the brake rods used roller bearings and also incorporated a self-limiting device to reduce wear. The finned edges around the wheel centre were aerodynamically tuned to a helix-corkscrew shape with constant angle profiles to direct airflow beneficially and cool the brakes.

With double-ignition by magneto (coil/accumulator), two spark plugs per cylinder in a three-valve per cylinder head, a cooled exhaust valve, balance weights on the massive crankshaft and connecting rods, and with twin carburettors mounted on one side of the engine and the impressive exhaust manifold mounted on the other, this was design brilliance. An extra braking mechanism was built into the transmission at the clutch drive shaft to assist the engine-braking effect.[7]

From special finishes, expensive alloys, over-engineering and an exquisite cabin, the Royale went far beyond even the excesses of, for example, a grand Voisin or a massive Packard as contemporaries. It might be argued that the Royale was too big for fast driving on tight rural French roads and was a true *grand routière* express car in its own genre.

On the bonnet, a Rembrandt Bugatti sculpture of an elephant rampant signalled the very special nature of the Royale as it approached. If that did not work, the purchase price of the Royale would. Just to add to the arrogance of the car, no sales brochure was provided, since it seems the Royale was beyond such common things. If you have to ask the price, please don't apply, could well have been Ettore's mantra.

Of the six elephant mascots featured on the Royale cars, only three cars used an original casting. So three Royales were solely originally fitted with the famous Rembrandt Bugatti elephant sculpture. Later, crudely cast and rather rough copies or 'fakes' were seen on other Royales. In the 1970s, the Bugatti Owners Club secured the damaged

The accurate facia or dashboard of the Royale (replica), somewhat *grande* and very *luxe*. Walnut wood and whale bone featured in the original; this one is an accurate replica of the Packard-bodied prototype that was built upon the original car's long discarded chassis.

Inside the former Schlumpf collection at the Cité de l'Automobile museum there lies this exquisite Royale, chassis #41100, now known as the Coupé Napoleon, which has had several bodies in its life. Re-bodies and out-of-sequence chassis number chronology seem designed to confuse the Bugatti student. Throw in accurate replicas, the Wheatcroft car, and less-than-accurate replicas, and the Royale story gets confused: six became seven then nine and more.

Jean Bugatti posing with the earlier-bodied Esders-type car. The scale of the thing is obvious.

elephant mascot from the crashed Weymann-bodied Royale and intended to repair it, and cast a series of copies. Somehow the original went missing.

Royale chassis #41100 had an original casting, but Schlumpf removed it in the 1970s. Chassis #41111, the original Esders car, was fitted with a 'real' elephant casting – the original casting.

The later copies appear to be gold finished but are not. However, the 'real' original casting made by the Valsuani foundry, was silver-plated over bronze and as such was smoother than the rather rough-hewn later 'gold'-finish copies. As for the stories of using rubies for the originally cast elephant's eyes, and the copies using paint, time may reveal more.

TYPE 41 ROYALE: OVERVIEW OF CHASSIS AND BODY/RE-BODY RECORDS

Note: Six chassis, one rebuild and eleven fitted bodies in total.

No. 1: chassis #41100: The prototype with 'bought-in' American-built Packard body fitted to the Bugatti chassis. Chassis soon to be re-bodied with a series of one-off bodies as follows:

No. 1A: Special experimental or concept bodies were fitted to the prototype chassis after the Packard body had been removed.

No. 1B: The bizarre 'Coupé' was a short-cropped 'stagecoach' cabin two-door body designed at Molsheim and next fitted to chassis #41100.

It was then re-bodied with an elegant 'concept' body built by Weymann of Paris. It was later crashed by Ettore and re-bodied using the same original chassis number on a renewed frame, which left the original damaged chassis extant and more recently cited as used in a 'replica'.

The next body mounted upon the original repaired car was the Coupé Napoléon (or *Sedanca de Ville*), designed and built at Molsheim, signalling more involvement in body design by Jean.

No. 2: chassis #41111: The second official chassis and first customer car to be sold. For some time it wore a stunning body designed by Jean Bugatti and built at Molsheim for the client purchaser Armand Esders. This was the 'Esders Royale', which was itself later re-bodied about 1938 as detailed below:

No. 2A: The next body to be fitted to chassis #41111 after removal of the Esders body turned the car into a Coupé de Ville designed and built by Henry Binder of Paris.

No. 3: chassis #41121: A drophead/cabriolet Coupé designed and built in late 1931 by Ludwig Weinberger of Munich for customer Dr Joseph Fuchs, who took it to the USA. It later passed to the collection of Henry Ford.

No. 4: chassis #41131: A four-door upright Limousine designed and built by Park Ward of London for customer Captain Cuthbert W. Foster for 1933 delivery. Its sumptuous yet restrained Edwardian-era style body aped Daimler design. Now on permanent display in the Musée National de l'Automobile in Mulhouse.

No. 5: chassis #41141: A two-door Coupé designed and built by Kellner of Paris, it was exhibited at the 1932 London Olympia Motor Show by L'Ébé Bugatti. It remained unsold in Bugatti family ownership until it was sold to Briggs Cunningham in 1950 and taken to the USA. Since 1987 it has been sold at least three times.

No. 6: chassis #41150: The final Royale was fitted with a four-door body of obvious Ettore Bugatti design motifs as a 'Berline de Voyage' Type. Owned initially by the Bugatti family, it too remained unsold after the war. It was bought by Briggs Cunningham in 1950 and was taken to the USA. Since then it has been sold several times, most recently to an anonymous European collector for an undisclosed amount.

It should be noted that Royale chassis numbers and dates are not chronologically or date consistent and vary due to numerous factors. The change of body, and chassis alterations, to more than one Royale has confused many recorders to date.

Ettore envisaged a short production run of built-to-order cars, perhaps up to 25, but only six were manufactured. Ettore threw most of what he knew at the Royale at huge cost, and the result remains something almost incredible upon the stage of supercar motoring.

TYPE 50, FROM LA ROUTE TO LE MANS

A Type 50 with the advanced and streamlined Jean Bugatti-penned *Profilée* Type body design was just one later aspect of the Type 50 story from 1930 to 1934, which produced a wide, even bizarre, range of ancient and modern in terms of body design over an interesting new engine type. The Type 50 could be had as a late-1920s style roadster, a grand saloon or as a sleek, low-set *Profilée* coupé looking towards the next age of design. But was it a grand touring car or actually a vehicle designed to enable engine development that was intended to re-establish Bugatti as a force to be reckoned with in the new 1930s era of motor racing?

Underpinning the Type 50 was an engine design that was supercharged from the outset. In the Type 50 we find a twin-cam, grand luxe of a car that could be had to suit the various categories of supercar description. Curiously, the Type 50 was designed and launched at the height of the 1929–30 global economic crisis, which had slowed down the sales of expensive cars. The only British buyer at the time for such a large and powerful car was the industrialist and baronet Sir Robert Bird. It is said that Bugatti's London agent, Colonel W.L. Sorel, did not think that the average driver could handle a Type 50.

The Type 50, in typical Bugatti fashion, repurposed existing parts such as the chassis and drivetrain. The 5.3-litre engine of the Type 46 series (specifically the Type 46S) was replaced by an engine of new design and lower capacity. Without getting into the minutiae of why certain Type 50s have shorter or longer chassis than others, we can say that the Type 50 offered an intriguing range of specifications and configurations beyond the basis of that engine. The drivetrain, notably, was of semi-transaxle configuration, inspired by the Royale.

With a capacity of 4972cc, the straight-8 had a plain bearing crankshaft (nine bearings). The Type 50 took new steps for Bugatti, with the marque's first application of twin overhead camshafts and of inclined-angle, rather than vertical, valves in a big Bugatti engine. Complexity was taken as read – you had to take the engine out and disassemble it to get to the valves – due to the fixed cylinder-head construction of a massive cast-iron one-piece block of great depth. Aluminium alloy covered not just the head but the entire engine right to the bottom. It was a work of Bugatti art, yet one designed to deceive the eye of the beholder. Even the sump box was artistically 'alloyed'.

This meant that servicing the valves, which was a regular task on engines of the era, was a complex and labour-expensive procedure, typical of Ettore.

Taking a cue for the design of the American, Miller-type engine, no doubt at the urging of Jean Bugatti, Ettore took the plunge and in doing so created a new series of large Bugatti engines. Aping the hemispherical-head design

Mike Preston at the wheel of the stunning Type 50, one of only 40 short-wheelbase Type 50s. DAR 349 was the fourth Type 50 to go to Le Mans, this time as a privately entered car.

in the cylinder heads and using inclined valves allied to a more finessed bore and stroke ratio led to an engine that 'breathed' better and was more dynamically efficient. A very expensive oil pump shaft-drive mechanism with bevels, gears and shafts also increased the engine's lubricity, which used to be a Bugatti issue.

A similar mechanism was used to drive the engine's supercharger off the front of the engine. At a heady 4,000rpm this engine pumped out nearly 200bhp. Torque was key to the engine's performance as transferred to the road.

The later Type 53 four-wheel drive of 1932 and the Type 54 Grand Prix cars used the earlier 'standard' Type 50 engine, but with a touch more power added, 275bhp being rumoured for short, one-off races. The Type 53 was an early experiment into four-wheel drive and predated many subsequent series production types using the four-wheel-drive mechanism, let alone its use in a racing car context. Ettore had the idea after dismissing early research into front-wheel drive by Alvis and Citroën. The Type 53, however, was reputedly the first four-wheel-drive racing car.

Only three examples of the Type 53 were built. Although successful at hill climbs, including the La Turbie event in 1932, the 4.9-litre car was rather long and large, and not as nimble as a Type 35 or a Type 51. Jean Bugatti crashed his Type 53 at Shelsley Walsh; this is believed to be the car later restored by Uwe Hucke.

Dreyfus broke the La Turbie record in a Type 53 in 1934, but the Type 53 had unresolved issues in its drivetrain and suffered from torque-steer, which was both exhausting and potentially difficult for the driver to tame. The new Bugatti practice of having the (three-shaft) gearbox mounted at mid-point in the chassis and connected by forward and rearward propeller-drive shafts was a Type 53 feature.

The Type 53 had twin upper and lower transverse leaf suspension at the front. With 300bhp on tap, and no torque balancing couplings or constant velocity joints, the car was a handful that ultimately diverted Bugatti's time and money.

Back with the Type 50, its engine was further developed with a light alloy crankcase and other changes into the type 50B engine, as used in Bugatti's later racers, not least the Wimille Type 59/50B car.

Beyond its engine, much of the Type 50's engineering running gear, from clutch to gearbox, to brakes and suspension, were 'paid for' carry-overs of existing toolings from the Type 46 series.

The Type 50's chassis was stiff with traditional Bugatti I-section outer side rails and tubed and box-section cross-members. Beyond that engine and the fact that it was then the fastest Bugatti money could buy for the road, interest

Bugatti supercars are for driving and Type 50 DAR 349 is seen hustling up Prescott with an enthusiastic load.

This Type 50 simply reeks of original Bugatti excellence. Bentley enthusiasts are invited to look away now.

in the Type 50 lay in the array of differing body styles with which the car could be ordered.

Coachbuilders went to town with the Type 50 series. From open roadster, to fixed head cabriolet, to sober saloon or a touring convertible, the big new Bugatti of 1930 could be very effectively tailored to the buyer's requirements to bring out the best in its power, handling, speed and sheer presence. One perhaps bizarre coachwork choice for a Type 50 was the Weymann of Paris-bodied two-door car with a hybrid Coupé and Fiacre style design that was finished with imitation canework. Sixty-five Type 50s (of various body fitments) were built in total.

Many Type 50s were bodied by Bugatti at Molsheim or by Gangloff down the road at Colmar, but the usual coachbuilder suspects included James Young, Freestone & Webb,

Gaston Grümmer, Graber, Kellner, Paul Nee, Schumann, Vanvooren and, unusually, by Antonin Tomáŝ of Prague, who built a very elegant Type 50 open tourer and several others.

Jean Bugatti, just 30 years old as deliveries of the Type 50 began, explored his styling ideas with the Type 50, but arguably not as definitely as he did with the Type 55 body design. There can be little doubt that styling influences from the dawn of the American industrial design movement, such as low-roofed coupés or 'coops', were evident in some of Jean's Type 50 body ideas. Yet Jean also came up with what many argue is his most perfect, most integrated European-looking design: the full, fastbacked Mk2 *Profileé* coupé, albeit with the two-tone graphical paint scheme that was part of the American design language as seen on a Duesenberg, the company that had previously built Bugatti engines.

Type 50s equipped with open touring bodies and looking somewhat like a Bentley formed a Type 50 racing trio that took on the greats in Europe, entering Le Mans in 1931 and 1933–5: a fourth Type 50 would go to Le Mans in 1935 as a private entry (see below).

The quality of the Type 50's engine enabled Bugatti to send a works team to Le Mans for the first time in nearly a decade. In 1931 the Type 50s went to the Sarthe and ran at Le Mans. The cars were piloted by Louis Chiron/Achille Varzi, Albert Divo/Guy Bourait and Count Caberto Conelli/Maurice Rost. Following issues with the tyres (Michelins rather than the earlier Dunlops), problems manifested in the race when Rost crashed due to tyre failure.

Rost survived (he did not race again) but spectators were killed and injured and the Bugatti team withdrew from the race. Yet the Type 50s returned to Le Mans in 1933, 1934 and 1935, taking some top ten places. However, it would be 1937 before a Bugatti (a Type 57G Tank) would win Le Mans.

The Type 50 chassis #50143, which is registered as DAR 349 and featured in the accompanying photographs, is one of those cars and has a gripping history and authenticity. Only two of these four cars remain. DAR 349, which is still driven regularly on public roads, is one of only 40 short-wheelbase Type 50s. It was the fourth Type 50 to go to Le Mans, but as a private entry car. First owned by Antoine Schumann, the car was sold to Richard Delavau who, with help from Maurice Rost, brought the car up to Le Mans specification for entry in 1935 with revised axle ratios, twin racing carburettors and magneto ignition. The co-driver was Jacques de Valance de Minardière, who crashed the car in practice.

The car was subsequently imported to England by Jack Lemon Burton, and later owned by Jack Crowther, Kenneth Bear, Stafford East, Ann 'Mouse' Davis and the Preston family, with whom the car remains today and is used for full enjoyment as well as to go up Prescott Hill. The car wears its wonderful cast-alloy wheels, similar to those on Royales, and short-bodied authenticity in a superb manner.[8]

As this Type 50 powers away, we can see the 'Royale' type alloy wheel mounted on the boot.

TYPE 54 AND OLDŘICH UHLÍK'S BUGATTI SUPERCAR

This series, introduced in 1931 and equipped with the powerful 8-cylinder, 4972cc, double overhead camshaft, twin-carb and supercharged engine of the Type 50, provided well-heeled buyers of a larger Bugatti with some interesting cars. The short-lived, high-powered Type 54 Grand Prix Racer design did, in its limited numbers, become the true 'beast' of a dedicated Bugatti racing car. But there was more you could do with its larger engine and chassis.

Among the rarer highlights were the cars bodied by Czechoslovak coachbuilders, notably the Uhlík-designed and built body on a Type 54 Grand Prix racing specification chassis, which was the first of the type delivered to a client.

Today, after having been 'restored' in another form, it wears an original and provenanced body by Oldřich Uhlík (1888–1964), but the provenance of the chassis is, shall we say, debated. However, in its time it has been owned by Zdeněk Pohl and later by the esteemed Bugattiste Uwe Hucke.

In the 1930s Oldřich Uhlík was a famed *karozar* (carrossier) in the Strašnice district of Prague, who had a list of wealthy and aristocratic clients for his coachbuilding business and drove a Bugatti himself.

Contrary to certain sources, Oldřich Uhlík was not a 'small' or insignificant coachbuilder and he certainly knew Jean Bugatti well: he spoke French and visited both Paris and Molsheim. Uhlík employed over 100 workers in his business. Alongside Josef Sodomka, Uhlík achieved fame providing bodies (often of 'streamliner' design) for all the top 1930s marques, including Bugatti, Mercedes-Benz, Imperia and Tatra. Uhlík also designed one-off bodies for cars including MG, Rolls-Royce, Lancia and an Isotta-Fraschini. He also worked with Parisian carrossiers and clearly had huge talent.

In 1948, just before the Communist Party took total control of the country, Uhlík was negotiating a car-body building contract with Donald Healey; the deal was to be stillborn, but one Uhlík-designed Healey body was built. Tragically, Uhlík was persecuted by the Communist regime and his final years were spent in some distress. In the 1930s, however he was a major figure in central European car design and certainly not the 'small' coachbuilder so grievously cited by the Mullin Automotive Museum in its Bugatti display information.

Uhlík had trained with the respected Czech company of Laurin & Klement. One of his first customers after starting his own business was the famous Bugatti racer Eliška Junková-Khásová, often better known as Elisabeth Junek.

The Type 54 has a very interesting and complex history. It was originally a 1931-built Type 54 Grand Prix-bodied racer purchased by Prince Jiří Kristián Lobkowicz through the Czech Bugatti dealer in order to race on the celebrated AVUSrennen race circuit in Berlin in 1932.

Tragically Lobkowicz suffered a fatal crash in the race. The wreckage was sold to Zdeněk Pohl and returned to the factory for repair and rebuild using the usual confusing Molsheim practice of incorporating new or nearly new parts, even of a chassis (here suggested as being from chassis #54201), but keeping the *original* chassis number. Rebuilt as a Type 54 Grand Prix with a racing body, the car proved a handful for Pohl, who decided to have it converted to a road specification roadster. The stunning new body was designed and built by Uhlík who, it is reputed, liaised with Jean Bugatti over the design, which included extravagant flowing side wings (originally with raised metal seams, as employed by Jean Bugatti for the Type 57 Atlantic), which have now sadly been discarded from the Uhlík body, as well as other hints of later Bugatti bodies from Jean's pen.

The history of the chassis number is that the damaged chassis became a restored Type 54 Grand Prix-bodied car, and the Uhlík re-body on a new factory chassis became an 'original' Bugatti that had a non-matching number following its multi-layered provenance of rebuild and re-body. Purchased and exported to England by Peter Hampton in 1970, the Uhlík-bodied car was to be somewhat controversially modified in the 1970s by its owner. The Uhlík body was removed and sold to Skip Berg in the USA, only to be later mated to another chassis (via Uwe Hucke). Meanwhile the original underpinnings of the car were rebodied as a Type 54 Grand Prix racer.

The Bugatti Owners' Club then gave the Uhlík-bodied car an official chassis nomenclature of BC-70.

Peter Mullin's Type 54 'resto' with Oldřich Uhlík's Bugatti supercar body design and a 4.9-litre under the bonnet: a car with an interesting history.

You would expect nothing less than dashboard delight on this Type 54.

Reputedly, two versions of cars as chassis #54201 existed, and one of them was DNA linked to chassis #54202! The actual bodywork (as opposed to chassis frame) count was by now three and it is possible that a further version of the Grand Prix body 'replica' was mounted on the ex-Hampton chassis.

As with certain other Bugatti chassis, body (and engine) combinations, the story gets complex when the intricacies of original chassis, old chassis and new chassis, and 'new' bodies are researched. Once again, more than one car has emerged in the story of this car's original chassis number using a new replacement chassis, and another variant using the once-damaged original chassis, and thence for its body to be sold off and subsequently re-chassised. Confused? Bugatti lore is marked by such quandaries; it is a minefield for the researcher.

To surmise, through several subsequent owners and a highly complex story, this Uhlík-bodied beauty entered the ownership of the Mullin brothers. 'Restored', it is now in the Mullin Automotive Museum in California. The complex story of the stunning work of Uhlík's body design has been laid out by the suitably well-informed Miloslav Plášil, who knew Zdeněk Pohl, in an article for the *Bugatti Revue* that does not hold back on his opinions.

Peter Mullin's Uhlík-bodied car *is* therefore allegedly a true Bugatti, but does not match its original factory numbered components. But it is not alone in such a condition – think of the 'Itier' car and the 'creations' by Peter Hampton and others. As can be seen in the accompanying photos, the Uhlík car has been 'restored', although whether it has been 'over-restored' is a matter of opinion. Whatever your view, it's a beautiful Bugatti supercar and a mark of Oldřich Uhlík's true talent as a Czech car designer. There is also a twist in the tale: Prince Lobkowicz had another Bugatti, a road-going Type 46 chassis #46409, which he had modified because the entrance way to his castle was too narrow to be able to open the car's doors. He had Uhlík modify the doors from a hinged outward opening to what may be the first use of sliding doors on a car, making it probably the only Bugatti with sliding doors.[9]

Oldřich Uhlík also bodied other Bugattis. One, based on a Type 43 chassis, had an American, Art Deco-inspired coupé design with extravagant chromed decorative strakes on the nose, which looked as if they could have come straight off an American railway locomotive. This feature was potentially about twenty years ahead of later American 1950s car design.

TYPE 55: JEAN BUGATTI AT THE LEADING EDGE

If it was the new twin-cam engine being tested in 1931 that set Jean Bugatti thinking, he was not only thinking about engines or a new era of sports Bugattis. For within the story of the Type 55 there may lie arguably Jean's greatest moments of artistic triumph: the bodies of the Type 55 roadster and, perhaps with even more confidence, the Fixed-Head Coupé (FHC) design.

Jean's Type 55 roadster and fixed-head coupé designs rank among the finest of his handiwork. Yellow and black was Ettore's favourite livery.

As a result of the downturn in sales that came with the global recession of 1929–31, a great deal of parts-bin kit was littered around the Molsheim factory. This included fully built but unused chassis, engines and gearboxes and various stocks of expensive components, such as brakes, hubs, axles, suspensions, interiors and trims. In fact this comprised most of what had not been used across the range of Types 40, 43, 46, 47, 50 and 54, all of it hand-crafted and hand-wrought in the Bugatti metalworks using very expensive machinery and tools. Could a use be found for the parts?

A new 'Super Sport' prototype was born from thinking about, and tinkering with, these parts. Making up a 2.3-litre twin-cam engine of single-block straight-8 supercharged specification (effectively a retuned Type 51 Grand Prix car engine), using a modified ex-Type 47 chassis – in the twin-railed, increasing-depth parallel side-arm type frame – adding ideas from the former 16-cylinder project, a gearbox from a Type 49, and re-purposing key suspension bits, the Bugatti Type 55 was born. An Atmos-type fuel injector was fitted (operated via the dashboard controls) and connected directly into the manifold. A magneto control on the dash was standard Bugatti fare.

The gearbox was mounted aft of the engine bell housing in a hint of transaxle-type configuration. No doubt this aided stability and centre of dynamic fulcrum behaviours.

As a rolling chassis, it was, despite its parts-bin origins, state of the art because what had been in the parts bin had been so special.

Mounted upon this chassis was an open two-seater body of sublime proportions quietly and elegantly expressed in a body design that was totally integrated and wholly 'organic' in styling instead of a riot of compound curves or ellipses. Jean had created something radical yet restrained; a true masterpiece that was perhaps one of the most beautiful cars, not just of its era but of all time.

In 1931 here was a stunning car that could also reach 180km/h (112mph) with 5,000rpm and cruise at nearly 160km/h (100mph) with ease and sustain it. The new twin-cam engine was less likely to foul up its plugs than the needy octane-rich earlier big Bugatti engine. The engine pulled strongly from low revs and did not have a 'peaky' torque curve, unlike certain racing car engines.

The car was low, not least to the low-line chassis and a cranked front axle that 'dipped' in the middle to allow the engine to sit lower than normal with a dynamo mounted off the front of it. The low stance and centre of gravity gave great poise and handling too. Hartford-type shock absorbers ('Tele-control') aided the ride quality and could be adjusted from inside the car via cable mechanism. The 100-litre (22 gallon) fuel tank sitting at the rear between

The Type 55 in 'art deco' black and dark red looks classier in the opinion of many.

the 'dumb' ends of the chassis gave long range although the positioning might be a cause for concern, but that is where people put fuel tanks in those days.

Climbing inside the dainty FHC's cabin, however, was not easy for tall people.

Are the Jean Bugatti-designed and built factory Type 55 roadsters and FHC cars the most spectacular? We have to say yes, but external coachbuilders had a go at clothing the chassis too. Figoni & Falaschi and Weymann, both in Paris, made a pretty good job of it too, as did Vanvooren. Some people rate the Figoni-bodied Type 55 as equal or better than Jean's roadster, but these things are all opinions and should not be presented as fact.

Jean's design had flowing mudguards, perfectly matched curves, and a bonnet-to-roof A-pillar and 'hip' line that was utterly pure and perfect in the FHC hard-top version. Yet a hint of America and 1930s industrial design was obvious in their body shape and flamboyant two-tone paintwork design. The roadster was pure class, but the FHC hard top without a doubt came with a further hint of the American 'coop' low-rider look. The touch of Americana was not a copy or stolen from anything specific, it just had a touch of confidence and glamour missing from early 1930s European styling output.

Seen from the rear, Jean Bugatti's exceptional styling is obvious. This is Rupert Marks' Type 55.

The Type 55's dashboard and instrument cluster was another defining design moment for Bugatti.

The Grand Prix type polished alloy wheels, leather, wood and alloyed interior, chrome work and fittings just reeked of the most amazing piece of design.

The car drove wonderfully of course, even if the gearbox might be a bit thick when cold. The through-the-gears, mid-range acceleration was astounding, giving real overtaking prowess. The cable-operated brakes worked well, but then they were Bugatti brakes and not really up to hauling the car down from 185km/h (115mph).

First announced in late 1931 at the Paris Salon, 23 Type 55s were delivered in 1932. Production continued for nearly another three years. As usual with a big 1930s Bugatti, this car cost more to buy than a house in Mayfair, London. Was this car the perfect precursor to even wilder things such as the Type 57 Atalante and then the Atlantic? Probably, but it was perfect it in its own right.

TYPE 59

Intended as a final throw of the grand prix racer specification by Bugatti, and briefly a shooting star from 1934 to 1936, this car is sometimes cited as a Type 35 or Type 51 offshoot, yet the Type 59 was in fact different in chassis and body, not just a different engine, so it deserves to stand alone. Only the cylinder block was common to any other Bugatti. In the 1930s the Type 59 was known as the '3,300 Grand Prix', which said much. Most Bugatti Grand Prix type connoisseurs say that the Type 59 was far more of a leap in design terms from the Type 51 and Type 35 DNA than has generally been held. Park a Type 59 next to a Type 35 or a Type 51, and you will see just how very different this much lower-built car is: wider, longer and of a different scale to its ancestors.

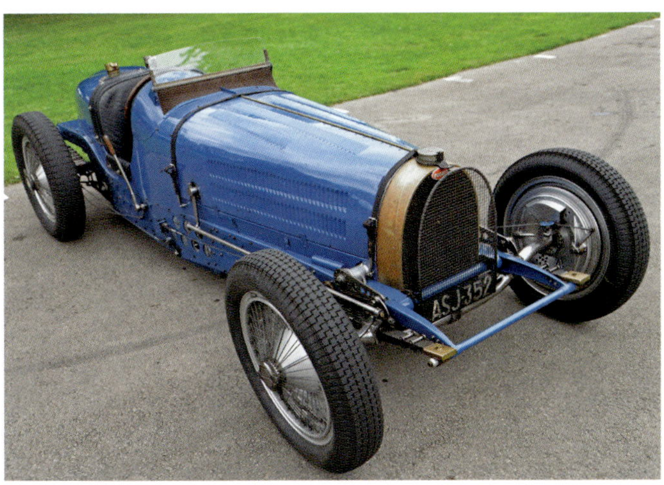

This Type 59 shows off the type's lower and wider stance compared to a Type 51 or Type 35. Of the handful that were built and remain, certain provenances apply. The rarest original car must be the King Leopold car, yet the most intriguing might be the so-called 'Benoist' 1945 Type 59/50B or S, which was also the Type 56/50B 'offset' car re-assembled and restored using original Bugatti parts, including those from the supply of Bugatti's last parts manager François Seyfried.

Very much a Jean Bugatti project and readied for late 1933, the Type 59 was therefore not a direct Type 35/Type 51 derivative, but a next step that was visually related to and of similar design thinking as the original Type 35 race car. Derived from a similar engine-type baseline as the Type 57 road cars that were then being developed, the Type 59 was only built in small numbers: originally only six were made but further factory chassis cars are mooted and a later car built from original parts is certainly well known. Experts still argue, citing the chassis frames and parts that have appeared, whether there were six, seven or nine Type 59s. Bugatti's attempt at a new, works racing team using the Type 59 remains shrouded in claim and counter-claim. The rise of Alfa Romeo's Tipo B racing car and the risk of German rivals from Mercedes-Benz and Auto Union had set Ettore thinking: the Type 59 in all its glory was his answer.

The Type 59 had a supercharger fitted to the 3.3-litre engine and yet relied on mechanical parts from an earlier generation, such as cable-operated brakes and a suspension design, all honed and set up for speed: one example owned by Francis Curzon, 5th Earl Howe, for example, lapped Brooklands at 222km/h (138mph). Such exploits

The same Tula-built Type 59, owned by Rupert Marks, seen from the stern, which is very boat-like. This is a squat and powerful car of huge power and torque. Note the 'spine' seam on the rear bodywork.

came after a disillusioned Ettore Bugatti had sold off his Type 59s to selected private owners, several of whom were British.

Before that happened, the Type 59 was the last Bugatti Grand Prix car offered for sale as a production car to privateer racers, public touring-spec drivers and those who thought they could handle it. The 1934 racing formula rules and weight limitation regulations lay behind this low, lighter 750kg (1,653lb) car, hence the drilled chassis frame and lightened body panels. Even the dashboard instrument display was kept to the minimum. The car cornered very well indeed due to its lower height, wider footprint and more focused component set-ups.

The Type 59 was a last blast at a racing car and road-legal high-performance device of minimalist design, echoing the Type 35 but actually wider and on a lower chassis, making it a different animal.

Beautiful yet brutal, this two-seater was a true early supercar. Initially built with a straight-8, 2.8-litre engine, which was replaced by the essential straight-8, multi-valve 3.3-litre, it was less of a handful than the 4.9-litre Type 54. The one-piece 8-cylinder block borrowed the Miller-inspired design elements relating to valve and cylinder head design, but added a clever valve operating mechanism rather like rockers or keys, which could be pivoted to operate very smoothly off the camshafts. This engine used six plain non-roller bearings for the crank and pressure-fed oil lubrication from a dry sump and twin oil pumps in an attempt to aid reliability in high-stress competitive applications. The supercharger was reversely rotated in comparison to its fitment in the same engine in the Type 57 cars (the carburettor was mounted higher) and the supercharger driven off a right-side gear drive; downdraught carburettors were fitted to the breathing and forced induction mechanism. The spark plugs were centrally configured in the cylinder head and sat within a steel shell.

The rated output was 230hp, which gave the car real ability and a high sustained top speed. Performance was sadly not reflected in the car's competition record.

Unusually, the drive or propeller shaft was lowered by use of a double reduction rear axle. This allowed the car's low stance, including for the twin-seat cabin accommodation. The usual outside-mounted gear lever still had its curious layout with both first and top gear engaged by shifting the lever forwards. Nearly all the Type 59s suffered from some form of transmission problem and Jean Bugatti had to come over to the Brixton Bugatti base in London to help resolve whatever it was that was plaguing the transmissions. The Type 59 gearbox was also often troublesome. Was the complicated double-reduction axle and propeller-shaft driveline the issue? There were rumours in the 1930s about re-designed parts to cure the issue.

The low chassis, which was not waisted and had a full-width spring base at the rear, was of new design but still used the Bugatti rear quarter-elliptics and leaf springs on the front suspension. Some rather nicely made front radius arms transferred torque back to the chassis, while also acting on the de Ram hydraulic friction shock absorber mechanisms. Ancient cable-type brakes still ruled!

The lightweight body was in aluminium alloy and of the usual forensic Bugatti detailing and beauty. Those unique and innovative Bugatti-patented wheels carried radial loads through radial spokes, but the drive torque (and retardation loads) went through the flanged and toothed mechanism circumferentially around the wheel's rim. A large cast built-up hub was heavy duty, but other wheel parts were lighter, such as the attached aluminium braking drum. There was a detachable wheel rim to allow for tyre fitting. Metal back plates added for stiffness, due to the light gauge wheel rim.[10]

The very clever wire and web wheel design of the Type 59.

Rupert Marks fettling the car's wonderful twin overhead cams, plain bearings and a dry sump set-up.

The sheer level of Bugatti engineering artistry is captured in this detail of the Type 59's front suspension and mounting design.

The 'King Leopold' Type 59 had an 'aero' nose cone. Its black and gold livery was unique for the type, although a Type 13 Brescia finished in Bugatti works black and with gold coachlines was reputed to have been created by B.S. Marshall in 1924.

The rear body or 'stern' featured a riveted central seam, perhaps hinting at the 'spine' on the Type 57 Atlantic that was to come.

Despite its beauty and brawn, the exquisitely engineered Type 59 was a stepping stone rather than a huge success. It was also a hybrid of Bugatti parts-bin items. Its abilities, not least those of the engine and structure, were somewhat hampered by the suspension and braking traditions of Ettore's 'old school' thinking. Despite a couple of grand prix victories, several podiums and placings, the Type 59 was not the dawn of a new era for the 'grand prix' type Bugatti nor its works team.

Jean-Pierre Wimille won the 1934 Monaco Grand Prix in a Type 59 and Robert Benoist won the 1935 Tunis Grand Prix in his. Wimille won again at Deauville in 1936. In 1937 Wimille won several other races in an unsupercharged Type 59, which was a curious and revealing feat in the face of ever-increasing competition. Wimille also won the prize of FFr400,000 at Montlhéry for lapping at an average speed of 146km/h (91mph). Benoist, Varzi and Piero Taruffi were among those who got their hands on a Type 59 in competition. Tazio Nuvolari, Dreyfus and Benoist drove Type 59s at Montlhéry in 1934.

The road/touring specification Type 59 that went to King Leopold of Belgium was a 'conversion' from a race specification car – one that has stood the test of time.

Numerous reports of Type 59s achieving over 241km/h (150mph) confirm the car's design efficacy. Many feel that given the correct servicing and fuel mixture, and the right top-gear ratio, a Type 59 might nudge 273km/h (170mph) on a suitable straight, although stopping might take some perseverance.

Wimille owned a personal 'Touring' Type 59, as did Earl Howe, and the cars were a stunning sight around the Brooklands banking: Howe's time around the Brooklands outer circuit track in his Type 59 made him the fourth fastest driver there ever. Tragically, the 9th Duke of Grafton died at the wheel of his Type 59 at the 1936 Limerick Grand Prix.

More recent Type 59 ownership luminaries have included Stafford East, Neil Corner and Ralph Lauren.

During the 1960s and 1970s Neil Corner was one of Britain's leading historic racing drivers. His highly competitive exploits in his Type 35B are well known, but he also owned a Type 57 chassis #59123 (the ex-Ronnie Symondson car, which may have been the one driven by Dreyfus) and a Type 59 (Earl Howe's Brooklands car, no less). Corner has driven, and owned, many of the greatest historic racing class cars and has publicly stated that in his view the Type 59 was the ultimate Grand Prix Bugatti. He last drove the Type 59 to victory in the Vintage Sports-Car Club's all-Bugatti race at Silverstone in 1986. Corner's son Nigel went on to race Bugattis and other cars.[11]

But was the Type 59, this limited-edition, pure racer-cum-touring beast, a true supercar as well as a true racer? In terms of design and performance, we must give it that accolade.

Long, low and squat like a hotrod, the Type 59 truly made its mark during the brief years of its racing life, which included appearances on the banking at Brooklands in the hands of British owners.

The rare and valuable Grand Raid Type 57 was first seen at the Paris Salon in 1936.

CHAPTER 5

TYPE 57: THE BIRTH OF THE 1930s SUPERCARS

If I was asked to give my opinion as to the best all-round super-sports car which is available on the market today, I should without hesitation whatever, say it was the 3.3 [Type 57] Bugatti. It is in a class by itself.
Sir Malcolm Campbell, *The Field,* 4 September 1937

Was the Type 57 the first true big grand touring or GT 'supercar' for the road, as opposed to the track? This car was not derived from a racer yet it is not without race driving DNA and all its resultant dynamics. It was so special that no less a figure than Sir Malcolm Campbell not only purchased one (chassis #57531), he also designed and built his own body for it, using Corsica-built coachwork, and called it Blue Bird, although by this stage he had switched his attention to water speed records.

However, if we recall that famous 1920s racing driver Woolf Barnato, one of the 'Bentley Boys' who had the bragging rights to driving Bentleys fast, and who not only financed Bentley and won Le Mans three times in a Bentley, did in fact order a Bugatti Type 57C, bodied by Gangloff, for his personal use in 1939, we might begin to gather just how much of a landmark car the Type 57 was. Given that Bentley and Bugatti were commercial and racing rivals (Ettore was rather rude about the heavy Bentleys), the one-time racer and chairman of Bentley buying a Bugatti Type 57 should not be underestimated.

Barnato drove his Type 57 hard on the supercharger and perhaps unsurprisingly the engine seized after just under 2,000 miles of hard charging use. As a friend of Ettore Bugatti, Barnato wanted the Type 57 repaired by the company, but the start of World War II prevented the car's repair once it was no longer possible to get parts from Molsheim. Barnato's daughter was the famous wartime Air Transport Auxiliary delivery pilot Diana, famed for her beauty, intelligence and ability to fly a Supermarine Spitfire better than almost anyone. Diana drove the Bugatti too, saying it was much nicer to drive than a heavy Bentley and she described Ettore as a 'charming man'.

Another example of the esteem in which Bugatti and the Type 57 were held was the Corsica-bodied Type 57S Tourer that was delivered new to Maurice Fox-Pitt Lubbock: a decade later, upon becoming Vice-Chairman of Rolls-Royce, he was reluctantly 'persuaded' to sell it by the Board.

The British Cholmondeley family were serial Bugatti owners and a rare one-off Type 57 with a four-door fastback coupé body by Figoni & Falaschi of Paris was commissioned by Sybil, Marchioness of Cholmondeley. Despite its free-standing front wings, the body and its rear end had shades of the design by Flaminio Bertoni of Citroën for a large car, the *Voiture à Grande Diffusion* (VGD) project, which developed from the Traction Avant to become the DS but was delayed by the 1939–45 conflict. There were also hints of the later styles found in 1950s Bentley and Bristol car offerings. Her husband, George, 5th Marquess of Cholmondeley, kept a Type 57 Atalante (*see* below).

A unique one-off Type 57 cabriolet three-seater design was bodied by the Belgian coachbuilder Albert D'Ieteren in 1938 and acquired in 1952 by the painter André Derain, who had owned fourteen Bugattis and had his Type 55 chassis #55227 converted to a unique lookalike Type 57 body style. Derain owned four 'real' Type 57s too.

The Shah of Persia drove a Figoni-inspired but Vanvooren-bodied Type 57 of outrageous design. Various European aristocrats, and the nouveau riche and the bourgeois also gravitated to Bugatti in the 1930s. Such was the world into which the Type 57 was born and upon which it made its mark.

The Type 57 was not just an engineering event and a driving delight, it was one of the earliest (if not the earliest) that met the definition of a 'supercar'. It defined a distinct automotive marque that represented a branding creation. Branding is not just a modern cliché, and the Bugattis were among the earliest brand creators.

Hundreds of Type 57s were built, which is more than you can say for some of the even more esoteric French or Italian exotics of the 1930s. This car was the stepping stone away from the design of the Type 46 and earlier Bugatti *grand routière* vehicles and onwards to a new dawn in Bugatti design and driving.

In the Type 57 lay the true 'GT' supercar of its age and era. Some of its technical details, such as the suspension and brakes, might have been later eclipsed by certain competitors, but as an overall package it surely was a significant and defining car, a true early supercar.

The Type 57 has to be the origin of the exotically engineered superlative car or supercar. Yet paradoxically is it, at least in part, an ultimate development of a 1920s ethos, rather than a near-1940s new era of engineering? Is it, in an appropriate aviation analogy, an equivalent to the chassis-based, frame and girder Hawker Hurricane (essentially a biplane with the top wing chopped off and a new engine installed), rather than a 'new-age' alloy-monocoque, stressed-skin, self-supporting, all-in-one Supermarine Spitfire, super sleek and expensive to build and repair?

Or is the Type 57 a bit of both, straddling two worlds, two eras, as many think it does?

In the words of a leading Bugatti authority, 'Only a fool would dismiss or ignore the Type 57 in the history of the supercar'. Indeed, for the Type 57 (or the Types 57 in their various iterations) represents not just advanced thinking, they also capture the spirit of Bugatti – via Ettore and, of note, through his son Jean.

As Bugatti expert Hugh Conway Snr stated: 'The Type 57 was the most celebrated non-racing car that Bugatti ever produced.'

Yet somehow the Type 57 was more than that, a pioneer of automotive design, engineering and driving. The car was a real landmark, not a clichéd icon, and it was created by a son (Jean) channelling the influence of his father (Ettore).

JEAN'S HAND

Jean Bugatti, born in Cologne, Germany, in January 1909, was officially Gianoberto Maria Carlo, but became known worldwide as Jean. Clearly none of these names were German despite his birthplace. Jean became immersed in his father's company and his design philosophy and language. He would emerge from around 1930 as its future leader, yet his career, and his impact upon the marque, never reached its full fruition owing to his early death in 1939 in a road accident.

The step forward in Bugatti engine design about 1930 that followed the first twin-cam engine for the Type 50, which

The oh-so-pure Jean Bugatti design of the Type 57 Ventoux combined style, power and something incomparable. JKX 767, a 1935 car owned by Allan McNab, is a true Bugatti supercar, seen here on the hill at Prescott.

The Giles brothers' Corsica-bodied Type 57SC seen with its very unusual glass-topped canopy. The fate of this add-on canopy is unknown.

deployed lessons learned from the American Miller-91 engine, offered an opportunity for the company's engines to advance, which Jean eagerly seized. Bugatti had made a major statement with the 1927 Type 41 Royale, and in 1932 Jean made a mark with his own Royale in its Esders Roadster variant (designed for Dr Armand Esders), notable for its 8-cylinder 12.8-litre engine and exotic design.

Even though work on the Type 59 racer took precedence, early drawings for the Type 57 are dated 1932. Early on Jean envisaged truly independent front suspension for the Type 57, but it was not to be, as Ettore insisted on a 'proper' front axle. Yet the Type 57 would be a natural corollary of all this learning. Ettore's Royale of *Sedanca de Ville* body type was truly exceptional (not least in its early use of alloy wheel design) and would signal huge intent for Bugatti.

With his father Ettore away in Paris designing railway stock (locomotives and power cars for the autorail project), and the company under financial pressure, not least from the late-1920s global economic crisis, the end of the Type 35 production run, the prospect of only a handful of Type 59 racers and the costs of the Royale, Jean Bugatti had to come up with not just design ideas but a model and engineering strategy to make Bugatti more successful and viable. One of his strategic thoughts was to use a single engine and chassis type to create a single 'platform' as a cost-effective base for a series of differently bodied cars. Today, car manufacturers have embraced such an idea to great effect; was Jean Bugatti the originator of this philosophy?

The expensive and somewhat messy Bugatti model range up to 1934, with all its costs and individual development requirements, had expended a lot of money. Rationalisation of the model range and the expensive engine and chassis toolings was urgently required. Perhaps above all, this was the quiet effect of the Type 57 'platform' sharing strategy.

The last examples of the Type 55s were built for mid-1935 delivery, after which the focus would be on the Type 57, launched in 1934, which was intended to be the new car to define Bugatti, and maybe even save it.

DESIGN

The 2.8-litre test engine was to become a 3.3-litre 'standard' twin-cam engine putting out 140bhp at a reasonable 5,000 rpm. Even though Ettore had vetoed the development costs

KEY TYPE 57 FEATURES

- Shared platform and engine drivetrain in range of in-house and externally supplied bodies of varying designs
- 3.3-litre (3257cc) straight-8 of 135–140bhp at 5,000rpm rated engine with overhead camshafts with helical drive taken from the rear of the unit
- Five main-bearing crankshaft (sometimes cited as six)
- Two valves per cylinder inclined at 94 degrees
- Twin-coil ignition (Scintilla distributor)
- Integral gearbox and single-plate clutch that replaced Bugatti multi-plate practice
- Single prop shaft with a Bugatti torque arm
- Bugatti articulated, split-beam axle. Quickly modified to single-beam, on-going suspension developments
- One original chassis length only 3,300mm (130.5in)
- Cable-operated brakes (later hydraulic)
- Spoked wheels instead of cast alloy; later-series wheel design also offered
- Hallmark radiator design with adjustable slats
- Unique and innovative aerodynamic bodies and paint schemes reflecting Bugatti industrial design and artistic heritage

The stunning Stelvio body design on Sir Michael Kadoorie's Type 57 sweeps away from another Bugatti day out. Two-tone blue at its best.

The Type 57 Stelvio's interior in classic tan leather and wood. Pure class.

JOSEPH WALTER

Joseph Walter had trained as a woodworker and was highly skilled and intuitive. He took ideas from Carlo Bugatti's wooden furniture and translated them, through Jean's own designs, into wonderful scale wooden styling models to assess and finalise the body designs prior to full-scale build. It appears that Joseph Walter and Jean Bugatti collaborated on the body designs to be offered, although some observers suggest that Walter was the stylist on some, while Jean was the lead on others.[1]

One body for a Type 50 is thought to have been all Walter's work and may indicate his growing confidence and esteem at Molsheim as work on the Type 57 progressed.

After a few Type 57s (some say three) had been built, the old Bugatti radiator design was dispensed with and a new vee- or 'vee'd' shape radiator was installed to become the new Bugatti hallmark or motif. Some say it was purely Jean's idea, others think that he and Walter created it together and that the inspiration may have been a very similar shape or motif seen in furniture by Carlo Bugatti.

After the death in 1927 of Felix Kortz, Ettore's favoured chief draughtsman and old colleague from before 1914, Ettore hired new people, several of whom had worked for FIAT or other manufacturers. Key names who assisted Jean in the realisation of the Type 57 range were Ettore's close friend Bartolomeo (Meo) Costantini and Antonio Pichetto.

Another name in the design office was Edouard Bertrand, an engine specialist who had joined Bugatti in 1924. Noël Domboy worked on the Type 57 design but soon found himself working with Ettore and his railcars in Paris. Adolph Nuss worked on the 16-cylinder engine design and the Type 57 development. The likes of racing drivers René Dreyfus and Robert Benoist were regulars at Molsheim at this time, Dreyfus being the Type 57 development test driver.

Jean had already penned the stunning yet petite sculpture that was the Type 55 in both its open and fixed-head forms, which could be said to have given him the confidence to produce the Type 57. When looking at the Type 50 *Profilée*, however, it is easy

The Baran family brought their Type 57 Ventoux to Europe for a road trip. Used and enjoyed, this is a supercar classic on the grandest scale.

to translate its design to the Type 57 Ventoux, although we should not overlook another of Jean's earlier and radical designs, the other *Profilée*, the fastbacked Coupé sometimes called the Type 46, which was perhaps even more cohesive and radical than the Type 57 Atalante, if not the subsequent Type 57 Atlantic itself.

From the grilles and radiator shells, to the proportions, scaling, side panels and the paintwork graphics, the Type 57 factory bodies set a standard that subsequent external coachbuilders had to match or exceed. Of note, the Type 57 of Bugatti design deployed precursors of European and American styling ideas that pre-dated coupé, razor-back and Empire-line themes in the later 1930s and 1940s.

The Type 57 would also handle like no other large car and have delightful steering and suspension dynamics: only the somewhat 'vintage' feel of the non-synchromesh four-speed gearbox was less than perfection for press-on driving. And yet a Type 57 would compete at Le Mans in 1937.

Developed in drawings commencing from July 1932 for launch in 1934, this was a car that soon evolved into a series of variations under the overarching 'Type 57' legend (sometimes referred to as the T57).

Created over a Bugatti chassis that was a work of sculpture in its own right, with massive twin-main tapered side longerons and clever crossmembers, upon which sat an original body design styled by Jean Bugatti, the Type 57 had a tubular front axle suspended on half-elliptical members and a rear end that deployed quarter-elliptics. The articulated beam front suspension, which was in some sense partly independent in mechanism, was a design by Antonio Pichetto, who had had much Bugatti drivetrain and suspension experience and also contributed to Bugatti body design, notable the Type 57G Tank.

Bugatti was beaten in terms of suspension design by the independent coil and wishbone system that Mercedes-Benz introduced in 1933, a year before the launch of the Type 57. By 1937 most of the Type 57's direct competitors had more advanced 'independent'-type suspension mechanisms. Citroën's torsion bars with wishbones would soon be significant in its Traction Avant, although a V8-engined coupé version known as the 22CV, which might have provided the Type 57 with some form of competition, failed to materialise.

Low-slung and long-nosed, the Type 57 had driving dynamics that defied its size. A straight-8 engine of 72mm bore and 100mm stroke with a capacity of 3257cc simply delivered torque and output of a kind that Bugatti excelled at. In fact its origins also lay in the Type 59's engine, but at its launch the Type 57 did not have a standard-fit 'blown' forced induction system in its configuration.

The unusually stark interior delivered a design motif of exquisite simplicity as opposed to the in-your-face 1930s equivalent of bling. But it was the coachwork options that were astounding. You could have a Type 57 to fit your needs, not just your idea of fashion – or rather a coachbuilder's idea of prescribing fashion as perceived wisdom.

Bugatti arranged for the Type 57 to be available with its main body design factory-built and supplied, or with Bugatti-commissioned coachwork options, in five main body styles and a further (sixth) as the differently chassised Type 57 Atlantic, which should not be confused with the earlier Type 57 Atalante. The Type 57 Atlantic was a Type 57, but it existed beyond the original Type 57 platform idea and cost more to design, manufacture and to purchase.

The first series of the Type 57 was available in three main body types, named after the Galibier, Stelvio and Ventoux Alpine passes. A further series of versions followed from 1936, including the defining moment of the Atalante notchback coupé, and a third series from 1938, including the rare Aravais convertible.

of fully independent suspension, Jean had still managed to build a running prototype with properly independent (transverse springs) front suspension. Add in the use of helical gear-driven timing and various alloy-rich components, it was evident that the Type 57 was over-engineered to the highest standards. Even the castings were artistic in their exquisite quality and design.

The gearbox was integral with the engine, a first for Bugatti. It had a ball-type change mechanism and helical constant-mesh gear mechanism for reduced noise and vibration – all the more reason for us to revel in the sound of that engine and its induction process and output.

In their styling of the Type 57's body design, Jean Bugatti and the Bugatti company stylist/draughtsman Joseph Walter created a stunning array of road-going sculpture, imagery and what modern designers call 'down-the-road graphics'. It was Walter who was credited with inventing the use of the riveted spine on the Aérolithe.

The Madame Itier car, a real Bugatti created from a parts trail that started with a pre-war re-body on a 'new' chassis that Bugatti had previously enjoyed himself. Seen here surrounded by modern supercars, this Bugatti is top trumps!

The Grand Raid seen outside the Bugatti château. Note the 'EB' logo in the railings.

GRAND RAID/USINE

Unveiled at the Paris Salon in late 1934, this Type 57 derivative was a short-lived luxury or grand luxe two-door sports roadster named 'Grand Raid' and was offered in the Type 57 range, but few beyond the knowledgeable Bugatti brigade are aware of it today. Designed for high-speed road and competition use by privateers, of course, the car's name refers to the French term for a rally over differing terrain. The Type 57 Grand Raid was the rarest competition-specification car in the range and effectively its niche car before the appearance of the ultimate Type 57 Atlantic. Changes to the steering column, gearbox shift, pedals and driving seat gave a more sporting driving position.

Four Grand Raid chassis were delivered to the London Bugatti concessionaire on the Brixton Road and, as shown by the records, Colonel Sorel purchased one direct in July 1935. An elegant but rather tame Corsica-built body was fitted to chassis #57324. Having spent much of its life with a single British owner from 1961 to 2002, its new owner entrusted restoring the engine to Ivan Dutton and the coachwork to I. Wilkinson & Son of Derby. Grand Raid chassis #57326 was also bodied by the Corsica works in 1935.

The most unusual aspect of the Grand Raid, the rare super-Bugatti of 1936, was the twin podded rear strakes that flowed off the headrests and down to the boot. Was this design copied for the Batmobile?

Italian tan leather and wood set within Bugatti black and yellow might be a bit bright, but once the patina sets in it should tone down a bit.

A notable and very rare 1935 Type 57 Grand Raid, chassis #57246, was rather unusually bodied by Carrosserie Worblaufen of Switzerland to a design by the Ramseier brothers. Another Grand Raid that was commissioned from Worblaufen in 1934, chassis #57260, has recently been displayed on the international Bugatti scene after a major restoration by Rod Jolley Coachbuilding.

Even rarer than the handful of Grand Raid cars was the original 1934 Paris Salon Grand Raid 'Usine' (meaning factory). This was reputed to have been a Bugatti/Gangloff design with spectacular rear bodywork incorporating lobed fairings running from behind the occupants' heads down into the tail. Various aerodynamically faired-in headlamp treatments were tried, as were rear wheel spats and an angled windscreen frame.

Built on chassis #57222 (or, as some say, #57221), the Usine roadster was alloy panelled and lowered. With a lowered seating position and steering column, and modified

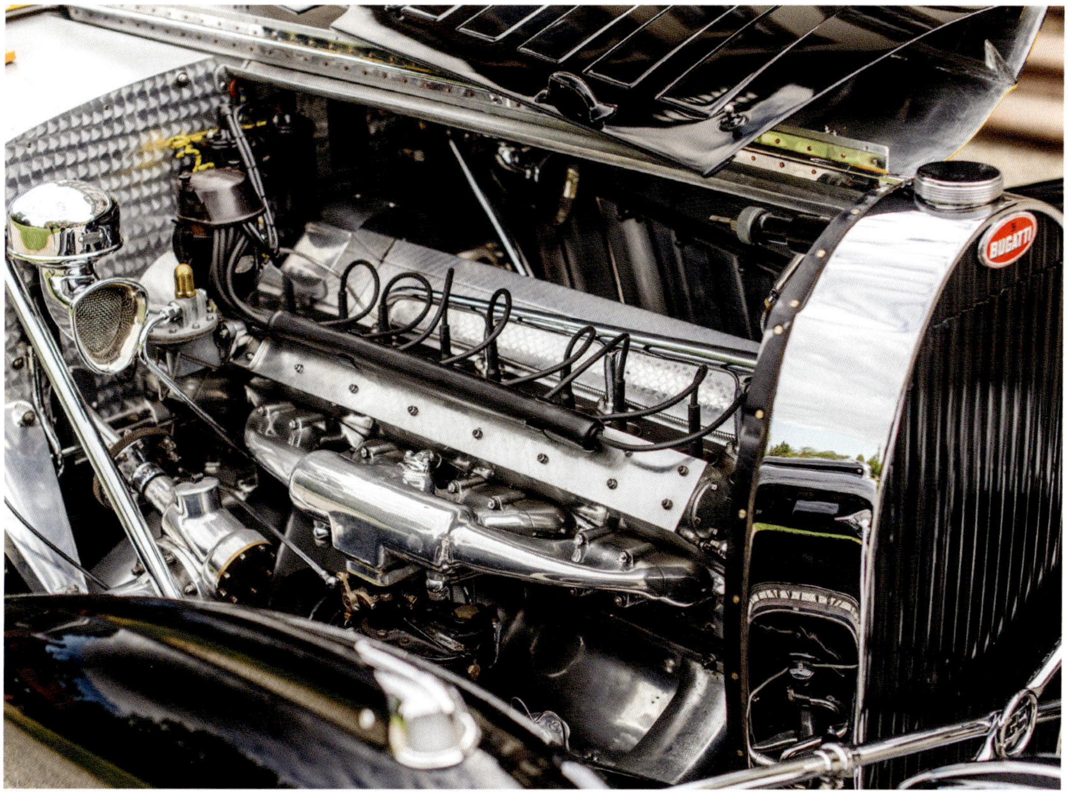

The true Bugatti obsession with perfection is captured under the bonnet of the Grand Raid. The alloy 'dressing' even extends to the engine block.

Designed like no other, the Grand Raid had a defining design language and massive style, as shown by this rear view.

bodywork, notably a spectacular vee-cranked two-piece angled windscreen, the Grand Raid Usine had the elements to define something special even by Jean Bugatti standards. The car was driven in competition by Pierre Veyron and Lucien Wurmser in the Paris-Nice Rally and then by Robert Benoist, who took the car to victory in the 1935 Chavigny hill climb.

Only ten of the Grand Raids were built and several chassis were reputedly used to build the first Type 57 Atalante bodies.[2] Today several Grand Raids are known, but the unique and very special original Bugatti/Gangloff Usine resides at the famed Louwman Museum in The Hague.

Further coach-built, standard Type 57 body designs would come in varying numbers from a range of coachbuilders including:

Belgium: Bertelli
Czechoslovakia: Sodomka
France: Fernandez & Darrin; Figoni & Falaschi; Franay; Gangloff Colmar; Guilloré; Letourneur & Marchand; Saoutchik; Vanvooren
Switzerland: Graber; Tüscher; Worblaufen
UK: Corsica; Maltby; Rice & Harper; Vanden Plas; James Young

TYPE 57 GUILLORÉ

A rare and intriguing Type 57 can be found in the elliptically tailed, swept fastback body of the 1938 Type 57 by Carrosserie Guilloré of Paris. The car (chassis #57651) looks stunning, especially when seen from the rear three-quarter angle, and possesses all the classic Bugatti factory ingredients of form allied to function in a just about restrained riot of teardrop, or torpedo, curves.

Guilloré supplied the body to the Molsheim factory but the war intervened and it was only afterwards that the body was offered up to a Type 57 factory chassis by Kurt Kiefer, the founder of the German Bugatti Club. The Guilloré-bodied Type 57 has all the drama of a true supercar.

Gangloff, the coachbuilders who were closest to Bugatti, both geographically at Molsheim and in terms of a relationship, offered three differing two-door roadster body designs for the Type 57 in 1936, in order to cater for the different chassis types used on the Type 57 production run, including those that were shorter or lower.

We should note that whilst many bodies were commissioned by customers for a bare running chassis, the Bugatti factory often used such coachbuilders to build the complete factory-supplied and commissioned car with bodywork.

Some cars had fold-flat windscreens, but later series cars dispensed with wooden windscreen pillar frames and used steel. Various changes and differences in chassis and body dimensions were found across these hand-built cars as they evolved.

BUGATTI, GANGLOFF AND LUCIEN SCHLATTER

Of all the coachbuilders that supplied Bugatti with bodies, it was Gangloff that perhaps had the closest relationship with Molsheim, and especially with Jean Bugatti, in the Type 57 story. Gangloff were integral to the Bugatti design legend and built many hundreds of Bugatti bodies directly

This very interesting Type 57S is an original chassis and engine topped off by a Dubos-designed Le Mans style body and is being driven by Tim Dutton, under whose auspices the car has been restored to a wonderful life. The Dutton family (now as Ivan Dutton Ltd) have been associated with motor racing, Bugatti and car restoration and refurbishment for nearly a century. The first reliable, high-quality and accurate replacement cylinder block for the Type 35 stemmed from Ivan Dutton.

for the marque as opposed to private customer commissions, which was the normal mechanism for a coachbuilder. Gangloff's chief designer from the mid-1930s was Lucien Schlatter, whose name is probably little known beyond the ranks of the most dedicated Bugattistes.

In 1927 the Swiss-based coachbuilder Gangloff had purchased Wiederkehr, a long-established engineering and coachbuilding company in the town of Colmar. Overnight Gangloff had a local office and was closer to Molsheim. Who then knew that from such humble offices would stem some of the greatest Bugatti car body designs ever seen?

The Gangloff brothers had founded their carriage building and coachbuilding concern in 1878, but separated their affairs and business interests in 1903. The resulting Georges Gangloff SA company moved to Colmar and worked with several car manufacturers to supply them with bodywork, including the legendary Voisin. Through Gangloff's lead managers Gottlieb Moor and Paul Horlacher, the company's relationship with Bugatti blossomed, producing up to five Bugatti bodies per month. Gangloff bodies for the Types 40, 43, 46 and 49 featured widely. There then came the expanded Gangloff headquarters based in Colmar and an even closer tie-up with Bugatti for the Type 57.

Perceived wisdom is that Jean Bugatti was not just instrumental in the later Molsheim-built Bugatti bodies, but that he also set down the parameters for Bugatti's 1930s design language. Whilst Jean's Molsheim factory design work is accepted as described, it is time that the design contribution of Gangloff's lead designer and draughtsman Lucien Schlatter is more widely recognised. Schlatter, who was but sixteen years old in 1935, is credited with leading the Gangloff 'design language' and the specific Gangloff-designed Bugatti body output.

The picture is somewhat less clear, however, regarding the Bugatti factory designs such as the Type 57 Stelvio, the Atalante and other in-house Bugatti bodies of the time. Admittedly Jean Bugatti designed them, but Gangloff built them, so how much of the design was down to Gangloff and Schlatter? The answer is that Jean is credited as the designer, but we must navigate a careful narrative when it comes to how his factory body designs, such as the Atalante, were put into production.

In interviews near the end of his long life Schlatter was clear that Gangloff followed Bugatti's instructions for Jean's Type 57 designs, as opposed to the Gangloff commissioned designs, yet he seemed to suggest that, other than sketches and discussions, few finalised, draughted and definitive Bugatti Type 57 bodywork designs were set in stone – before Gangloff 'designed' them as tooling-ready drawings, scaled renditions and models that could be employed for the production of actual Type 57 Gangloff cars. Schlatter was not an ego-driven car designer and he signed his Gangloff design/styling drawings as 'Scr' under the title of 'for Carrosserie Gangloff'.

For clarity, perhaps we should separate the Jean Bugatti penned and credited factory-built body designs that were part of the Gangloff-built Type 57 body output from the wider and more numerous designs from Schlatter's pencil. The names of the lead bodyshell developers and constructors at Gangloff are believed to have been Messrs Zuben and Schmitt.

As for Schlatter and Gangloff's effect on the actual designs handed down by Jean as his own, it is a contentious area, although it is certain that not only did the Bugattis trust Gangloff, they definitely relied upon them.

But clearly the man behind the creative Gangloff process that put Jean Bugatti's ideas into effect was Lucien Schlatter, despite his youth (he was born in 1920) – and he kept his drawings to prove it. Schlatter had joined Gangloff as a fourteen-year-old apprentice. He was a natural stylist and designer draughtsman with a great eye for scale and sculpture, making him a 'natural' for Bugatti. Quickly working his way upwards to the position of Gangloff's chief of design as the 1930s progressed, he was instrumental in the creation and production process around some of the Type 57's most vital body designs.

Schlatter left a significant imprint on the Bugatti marque, for which he is rarely given due credit. He designed some very significant bodies for Bugatti and had a notable role in the realisation of the styling of the Atalante, which, whilst credited to Jean Bugatti, was seemingly realised in 'the metal' and taken to production by Schlatter and just one other colleague at Gangloff. Certainly collections of his drawings for Gangloff, many of which have been sold at auction since 2005, are evidence of Schlatter's place in the process.

In 1936 it was Gangloff who presented Bugatti with a series of speculative designs (by Schlatter) for a shorter, lower, sleeker, streamliner type of coupé and roadster based on the shorter Type 57's chassis. In recent years one of these designs (the cabriolet) has been realised in the metal by the Museum Autovision at Altlussheim, Germany, headed by Horst Schultz and with the support of the leading Type 57 exponent Eric Koux.

In 1938 Schlatter styled a unique revised late-model Type 57 Stelvio Cabriolet (chassis #57731) of four-seat configuration, which, after completion in October 1938, appeared at the 1939 Geneva motor show and also became the company car and demonstrator of the Bugatti team driver Jean-Pierre Wimille. Schlatter incorporated a Type 57 Atlantic headlamp treatment for better airflow, a more steeply raked windscreen and a revised rear deck. As such this Stelvio was unique. This car became part of the Quattroroute Collection in 1964 and was sold most recently in 2020 for 770,000 euros.

In 1939 Gangloff was asked by Bugatti to design an updated Type 57 coupé-styled body for a client. This was penned by Schlatter and took the Atalante and Atlantic styling themes a step further into a more modern and prescient style that had shades of early 1950s American coupé styling a decade before that appeared. The special one-off Type 57 coupé had echoes of the Type 57 Atlantic and of Figoni & Falaschi's Talbot-Lago T150-C-SS 'teardrop' coupé and yet had a style of its own. This was in 1939 and the outbreak of war stopped the project in its tracks, as did Jean Bugatti's death a month before, but Schlatter had drawn everything up ready for building. Five decades later Jean-Marc Robert had that Type 57 coupé body built on an original Bugatti chassis and engine, and Lucien Schlatter helped him realise it using his own original design drawings for the body: how close to 'original' can you get?

The ill-fated Bugatti Type 64 4.4-litre engined concept (with a uniquely advanced, riveted alloy chassis underneath its body) was designed in 1938–9 to replace the Type 57 model line-up. With a gull-wing door design, alloy body and chassis and many new design features, the Type 64 was the design that Jean was working on when he was killed. It was a car that Jean thought might be the future for a revised Bugatti company, alongside the smaller, cheaper Type 68. Did he somehow know that the days of the limited-production, grand land-yacht were over?

It is hard to define how closely Gangloff and Schlatter were involved, yet the synergies of design language are very obvious. It is worth mentioning that the Bugatti Type 101 design from 1951, which was intended as a potential 'new' Bugatti, was built as a prototype (two bodies) by Gangloff themselves and as styled by Schlatter. The reader can surely begin to appreciate the bond between Bugatti and Gangloff in terms of design language. Perhaps Schlatter's exceptional youth at the time of this Gangloff Bugatti output in the mid- to late 1930s has caused some to be reluctant to credit him, yet the evidence of the original Gangloff drawings that bear his name is compelling.

Eight months short of his 100th birthday, Lucien Schlatter died in 2019. It seems incredible that the man who made notable contributions to the great moments of Bugatti Type 57 design and production of the 1930s should have been alive until so recently. Yet his name is often missing from the Bugatti story as told by many authors, not for want of evidence, but probably due for want of visibility. And of course, Jean Bugatti's own coachworks designs were the stunning product of the Molsheim factory, to which Schlatter did not offer any challenge. But it is clear he worked very closely on such cars' body styling and design.[3]

The Baran family Type 57 Ventoux captured in a classic English setting during its European tour with Matthew Baran at the wheel.

The same Baran family car seen from the rear with the classic '57' badge on its rump.

JAAP BRAAM RUBEN'S ULTIMATE TYPE 57 COLLECTION

Today, arguably the most interesting collection of Type 57s is that belonging to Jaap (Jack) Braam Ruben of Fine Automobiles in the Netherlands, who is a man who really knows his Bugattis. A Bugatti trader and collector who has known over 300 Bugattis, it was Jaap who handled the sale of the Bugattis from the Malmerspach Collection that had been handed back by the French Government to Mme Arlette Schlumpf. His personal five Type 57s cover the whole DNA of the range, but the Type 57 Atlantic is absent – not least as it was a different model on a different chassis to the 'standard' Type 57 – not that any Type 57 could ever be called standard. His original-condition Galibier saloon is simply captivating.

The Dutch seem to have as much affection for Bugatti as the British, with several significant names appearing among those involved with Dutch Bugatti dealing and collecting, including the Louwman Museum in The Hague and H. Groenewegen of Rotterdam.

The legend: the Type 57 with the bonnet open to reveal that powerplant. Note that the radiator louvres were adjustable by design.

Inside the Baran Type 57, the sheepskin seat covers must have made life more bearable during the long European tour. Note the exquisite instrumentation.

THE TYPES 57

The Type 57 range was produced in three distinct production series, with salon, coupé and cabriolet options, all with varying seating capacities and arrangements within the series set:

Series One (from 1934): launched as Bugatti's new straight-8, 3.3-litre, twin-overhead camshaft, non-racing grand luxe, grand tourer packed with exquisite and expensive engineering and design details. Small number of pre-production test-run cars had the Bugatti split-articulated front axle, but this was revised for production series.

Series Two (from 1936): new rubber engine mounts added, camshaft, timing, crank for charger changes all instituted. Chassis cross-bracing added. De Ram-type shock absorbers replacing earlier Hartford-type absorbers by Telecontrol.

Series Three (from 1938): added hydraulic brakes, telescopic Allinquant shock absorbers in place of de Ram-type. Higher front wings for suspension clearance. Engine and clutch changes.

Type 57 Tourer

1934. The factory-built four-door pillarless saloon body, which could nudge 160km/h (100mph) on a good day, evolved in stylistic terms into the two-door Ventoux. It was also available with other coachwork as a four-door in several body designs. Graber-styled and -built bodies were popular on the Type 57 and arguably incorporated certain earlier Type 57S Tourer themes from the Galibier. Of interest, the Type 57 Tourer was also made as an SC model. Only two

Type 57S Tourer chassis were to be bodied by Corsica of London and one of them (chassis #57512) was to be retrofitted with a supercharger (either by the factory or the London agent) to create an SC variant of the Tourer class.

Type 57 Ventoux

1934–8 (later with Series Three nomenclature). The Molsheim-built and body commissioned car of Jean Bugatti hallmark design. Two-door box-cabin with highly raked windscreen and a cut-off or truncated rear end design treatment. The angled windscreen and A-pillars were echoes of the outrageous angles of the Type 50 *Profilée* that Jean had designed in the early 1930s. Later fitted with hydraulic brakes.

Type 57 Stelvio

A convertible, the 1934 Series I cars had cut-away sections for the folded roof, a feature deleted from Series 2 cars onwards. Principally associated with chassis clothed by Gangloff of Colmar in a two-door convertible body style, the Stelvio was interesting in its details beyond the chassis and engine specification of a Type 57 base. Of note, it could be optioned with a folding windscreen and frame, which was very unusual for a grand-touring open-topped car.

Type 57S

These shorter-chassis cars are of note as the chassis was modified with a lowered centre of gravity and rear chassis rails, with the rear axle passing through the frame. The tuned engines, which could reach 170bhp even without a supercharger, had a higher compression ratio and dry sump system. Apart from the iron bits of the engine block and various pressings and component parts, this is a model with less in common with the Type 57 than is often realised. Throw in a double-plate clutch, a Scintilla Vertex magneto, aluminium coachwork, the V-shaped grille and better handling dynamics, and the 'S' embodied the magic and myth of Bugatti, let alone the Type 57 series.

Launched at the 1936 Paris Salon, the Type 57S (Sport) was available ex-works as a chassis or mounted with a Molsheim-sourced body. It was also available as a convertible from coachbuilders including Vanvooren and Vanden Plas of London.

Just 43 Type 57S chassis were built and bodied: 22 of these had factory-commissioned bodywork, comprising the seventeen Atalantes, four Atlantics and the one-off 'Paris' roadster.

Type 57 Atalante

Jean Bugatti's personal vision of what a sporting Bugatti could and should be for the 1930s. It should not be confused with the 'Atlantic' or the incorrect and mispronounced 'Atlantique'. The Atalante came first and has the lower centre of gravity of the Type 57S. The Atalantes are arguably the most stylistically desirable of the original Type 57 series. The single-carburettor engine was fitted with a Marshall or Roots-type supercharger, 8 cylinders and a four-speed manual transmission enveloped in the outrageous curves of supermodel elegance. The Atalante remains a standalone Bugatti despite the overshadowing halo of the three Atlantics that remain. The fitment of an Ettore Bugatti-patented carburettor to a Type 57 could only enhance its performance and desirability: seventeen examples of the Type 57S Atalante were constructed.

Earl Howe, president of the Bugatti Owners' Club, owned a spectacular Atalante (chassis #57502) that was not supercharged until sometime before 1960, when it was locked away and remained unseen until 2008. Restored by Ivan Dutton Ltd, the Howe Type 57S Atalante remains a pure thoroughbred.

Type 57C and Type 57SC

An early 1936 specification, the C (compressor) added a camshaft-driven meshed gear supercharger that increased the peak power by 25bhp to 160bhp.

The next variation was the Type 57SC, reputedly capable of 200bhp, which used the S series chassis and added a supercharger from the C series – hence SC. The SC is lower and used an ovaloid vee-grille design motif.

The C series had a higher compression ratio, modified valve timing and de Ram-type suspension shock absorbers. One of these cars was delivered to Eric and Godfrey Giles in London, whereupon they co-designed a stunning, rakish one-off body to be coachbuilt by the Bertelli concern. Eric Giles, an interior designer and natural stylist, had also styled a Type 57S. The streamlined body had an expensive vee-windscreen and various fairings and spats. Just as the design had been finalised, however, Bugatti launched the revised, lower chassis variant and this led to the Giles brothers modifying a similar body design as then separately built by Corsica of London.

The Corsica-bodied Type 57 of legend. To call it elegant would be an understatement.

Ettore Bugatti's own Type 57C Special was chassis #57335, engine no. 340, with a unique Gangloff-built coupé body and a style all of its own. If Bugattis are special, then Ettore's 'Special' one-off Type 57C tops a specific list, not least as it spent twenty years as a Bugatti company, factory car and development chassis.

The unique coupé coachwork was penned by Jean's own hand and realised by Lucien Schlatter at Gangloff. Not only were the coupé-style rear panels unique, there was also a two-piece glass roof (not dissimilar to those so fashionable now). This roof was removed at the factory prior to its sale into private ownership. Of note the front grille is the more traditional type, not the vee-type seen on certain examples of the Type 57S and Type 57 Atlantic.

Originally created with a two-tone green exterior and an exotic green leather interior, this car became the Patron's own car. It was not originally fitted with hydraulic brakes but did benefit from later-series Type 57 updates, including Rudge-Whitworth wire wheels and rubber engine mounting blocks. The car survived the war and remained in Bugatti family ownership until 1959 when things really did come to an end for the original marque. While still in Bugatti company ownership the car was fitted with a Durand steering box on the instructions of Noël Domboy. Today this car remains a Type 57 moment of great significance.

Type 57 Aravais

1938. With only twelve built and the factory directly outsourcing the bodywork to Gangloff and to Letourneur & Marchand, both of which built six examples, the Aravais demonstrated glamour a step beyond the Stelvio shape.

Details of Bugatti body commissions, coachbuilder invoices and customer payments became somewhat sketchy as the state of Bugatti's finances became more concerning. It seems that some cars were sold by their respective coachbuilder's showroom, rather than from Molsheim, as was usually invoiced. The last two Aravais, seen by some as the highlight of the Type 57 baseline range, emerged in the late summer of 1939 as geopolitical turmoil enveloped Europe and Bugatti itself.

Another 'interesting' Type 57 owner was Rudi van Daalen Wetters, whose stable of Bugattis after the war included a Type 57 Aravais. He escaped from the occupied Netherlands by sea in June 1941 and ended up flying Supermarine Spitfires in the Royal Air Force's No. 322 (Dutch) Squadron, completing more than 170 operational sorties from 1943 onwards. Soon after the end of the war he purchased his first Bugatti, a 1938 Type 57, chassis #57644, fitted with a rare and stunning open touring body designed by Carrosserie Letourner & Marchand. Years later, living in America, Rudi became member No. 22 of the American Bugatti Club (ABC) and purchased a very rare Type 57 Aravais, chassis #57768. He also owned a Brescia, a Type 40A and the Type 57 Stelvio, chassis #57609, with body by Gangloff. This car is now owned by Sir Michael Kadoorie.[4]

From 1936 Type 57 Series Two cars had new flexible engine mounts and a revised exhaust manifold; from 1938 hydraulic brakes were fitted as Series Three specification. Several Type 57 cars were returned to the factory for two-lobe superchargers to be fitted, although use of the earlier three-lobe Type 35 supercharge variant has been suggested.

We should not forget that the rare and much revered Type 57 Atlantic (of which three of the four built are still known) used a different and lower (*surbaisse*) chassis to that of the baseline series production Type 57.

The production numbers of the entire Type 57 range are surprisingly high given its costs and its complications: Bugatti built 687 of its Type 57s between 1934 and late 1939 (sometimes stated as into 1940, when the cars were first registered and by when the company had moved from Molsheim to Bordeaux). At one heady stage the factory was turning out up to 80 Type 57 chassis or complete cars a month.

Type 57S: a Tank chassis anomaly

The W.S. 'Bill' Turnbull car Type 57S, chassis #57503-16S, is a Corsica-bodied open tourer from 1937 that provides us with an example of a typical Ettore anomaly: this famous car has been shown categorically by its numbers to have been built on a chassis of Grand Prix type that came from a former Type 57G Tank, which had been raced in 1936. So it was a year-old chassis when used by the factory for the tourer commissioned by Robert Ropner, who had an eye for special cars and even more special Bugattis. From 1945 it was briefly owned by Rodney Clarke, who would found the Connaught grand prix team of the 1950s.

The fifth owner, from 1969 until his death in 2019, was Bill Turnbull, a well-known engineer originally from New Zealand, who later worked for JCB as Chief Engineer. When he came to strip down this English-bodied Type 57S for restoration, Turnbull discovered that the drilled chassis members matched the lightweight Le Mans Type 57G Tank cars' chassis, which were distinctly different to a so-called 'normal' Type 57S chassis. But was his car the rarest contemporary example of Bugatti recycling and upcycling at the same time? The chassis was stamped '1', but this had then been stamped over with an '8' when it was reused by the factory for a 'new' Type 57S – a *surbaisse* chassis model.

The effect of this is that a large number of Bugatti experts, including Julius Kruta, Pierre-Yves Laugier, David Sewell and David Morys, now accept that here is a Type 57S with a rare 'pre-used' Bugatti 'Tank' racing chassis, which has been proven to have come from a Type 57G Tank that wore number 82 in the 1936 French Grand Prix at Montlhéry and number 14 in the Grand Prix de La Marne at Reims, driven on both occasions by Robert Benoist.[5]

AUK 717: the curious coachbuilt Type 57?

Type 57 chassis #57495, with engine #390, was built in late 1936 to early 1937 and was invoiced to Colonel Sorel, the Bugatti dealer in London, on 5 February 1937. It was registered in England as AUK 717. Upon the chassis's arrival in London, it was bodied in a very stately, somewhat 'Empire-line' design by the coachbuilder Charles Clark and Sons. Fitted with a four-door, six-light (six-window) upright saloon body, the design would have been more appropriate on a landaulet from the Royal Mews, which hardly went with the sporting character of the car's chassis and its 3.3-litre engine. This body was removed during or after World War II and the car carried a basic body until becoming a rolling chassis.

After some time in the doldrums, AUK 717 was purchased in 1971 by Margaret Price, the wife of Barrie Price, the high-profile Bugatti owner and supporter who rescued the remains of the Lea-Francis brand. Barrie Price then drew up plans for a stunning two-door, two-seat (you could get three people on the front bench seat) tourer-roadster body that was inspired by design elements of a Type 57 Galibier saloon. He made the body himself: it looked so good, so original that those not in the know might have

The Type 57 Atalante had perfect scale and style.

assumed it was an original 1930s body coachbuilder design. Underneath its flowing yet restrained style remained a Type 57 engine and chassis with matching numbers.

Type 57 NBW 317 – the three-seat Atalante?

Recently purchased and restored by Sir Michael Kadoorie and under the care of the renowned specialists Ashton Keynes Vintage Restorations, this unique Type 57, chassis #57501, has a single transverse-aligned third seat across a small bay in the cabin behind the two front seats. This was an original feature of the car, together with a raised roof line that adds a degree of the bulbous to the more usual Atalante cab that accommodates that passenger. The body was built by Gangloff and the special cabin design was by Lucien Schlatter.

During World War II this car was commandeered in France by the Nazis, yet survived. In contrast it was raced at Prescott in 1957 by its French owner. It is also known as the car that 'got away', because having been scooped up by the Schlumpf brothers, they sold it (a rare event) and this unique three-seat supercar eventually went to the USA before its current ownership.

Type 57S Le Mans

Chassis #5722 is particularly interesting as it now wears a stunning and to all appearances seemingly original body design and has recently been subject to restoration by the Dutton concern in England. Yet this car is wrapped up in a riddle. The car was originally delivered with engine #18S for Raymond d'Estrez de Saugé and raced at Le Mans in 1937, but retired from the race with gearbox issues.

In the course of its life it has been modified several times. Sold in France and taken to the USA, rather curiously it ended up being rebodied more than once, eventually with a privately built 'low-rider' body of Packard roadster look. That body has also been (confusingly) linked with chassis #57512.

There may be some fog lingering around the various iterations of this car, but that should not be allowed to detract from its authenticity. Chassis #5722 is real, is traceable and did compete at Le Mans. It contains a high level of original, provenanced Bugatti parts and the fact that it now wears an authentic-looking, though recently procured body that looks far more the part and is far more accurate, is hardly reason to look down up it.

CHOLMONDELEY BUGATTI AFFAIR

Sybil, Marchioness (Lady) Cholmondeley's Type 57, bodied in a very elegant fastback four-door saloon style by Figoni et Falaschi upon chassis #57739 in early 1938, was stunning in its own right, being classic yet also very *moderne*. It was elegantly sensational and sculpted, and it topped off over a decade of Bugatti ownership by the Cholmondeley/Rocksavage family and title holders – they owned seven Bugattis in 1921–39.

By 1939 Sybil's husband, by then the 5th Marquess of Cholmondeley, simultaneously owned a glorious Type 57 Atalante, which, according to the family, was urged upon them by Ettore but not 'gifted' as some have suggested, although Ettore would have loved the thought of hobnobbing with the aristocracy; we might suggest that Ettore was a bit of 'snob' and that the Cholmondeley family may have got a good deal out of Ettore. David, the current Marquess of Cholmondeley states that his grandparents visited Ettore in Molsheim in order to personally discuss the trims, colours and specifications of the cars they ordered. In the 1930s the 5th Marquess struck up a friendship with Jean Bugatti and attended Prescott Hill Climb when the Bugattis visited the event. The Bugattis stayed with Bugatti owner Earl Howe, which was to be expected.

Obviously keen Bugatti enthusiasts, the Cholmondeley family had taken delivery of the first-built Type 50 just before Christmas 1930. In 1921, the family had taken delivery of an ex-Paris 1919 Motor Show Bugatti Type 22, chassis #777. The Cholmondeley family then received the Type 35 chassis #4394, built for private use as opposed to motorsport competition (at this stage the later 5th Marquess was still Lord Rocksavage). This car found its way from Molsheim, being delivered direct to the Cholmondeley villa in the south of France, only later to be driven back to England. There, it was locally registered to the family area at Houghton Hall, Norfolk. The Marquess won the La Turbie hill climb in the car on 15 March 1925. It was later sold to Malcolm Campbell.

In 1929 the Cholmondeleys took delivery of a Type 44 chassis #44879 with the factory designed four-door *Berline Fiacre* body; the first family Bugatti that the Marchioness is reputed to have influenced the style of, not least the wickerwork applique effect on the sides of the car. Next came a 1930 Type 49, chassis #49175, that looked almost identical to the family's Type 44 with the

Lady Sybil, the Marchioness of Cholmondeley at the wheel of the unique 1930s Figoni et Falaschi-bodied Type 57, in the styling of which she had a hand.

The stylish and aerodynamic rear aspect of the car displays its futurism – remember this is pre-World War II. Shades of Flaminio Bertoni's 'VGD' and certain 1950s supercars are hinted at.

Marchioness' design input. The car was fitted with the finned-alloy wheels of a design taken from those used on the Royale.

In 1930, the family purchased a Type 50, chassis #50116, also with the *Fiacre* type coachbuilt style and extensive specification. Of note, the finned alloys wheels boasted a unique, applied, design motif that reputedly was the Marchioness's work. That car still exists today. Next came the ordering of a Type 57SC Atlantic by the Cholmondeleys – the second British order for the car brand new ex-factory. Strangely, the order was cancelled despite chassis number # 57612 being reserved. Jean Bugatti wrote to the Marquess and somehow cancelled the order and steered his lordship away from purchasing the Type 57 Atlantic supercar. Nobody knows why. Instead the family took a Type 57 Atalante, chassis #57698, direct from Bugatti. It is sometimes claimed that the terms meant it might have constituted some form of deal to the family, although it was invoiced at 130,750 francs and the family today insist that Bugatti did not 'give' them cars.

Still at the Cholmondeley family seat of Houghton Hall, the side profile of the car shows off its advanced design.

The 5th Marquess's Atalante was in black and with gold-striped detailing, and he became a well-known figure in the late 1930s British motoring scene with the car. Curiously, the Atalante's matching numbers for chassis, engine and gearbox were somehow latterly swapped in 1938 to a Type 57 Stelvio, chassis # 57679, that was supplied to the leading Bugatti supporter Earl Howe in late 1938. Recently, the famed Bugatti collector Jaap Braam Ruben was the man who sorted out this paper trail and correctly re-identified each car and the respective components. The Atalante was more recently owned by the actor Nicholas Cage.

Back in February 1939 the Cholmondeleys took delivery of a rolling Bugatti Type 57 chassis, #57739, to be fitted with the stunning, fastback, four-door coupé body of Figoni et Falaschi in Paris. Contrary to rumour, it was not an overly high-roof car to accommodate the Marchioness's height – she was not as tall as the story suggested. This is the car that looked a bit like a Flaminio Bertoni late-1930s sketch for the new Citroën large saloon proposed as a Traction Avant replacement – the *Voiture à Grande Diffusion* (VGD); such a design later metamorphosed into the Citroën DS.

The car was registered as FUW 180 and the Marchioness, Lady Sybil, definitely had a hand in the car's black and yellow livery, and principally the interior design that used a uniquely dyed shade of primose yellow leather; this was accentuated by the intriguing used of black and yellow gold highlights to the exterior. It is unlikely she 'styled' it in its totality, but she may well have influenced its looks and scale, and she visited Paris to discuss the car and its design with Ettore, whom she clearly found an interesting personality. Ettore must have revelled in the upper class association of course…

The Cholmondeleys were some of Ettore's most elite customers and he ensured that they remained loyal; they also amassed a collection of personal Bugatti memorabilia.[6]

More recently the Pageant of Speed at Cholmondeley Castle has seen modern Bugattis featured as well as earlier examples. Eight decades on, the Cholmondeley-to-Bugatti relationship endures and the family archives contain many interesting details and notes relating to the family Bugattis from the 1920s to the 1930s.

Thomas Pitt Cholmondeley Tapper

British-domiciled New Zealander Thomas Pitt Cholmondeley Tapper, a distant relation of the Cholmondeley family (above), had a separate tale of amateur Bugatti racing in the 1930s. He is cited as New Zealand's earliest competitive international racer. Cholmondeley Tapper was a well-known and dedicated Bugattiste and authored *Amateur Racing Driver* in 1954 (G.T. Foulis). He served in World War II, flying for the Air Transport Auxiliary service, had skied professionally in the British ski team and was a Cambridge University graduate. A 1930s friendship with Peter Churchill, and also with no less a figure than Winston S. Churchill, led him to set up a flying school at Haddenham airfield, Oxfordshire. But Bugattis (and the occasional Maserati) were his thing. He also developed a friendship with the Bugattis, visited Molsheim and knew Aumaitre at the factory.

He purchased a second-hand Type 37 for privateer racing and modified it extensively (into Type 37A supercharged specification). However, some Bugattistes have suggested that Cholmondeley Tapper rather made the most of using a co-driven Type 37 that may have been 'shared' with Eileen Ellison, the wealthy and highly competitive and successful British privateer Bugatti 'queen' who – being a women in a 1930s male hierarchy – had to fight harder for recognition. This moneyed pair travelled the world with the Bugatti (towed behind a Type 40) and even raced in South Africa, where Cholmondeley Tapper also competed in an Alfa-Romeo. Cholmondeley Tapper's last major race was at Brooklands in 1937 where he finished third, behind Malcolm Campbell in a Bugatti.

The one-off 'Shah of Persia' wedding-gift, a 1939 Van Vooren-bodied 160hp twin-cam Type 57C #57808, with design homage to Figoni. The windscreen and frame can be hand-cranked down into the body. On display at the Petersen Museum.

Atlantic style captured in the Amalgam Collection scale model of exquisite detailing.

CHAPTER 6

TYPE 57: AÉROLITHE AND ATLANTIC

If the Type 57 series was not stunning enough, there then came the combination of aero, auto, industry and art that was the two-door, fastbacked, aerodynamic and industrial Art Deco-esque device that Jean created as the ultimate supercar, one that cost a very significant amount of money to purchase. It was in effect a different type of Type 57, a stand-alone car in its own right.

Taking a Type 57 engine and chassis, yet clothing it in a body created at not inconsiderable development cost, does not adequately frame what might as well have been an advanced concoction of aviation design and biomorphic homage to nature that had landed from space – indeed Aérolithe means 'stone from the sky' or, more colloquially, 'meteorite'.

The Type 57 Atlantic did not come from out of the blue. It stemmed from the Aérolithe concept car of 1935, which, it should be noted, was higher built and had a bonnet topline higher than the front wing line, whereas the subsequent Type 57 Atlantic had a lower body and a bonnet close to the height of the front wing line, making it much lower and very different in appearance. The Aérolithe radiator shell and bonnet line were actually lower than the standard Type 57 line, but not as low as those that would be applied to the Type 57 Atlantic production cars, and these differences are obvious in the metal.

Created and built by Jean Bugatti for 1934, the Aérolithe was a prototype Type 57S reiteration clothed in a dramatically sculpted, aerodynamic body replete with fairings (less spats and more blisters) to the rear wheels, a faired-in cabin turret and a tapered rear form of 'Gondola' type. The sheer extravagance of 'aero' design was taken not from results in a wind tunnel but from the 1930s design movement, yet the results were unique and in no sense derivative. The Aérolithe was like a sci-fi machine decades before that movement itself was to manifest.

The long bonnet, swept wings, cutaway doors and domed carapace of a cabin turret, leading through to an extended tail and fastback, were beyond stunning and represented car design taken to a new level. It may be possible to see faint traces of certain emerging 1930s American styling trends, but nothing about the Bugatti was a copy and nothing was vulgar. And surely American styling of the late 1930s and the 1940s, perhaps even the 1950s, was influenced by Jean Bugatti's designs and Figoni's motifs.

AÉROLITHE

The Aérolithe was one of the first car show designer concept vehicles, yet one that would very quickly become a production type, albeit in limited numbers.

Although the early Aérolithe prototype was touted as having a magnesium alloy body (perhaps in the fashion of lightweight aircraft of the time, such as the Heinkel He 70) and deployed the use of a structural 'spine' feature, the subsequent production cars would not be magnesium bodied. The magnesium alloy Elektron (or Electron) could not be easily welded at this time of its development and this was why Jean Bugatti used a riveted structural spine along the car. When building the production Type 57 Atlantics he reverted to aluminium, which could be welded by an expert using the right welding gases. The production series Type 57 Atlantic, however, retained the spine for design and aerodynamic reasons.

With the backing of Ettore, Jean's design lead, Joseph Walter's input and the reputed encouragement of Adrien Paul, then Bugatti's Sales and Commercial Director, the project from the Aérolithe to the Type 57 Atlantic began its journey.

Adrien Paul, the often forgotten 'other' name at Molsheim from 1926 to 1939, had been an engineering apprentice, a fighter pilot in World War I, an employee of Louis Renault and an early 'petrol-head', so it should come as no surprise that he gravitated towards the Bugattis at Molsheim and

On the grass at Monterey the Mullin Atlantic, an ice-blue beauty, says it all. Note the low-line headlamp valance/fairing design, but shouldn't the windscreen wipers be 'parked' in the other position?

moved there from Paris. After World War II and the winding-down of Bugatti, he returned to his love of aviation as a director of *Société d'Etudes et de Constructions Aéronautiques* (SECA) based at Le Bourget.[1]

After a second international exhibition at the 1935 London Olympia Motor Show, a road-going revision of the Aérolithe complete with prosaic items such as windscreen wipers and sidelights was built as Aérolithe chassis #2 and shipped for demonstration to Bugatti's then most enthusiastic and wealthiest customer market, Britain, most specifically to London, and into the hands of Colonel Godfrey Giles and the racing driver William Grover-Williams, often known as 'W. Williams' or 'Williams', who had won the 1929 Monaco Grand Prix in a Bugatti Type 35B.

On his first or second visit to London with the Aérolithe, Williams parked outside Giles's premises at 2 Queen Street, Mayfair. Passers-by stopped and stared at the Aérolithe, such was its extravagance and modernity of design.

During World War II Williams, who had grown up in France and was fluent in French, was recruited by the Special Operations Executive (SOE) and performed many acts of bravery in German-occupied France before his capture in 1943 and untimely death at Sachsenhausen.

The second prototype Aérolithe, sometimes tagged a 'Torpedo' model, was built and used for testing and development. For a year or two the Aérolithe created a major stir, not least in London and Paris, but was it ultimately too much for conventional minds, Bugatti's 'Punk' moment?

AÉROLITHE REINCARNATED?

Incredibly for Aérolithe fans, there remains an act of 21st-century industrial design inspiration in how a recreation of the 1935 Aérolithe was realised. This was built for Chris Ohrstrom over several years in Canada by the Guild of Automotive Restorers under David Grainger's lead. It has become a mobile global art exhibit that is constantly in demand, but we should note that it is *not* a Bugatti nor sanctioned as such. If it takes the name of Bugatti to a more diverse audience, however, then that is no bad thing provided they are made aware of what they are looking at.

Relying on some original photos, a handful of original plans and little else bar a Bugatti chassis for guidance, there has emerged an assumed replica of the original Aérolithe.

Constructed on Bugatti chassis Type 57 #57104, the 'new' car was built in magnesium, as originally specified, with the lead work on the metal forming carried out by Alex Plestid, who cut, rolled, heated and sculpted the sheets of magnesium into the form of this unique car. The resulting all-Bugatti reincarnation, in a rare hue of silvered green with a tint of blue (reputedly inspired by original Bugatti factory artwork by one of its engineers), sits on whitewall tyres that, however vulgar and 'American' some may consider them, attempt to reflect the Bugatti specification of 1935. White-walled tyres did not offend Jean Bugatti, it seems.

The car has toured the world, reinforcing and reigniting interest in Bugatti amongst the lay public. En route it was allegedly bent when an airline dropped it several feet, and it also went missing in a shipping container. Unlike the original missing Aérolithe, however, it came home to stun the assembled observers.

Looking at Bugatti's Aérolithe, albeit in its alloy reincarnation, can we see more obviously the hint of 1930s American 'style' at the dawn of the age of industrial design, a look that is less obvious in the more delicate, more Italianate 'real' Type 57 Atlantic itself?

Is it heretical to find hints of Pierce-Arrow, Cord, Chrysler, Ford and others in the look and stance of the original Aérolithe and its copy, or is this a new way of viewing the design of the Aérolithe and its effect beyond Bugatti? The new 'copy' Aérolithe is not perfect and there are certain recognised issues in its interpretation, but it does at least take the Bugatti message to a wider audience beyond the narrow confines of the authentic Bugatti movement and its quite understandable rules. While it cannot be a truly 'pure' representative of Bugatti, many consider it an admirable act of enthusiasm and commitment to Bugatti's design legend: no one is pretending it is *real* Bugatti – are they?

Within a year the two Aérolithe 'Gondola' tapered chassis prototypes of 1935 had been superseded by a modified variation as a production car in the Bugatti catalogue. This was the Type 57 Atlantic, available as an S model or a later SC model depending on where and when the supercharger was fitted or retro-fitted.

The true fate of both of these early Aérolithe prototypes remains an obscure and tantalising mystery. Jonathan Wood in his *Bugatti: The Man and the Marque* (The Crowood Press,

Grey seems a bit flat for an Atlantic. but who are we to argue? The 'Holzschuh' Atlantic chassis #57473 on display at The Bugatti Trust, as recently restored by Paul Russell and Company to its condition before it was struck by a train in 1955.

The Aerolithe was a stepping stone from Type 57 to Atlantic, being taller and more 'American' in its industrial design language.

1992) cites a tale of what sounds like the Aérolithe development car being found by an American serviceman late in World War II and being shipped off to the USA, never to be seen again, but that account remains folklore.

Effectively there remain two 'missing' Type 57 mysteries: the fate of that Aérolithe and of the production Type 57SC Atlantic chassis #57453, *La Voiture Noire*.

Before that, the Aérolithe became the Atlantic (not the 'Atlantique'). Some say this name was in homage to the French aviator Jean Mermoz, who crashed into the Atlantic Ocean in December 1936 whilst flying his Latécoère 300 seaplane *Croix du Sud*. No other explanation is known. We might have expected the Type 57 Atlantic to have followed Bugatti factory tradition and be named after an Alpine pass, but somehow a Bugatti Brenner, Gotthard, Grimsel, Timmelsjoch or Furka would have seemed inappropriate in late 1930s Europe as Hitler sounded his war drums.

The Atlantic that emerged from the Aérolithe was a lightweight, alloy-bodied, 3.3-litre twin-cam high-powered grand touring car with a redesigned *surbaisse* (lowered) chassis, which saw the rear axle pass through the main lowered chassis longerons. It was fitted with de Ram sports-specification shock absorbers, divided front axle, and the lower radiator and nose were streamlined to achieve 200km/h (124mph). Sadly, only four examples of this superlative supercar were manufactured, although later replicas have been created.

So began in October 1936 the story of the Bugatti Type 57S Atlantic. The ex-works factory list price was initially FFr117,000, which was FFr37,000 more than a baseline Type 57. Within a year, Bugatti was charging 150,000FF! Despite this frankly incredible price (you could buy several very large houses or a country estate for that kind of money in 1934), six orders were received and two cars were quickly delivered to England. An order for the Type 57S Atlantic came in from the Greek shipping magnate André Embiricos, but he cancelled his order and instead approached Carrosserie Pourtout and its designer Georges Paulin for what would be the 4¼-litre 'Embiricos' Bentley. We might argue that Paulin's Embiricos Bentley styling owed something to the earlier Type 57 Atlantic and the Aérolithe.

Some observers also cite a direct link between the styling of the Saab 92 UrSaab concept prototype of 1947 and the Type 57. Certainly the angle of the windscreen pillars and the carapace cabin turret leading into a vee-section tapered tail are all redolent of the Bugatti and Paulin designs. The Saab's seats also appear to have been very closely modelled on those of the Bugatti. Given that the Saab designer Sixten Sason had spent time in Paris and Turin in the early 1930s, the influences on his Saab 92 UrSaab prototype should not really be contentious. The effect of various '*Stromliner*', '*Aerodinamica*' and '*Aerodyne*' cars from such as Mercedes-Benz, Porsche, Alfa-Romeo, Lancia, Delahaye, Talbot-Lago, Tatra, Briggs and

From the rear, the longer-tailed styling changes on the 'Holzschuh' Atlantic, probably penned by Figoni, seem even more incredible.

FIGONI AND BUGATTI INFLUENCE

The 'teardrop' (Italian *goccia d'acqua* or French *goutte d'eau*) school of ellipsoid car design became a defining factor in this era of aerodynamic experimentation and its influence on industrial design and styling. The Bugatti company and their collaborators were at the forefront of this movement. The Type 57 (notably the Atalante) and the Type 57 Atlantic remain defining mid-1930s events in the creation of a design language.

The famed French *carrossier* Giuseppe (or Joseph) Figoni of Carrosserie Figoni & Falaschi of Boulogne-sur-Seine (Ovidio Falaschi being his business partner) was sometimes known as the 'Grand Couturier de la Carrosserie Automobile'. He devised the body for the Marchioness of Cholmondeley's Type 57 upon chassis #57739 in early 1938 and would later modify a Type 57 Atlantic in 1949 (see below). Prior to that, in 1933 Figoni had styled the body for a Bugatti Type 55, chassis #55221, which was originally a Bugatti racing car of conventional appearance that had failed to finish at Le Mans the previous year owing to a hole in the petrol tank. Figoni's restyle for the Type 55 (then owned by Jacques Dupuy) was utterly stunning in its sculpture, scale, paint, graphics and sheer impression of individualism. The car was later rescued by Geoffrey St John, who owned it for 56 years.

Figoni also bodied the Shah of Persia's Type 57 in flamboyant style. Jean Bugatti had pioneered lustrous two-tone graphical paint schemes in the Type 50 and Type 55 long before the American motor industry of the 1950s seized upon such a idea. Figoni used highly advanced paints to achieve the hues required in the two-tone technique he applied to his 1930s Bugatti coachwork commissions. It becomes obvious that Jean Bugatti and Joseph Figoni seem to have been feeding off some form of central design theme in developing their creations.

Amid all the design excitement of the era, Jean Bugatti and his small team would create four production Type 57S Atlantics and three remain: *La Voiture Noire* went missing from Bordeaux in World War II and remains yet another Bugatti enigma.

Gerin, as well as Paulin's Embiricos Bentley, should surely also be mentioned in relation to the Type 57 Atlantic, regarding both the influences on it and those that it influenced.

BUGATTI COUPÉ TYPE 57S ATLANTIC HISTORIES

Chassis #57374

Factory date: 2 September 1936

First owned by Lord Rothschild, registered as 6559 WW 20, then in England as DGJ 758

A car described in its factory documents as a 'Coupé Aero', as opposed to the other three cars, which were cited as 'Atlantic' in their factory paperwork. This car set a formula, with its low-mounted headlamps in pontoon from the wing/fender valance, and with windscreen wipers mounted below the windscreen on the scuttle panel. It passed through several British owners, including Leonard Potter, before being sold to the USA. Its long-term US owner Dr Peter Williamson then restored it to the original specification. It is now owned by Peter Mullin, the philanthropist, museum owner and Bugatti supporter, and is currently on display at the Mullin Automotive Museum. This silver-blue car may now be the most expensive Bugatti in the world because many feel it is worth in excess of $50 million.

Chassis #57453

Factory date: October 1936

This is the famous factory black Type 57SC Atlantic (compressor/supercharged by the factory from new), known as *La Voiture Noire* and registered as 58000 NV3, 9219 NV2 and 1521 NV4. It was the second Atlantic by chassis number, although for some time it was mixed up with chassis #57473. Its status was clarified by research to be a factory car resident in Paris and driven by Jean Bugatti, Benoist and Williams. The car disappeared in the fog of war in 1941 and no trace of it has yet been found. It has been conjectured that an estimated value of circa £100 million might apply if the car were found in good condition.

Chassis #57473

Factory date; 11 December 1936

Known as the 'Holzschuh' car after its first owners, Jacques and Yvonne Holzschuh, this car is the enigma of the Atlantic series. Variously registered as 3924 RK7, MC 2288, 6242 BA9, 32 AG 06, 1610 AV75, 7262 QF45 and BWV 75, the car was first exhibited at the Juan les Pins Concours d'Elégance on 31 March 1937. Various bodywork modifications started with a central, third front headlamp. Other changes included faired-in headlamps, an extended bonnet and, more significantly, a

The famous Atlantic 'spine'. There has been much debate about its development and use.

The windows of an Atlantic did not fully open and it could get hot inside without roof vents. This window design allowed some modicum of venting.

In the 1930s cars, aircraft and shoes had 'spats'. This chrome work at the front of the 'Holzschuh' Atlantic's be-spatted rear wheel enclosure reeks of pure Bugattism.

The interior of the later Gangloff-bodied post-Atlantic coupé fastback completed in the late 1980s under the supervision of its designer, Lucien Schlatter, using many original Bugatti parts.

pre-1949 reworking and rescaling to the wings and the tail by Figoni & Falaschi (according to research by Christian Huet and as published by The Bugatti Trust).

Raced, including by Robert Verkerke in Nice in 1951, the car was resident in Nice and Paris through a series of owners. In 1955 the car was struck by a train on a railway crossing and both occupants died. Contrary to claims made then and now, the car was not 'completely destroyed', but it was badly bent and broken up. The wreck was retained by SNCF in a railway scrapyard as the result of a legal wrangle until it was sold off a decade later. It was found by an interested enthusiast, Paul-André Berson, who carried out a lengthy restoration across a decade that failed to return the car to its pure original state, let alone its Figoni-modified form.

Further owners had the car restored (twice), including its time in the Seydoux Collection, where it was restored with the help of André Lecoq. The restored Seydoux car was exhibited at the Villa d'Este Concours in 2000 and it later went to the ownership of the Gonzalez Collection.

Almost incredibly, the original parts from the left side of the car damaged in the crash decades earlier had been purchased from Berson. After a stunning restoration by Paul Russell and Company, several vital body components were returned to the car, which was now in as near-original state as possible. It was seen at Pebble Beach Concours in 2010. The car now resides in England and it made an inspired appearance at The Bugatti Trust during 2022.

Chassis #57591

Factory date: 3 May 1938

Known as the Pope car, as it was originally owned by the 1930s tennis player and barrister Richard Pope. According to some commentators, construction began in late 1937, it was British registered as EXK 6 early in 1938 and road-ready in London by June. It was delivered in Sapphire Blue. Pope referred to the car as 'My Electron coupé', but of course it was not clad in Elektron (or Electron).

It was notable for its different front valance/headlamp design and cabin roof vents. It was also supposed to have had a cabin roof line that was curiously one inch higher than the others, yet no sign of a 'taller' cabin was evident during its restoration by Paul Russell in 1990.

The car was seen in the late 1930s with the driver's side windscreen wiper position on the header rail above the windscreen. This position was not a factory standard, and indeed the car was built with its wipers below the windscreen. It is suggested that Pope was unhappy with the rain visibility of the very poor wiper arc on the standard design and had the driver's side wiper arc rotated to offer a better sweep and view by inverting it off the header rail. Certainly it is impossible to accept that Jean Bugatti would have turned out a car with such a hideous feature as a top-mounted wiper!

There were also variations to rear wing/fender and tail design, and Pope preferred to run without the rear wheel spats. He had the car retro-fitted with a supercharger at the Brixton Bugatti dealership of Colonel Sorel. The engine was fettled after just 5,000 miles (8,000km) of running by the expert mechanic Emil Mischall, a key figure in the London Bugatti operations who had started work at Molsheim in 1917 and came to England in 1925 to work with Colonel Sorel at the Brixton Road depot. Mischall later joined British Messier, where H.G. Conway was Technical Director. The fettling further increased the car's GT performance, notably on Pope's grand European road trips. Thus the Type 57S (Atlantic) became a Type 57SC. Pope believed that the addition of the supercharger took the engine to about 220bhp at peak revs. A Type 57SC in the hands of Ernest Friderich reached 205km/h (127mph) at Montlhéry with a standard axle ratio. Pope mixed Benzol into his fuel and an upper cylinder lubricant. Suitable octane numbers must have been achieved!

Pope further refined his brakes with special pads found on the later hydraulically braked Type 57S range. Clearly Pope, who ultimately owned nine Bugattis, was a press-on driver who delighted in his Bugatti Atlantic, describing it in 1939, 'I consider the Type 57 SC the best of all Bugattis and the finest sporting car in existence.'

From 1967 the car was owned for a decade by Barrie Price, Chairman of The Bugatti Trust. EXK 6 then became the 'Bamford' car in 1977, as owned by Anthony Bamford, before it was sold to the Tom Perkins Collection in the USA. Since 1988 it has been part of the Ralph Lauren Collection and was repainted in black after a superb restoration by Paul Russell and Company.[2]

TYPE 64 TO TYPE 68

The Type 57 story does not simply end with the Atlantic series. The Bugatti Type 64 was the long-awaited replacement for the Type 57 series. It featured the Type 57 engine with quieter chain-driven camshafts and an advanced Cotal-type electrical gearbox of advanced electro-mechanical epicyclic activation, something that was to have been offered on the later Type 57S. The Type 64 went back to lightweight alloy for its major chassis components by deploying the new Duralumin alloy in a new chassis of U-shaped support members, which formed a box-section frame that was different to the Type 57 chassis 'longeron' and 'bearer' type design.

Intended to be launched in 1939, this two-door, two-plus-two was lower, wider and more modern than the Type 57 series. Two were built by Gangloff, with perhaps two more built as chassis or bodied chassis, yet the project went nowhere due to the death of Jean Bugatti and the outbreak of war. The fact that Bugatti was short of money at the time is best left undiscussed.

If Jean Bugatti had lived, it was entirely possible that Bugatti would have taken on a new identity, because Jean had realised that the era of the *grand routière* 'land yacht' type of car was over. The world wanted smaller and more efficient cars that were easier to own and to drive. It is evident that Jean had planned just such a smaller car, moving away from the elegant grandeur of his Type 57 and Atlantic designs. The Type 68 was already born as a new Bugatti design concept for a smaller, cheaper to own Bugatti that could have sold in vast numbers. Effectively Bugatti was planning for the war and the post-war years with a clever but complex 370cc 4-cylinder supercharged engine. Today, small 1.0-litre engines with three or four cylinders and a turbocharger and or supercharger designed-in are the accepted norm for low-capacity yet well-performing small cars. Eight decades ago, Bugatti had already thought of the idea and its application. Ettore also planned a mid-range 4-cylinder car, the Type 73.

The Type 68's high-revving (up to 7,500rpm), 370cc engine, which would have brought it into a low tax rate, was envisaged with an even smaller capacity than a Citroën *Deux Cheveux*, yet it had a twin-overhead camshaft, supercharger and four-valves per cylinder. Throw in a fluid flywheel complete with an in-built 'engine brake' effect and highly aerodynamic sculptured form, and the Type 69 was a typical piece of advanced Bugatti thinking. Finally unveiled in 1946, the project died before it became a 'baby' Bugatti supercar, although there was to be a later attempt to revive the concept (*see* Chapter 7).[3]

A rather ungainly Type 68 rolling prototype was built with a strange, two-door roadster body of somewhat perpendicular style. Yet by late 1940 the Type 68's secret of economy and performance lay in a planned bodyshell of curved, aerodynamic coupé design, whose low drag allowed its small engine to achieve high speeds. But by now the Type 68's originating stylist, Jean, was dead.

Atlantic 's interior had a sense of occasion and this Amalgam Collection example captures it perfectly. Since 2005 Amalgam have been official partners with Bugatti for the creation of stunning Bugatti scale devices.

Amalgam's scale Atlantic shown with the earlier bonnet louvres and low-line headlamp position as defining identifiers of the example. This 1:8 scale Atlantic is yours for £16,995.

Blue on blue with wood, and chrome trims – essential Bugatti cabin design from Jean Bugatti.

This view clearly evidences the 'carapace' shaped hallmark of the Atlantic's design language.

Jean-Pierre Wimille's command post: a very rare view of the original and unrestored Type 59/50B 4.7-litre single-seater seen in 2019 on the occasion of its first return to Prescott in eight decades. Thanks to Angela Hucke at The Bugatti Trust and Chris Rogers at the Bugatti Owners' Club, the author was present to record the event.

CHAPTER 7

MONOPOSTO AND MAGNESIUM

In the mid-1930s converting the Type 59 to a single-seat racing car body configuration was a quick and easy plan for Bugatti in its quest to increase its profile through motor sport. With deft changes carried out by the factory, the days of Bugatti's racing ace Jean-Pierre Wimille competing in a modified yet unsupercharged Type 59, complete with mudguards, were just a precursor to the power of a re-engineered Type 59. Yet before long cars such as that belonging to King Leopold of Belgium were surpassed by the re-engined Type 59/50B as developed for racing and then developed again for the new racing Grand Prix Formula that began after 1937.

Could Bugatti take on the German racing marques and beat the Alfa Romeos? To do so it needed a supercar racer – a single-seat one.

The works racing department at Molsheim started doing some mix-and-matching with chassis, bodies and engines produce in various limited numbers. From this emerged various re-purposed Type 59s and Type 57 chassis of confusing ancestry. As an example of the complex goings-on, a chassis from the 57S45, of which only two were made, seems to be the basis of a car fitted with the 4.5-litre type 50B.2 engine, yet referred to by many as effectively a Type 59 with the type 50B engine. The definitive single-seater cars had a revised or altered chassis and body as described below. Yet 1939 also saw a much modified 3.3-litre-based 'Tank' Type 57G compete at Le Mans for the first time since a Bugatti Tank had won the race in 1937. It was to be the revised Type 59, however, with a new engine and new body that would become the single-seat 'Queen': the Tank was done with.

The in-line 8-cylinder type 50B engine was Bugatti's last pre-war racing engine and pumped out up to 186kW (250hp), and finally up to just over 400hp in supercharged form if you filled it with suitably enhanced (alcohol-based) fuel. Fifteen such engines were said to have been built, these being of 3.0 litres (suggested with twin-superchargers, but often with one and rather a troublesome engine), 4.5 litres and ultimately the supercharged 4.7-litre variation. Lead on by Jean, Edouard Bertrand as Molsheim's engine builder on the project applied forensic standards to the new engine's build specifications.

There is intrigue in the factory paperwork regarding these few engines; records held at The Bugatti Trust clearly show that Ettore personally specified in a typed note of 20 September 1937 that a small number of engine type 50B were to be made with magnesium components as the crankcase and cylinder liners. It is even possible that a magnesium block was hinted at, but it has not been located, nor is there any evidence for it to date. Bugatti gave the engines the written nomenclature '*Moteurs 50. B.1. and 50. B.2.*'. Ettore categorically refers to B.1. and B.2., not BI or BII.[1]

Magnesium was an expensive option and a new technology that required extreme precision and care when being built, but it was Ettore's usual practice when seeking perfection; he was going to body a car in magnesium, even at vast expense (*see* below).

Did he intend using the 'magnesium' engine for air racing as well as in a racing car when he specified such an alloy? The other type 50B engines used R.R.50 standard and A.P.33 aluminium alloy for such components.

Given that Bugatti as a company was in financial trouble and propped up by its railways contracts, such expense seems risky, but then Ettore always thought the money would materialise.

Ettore Bugatti had requested Louis de Monge to create an air racer. The new type 50B engine was, of course, the engine Ettore had in mind for that project and he was dreaming of 500hp output, hoping to get somewhere between 66 and 100hp per litre: even 66hp per litre was over 20hp per litre more than the rival Renault engine. Bugatti negotiated a French Government contract to build two of these aircraft, one with a smaller wing but of higher wing loading to be faster for sprint record attempts, and another with the long-distance speed record wing type. A 5.0-litre Type 50B engine was considered, but went no further.

The Type 50B engines No. 7 and No. 8 (not matched and with differing charge ratios) were fitted during construction of the Bugatti Type 100 aircraft, but this airframe was mothballed during World War II and it is recorded that engines No. 4 and No. 5 had been the actual engines intended for the first flight. This pair had technical differences and were directionally 'handed' in a different direction to engines No. 7 and No. 8 for their power delivery. This was a vital torque factor in the aircraft's handling characteristics, yet went against the then accepted wisdom of contra-rotation. The engine drawings indicate that these may have been the 'magnesium' block engines, as well as using magnesium cylinder

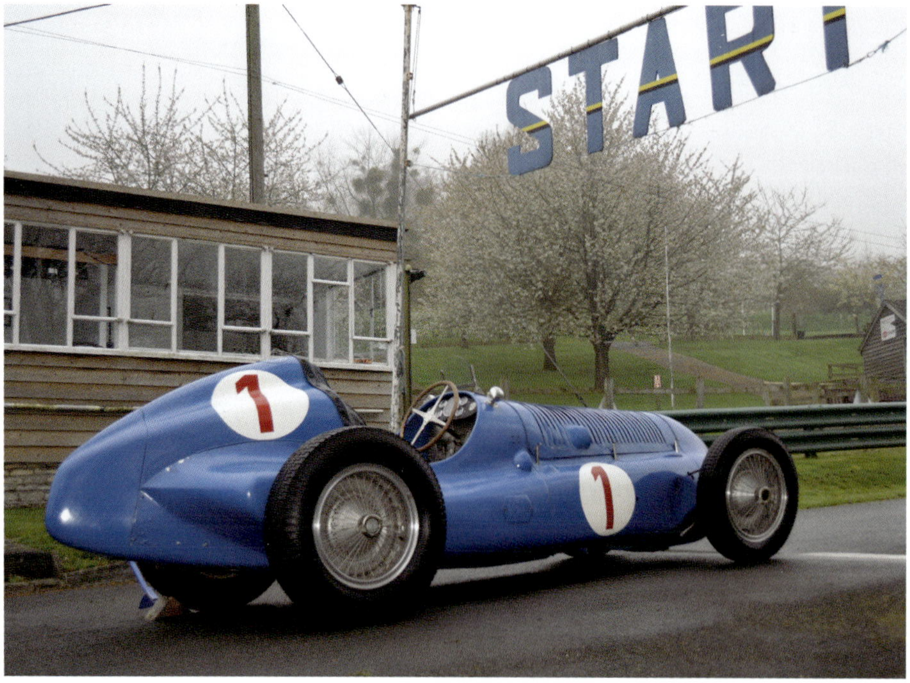

Captured on the starting line at Prescott, the true nature of a 'Grand Prix' Bugatti racing car makes its own statement.

Seen without the twin rear wheels that were tried at Prescott on its first visit, this angle of the Type 59/50B shows off the side profile and bulbous side fairing underneath which lay something rather concerning.

liners or crankshaft, but when examined later the engines did not tally with the records. Magnesium, however, was a valuable raw material, and the fate of the intended or realised magnesium engine parts is unknown.[2]

For the last of the Bugatti racers, a car with a larger capacity engine, a rather generic cowled nose and a new, slanted-back radiator cover and numerous tweaks, including an external exhaust, was ready. A single-seat 'monoplace' or *monoposto* Bugatti was a reality. It had a built-up rear and fairing behind the driver's head running down into a 'boat-tail' shape of supposed streamlining efficiency. The earlier Type 59 had now morphed into the Type 59/50B single-seater, which itself would appear in more than one guise, later with Type 57 Atlantic-style faired-in headlamps set into a curved frontal valance that protruded forwards of the chassis front crossmember.

Here was a one-piece 'pontoon' style body for a racing car, a style that lasted long into the 1950s for racing cars before the be-winged and space-framed Grand Prix cars of the 1960s. Unsurprisingly, the Jean Bugatti-penned Type 59/50B was elegant, sculptural, wind-cheating and just perfectly 'organic' from every angle. Here lay another great Bugatti design moment – in a single-seater racing car.

The type 50B engine's fame came from its use in Bugatti racing cars, notably at the hands of Jean-Pierre Wimille in the single example of the 4.7-litre Type 59/50B. First seen in competition in the 1936 Monaco Grand Prix as a lower capacity engine, the Type 59/50B cars would soon be developed to meet the new racing formula regulations. A reverse-engineered or de-rated Type 50B engine of 3-litre capacity, which reached 229.6km/h (147.2mph), would appear at Reims and then at the 1938 Cork race in Ireland.

The B-variant engines had a light alloy block with liners, which differentiated them from the earlier 'normal' type 50 engines. Versions B.1., B.2. and finally a B.3. were created. The supercharged engines gave power ratings of around the 400hp level, depending on the supercharger pressure: engine No. 7 was recorded in a test on 27 June 1939 as giving 404hp. Roots-type superchargers of increasing capacity were used. Jean Bugatti claimed that 480hp was achieved in bench testing using a special fuel mix, not far off the 500hp his father had touted to de Monge for the aircraft engine.

So evolved the new Grand Prix type of single-seat Bugatti racer, even though the 3-litre engine was less than reliable. That first car was also shipped to the USA to take part in the 1937 George Vanderbilt Cup at Westbury, New York, Wimille coming home in second place.

The engine would grow to 4.5 litres and then 4.7 litres supercharged, which was without doubt the most powerful engine to emerge from the Molsheim factory. The engine was firstly rebuilt to a normally aspirated 4.5-litre capacity in order to race in Europe. Jean-Pierre Wimille drove it to second place in the major race at Montlhéry in 1937, being beaten by a 12-valve Delahaye Type 145 driven by René Dreyfus. The new 1938 regulations affected engine cubic capacity (and bore and stroke) in terms of displacement restrictions across both unsupercharged and supercharged capacities. Bugatti effectively de-rated his earlier, larger engine back down to a supercharged 3 litres: this was the troublesome 3.0-litre referred to earlier.

Bugatti uprated the engine to the defining 4.7 litres with a supercharger, giving us the Type 59/50B car as a 'one-off' for Wimille to drive. This 1939 single-seater of 4.7 litres had a more-enveloping, more aerodynamic front end compared to the previous year's smaller-engined single-seater, and that is the visual clue to the car's difference. Of the two such cars, the 4.7-litre car depicted here shows the final 'faired-in' front end design.

Veyron, Benoist and Wimille had driven the racing Type 59, Type 57 and Type 59/50B cars respectively in this era, but it was Wimille who came to the fore in 1939 with the larger-engined and supercharged Type 59/50B (chassis #50180), which by now boasted much-needed hydraulic brakes. Various competition wins and placings, including a win at the Coupe de Paris at Montlhéry, signalled that the car was the class leader on an open circuit or road, but it was more difficult on tight, narrow circuits such as hill climbs.

The car came to Prescott Hill Climb's first international meeting and Jean Bugatti and Jean-Pierre Wimille made a

The same Wimille Type 59/50B captured during its first visit to Prescott in July 1939. Jean Bugatti chats whilst leaning against the car. Also present were chief mechanics Robert Aumaître and Lucien Wurmser. Earl Howe just happened to be standing there too.

mark with the Type 59/50B there at the Bugatti Owners' Club on Sunday 30 July 1939.

Wimille had just won at Le Mans for the second time in his career. Robert Aumaître, the Molsheim chief mechanic, came with them as did mechanic Lucien Wurmser. To be frank, however, the new car was too big – too long in the wheelbase and too wide, too unwieldy around the very tight bends at Prescott. The straights were not really long enough for the supercharged effect to come in, either, prior to heavy braking. A wet track, despite the use of twinned rear wheels, kept the blue Bugatti off the victor's place, but it came in second fastest of the day (46.69 seconds), behind the smaller, more nimble ERA of Raymond Mays, who claimed the fastest time of the day. Wimille and the Bugatti, however, had taken their Class record. But this was the first and only appearance of an official Bugatti of Molsheim entry at Prescott. The Bugatti entourage stayed at the Queen's Hotel in Cheltenham.

We might wonder if this late 1930s Type 59/50B set the rules for post-war grand prix car design. Owing to the disruption of World War II, the car only ran once more at the Coupe de Prisonniers in Paris in 1945. It later was acquired for the Schlumpf Collection in Mulhouse.

A perfect profile. The Type 59/50B was the last gasp of the Bugatti racing car. Wimille came second at the original event with a hill-time of 46.69 seconds but was beaten by Raymond Mays in the ERA by milliseconds, 46.14 seconds being the time of Mays's ERA.

The car, the last Grand Prix Bugatti prior to the 1939–45 conflict and also the last such Bugatti ever, somehow survived the war and was later acquired for the Schlumpf Collection at Mulhouse. Since 1982 the collection has been known as the Musée National de l'Automobile.

This same car, untouched, unrestored and fragile, yet of vital historic significance, returned to Prescott just once, 80 years later in 2019, thanks to the efforts of The Bugatti Trust, its trustees, and the support of the Bugatti Owners' Club. The author was invited to witness and record the moment of its arrival from France in the unique photos of the event presented here.[3]

Wimille won the first post-war race with this car in Paris on 9 September 1945 at an average speed of 114km/h (71mph). He then won the Grand Prix de Luxembourg in a different Bugatti chassis with the citation of #57-50B 'sports equipment'. Sadly Wimille was to die soon afterwards in a race in Argentina in 1949, but not in a Bugatti. His 'Prescott' car, the Type 59/50B was preserved, untouched, and reputedly never again sat in by anyone to this day. Its return visit to its old haunt in England lent a ghostly air to its legend. Bugatti car production and Bugatti Grand Prix car manufacture had effectively ended in 1939 in all but name. So this 'Wimille' Type 59/50B is both a stunning supercar racer, and effectively the last pure racing Bugatti.

Supercars do not get much rarer or more original. It is beyond price.

MAGNESIUM MAGIC

In the 1930s magnesium alloy was touted as the new lightweight, high-strength alloy for use in the building of aircraft bodies. It would prove to have several problems, including its easy flammability and its potentially brittle nature, which made it difficult to repair and weld. Curiously for an alloy intended for use in aviation, it did not like very cold temperatures of the kind found at higher altitudes (–50°C being the norm).

Jim Hull in the Type 59S 'Elektron' exits Prescott, taking the original chassis and toolroom-new body built using the original techniques for a run through the Cotswolds.

Variously known as Elektron or Electron, the magnesium-rich alloy was invented in Germany as *Elektronmetall* as early as 1910 and had been used in experimental engine castings. The infamous IG Farbenindustrie would take over the various small producers of Elektron in Germany; the British would also manufacture the alloy under licence from about 1923 whilst at the same time developing their own modified or improved variant.

The Zeppelin airships were the first major use of the alloy in aviation. The flammable alloy was also used in bomb casings by British and German forces, so Elektron has a somewhat colourful history.

Extruded metal was a new science in the 1920s. A very high-powered Air Ministry committee, led by Supermarine Spitfire aerodynamicist B.S. Shenstone, was funded and tasked in the late 1930s with investigating and developing such alloy techniques. Elektron alloy comprised approximately 87–90 per cent magnesium, up to 9 per cent aluminium and various smaller percentages of rare-earth metals including manganese, zirconium, neodymium and yttrium.

Intriguingly, Bugatti is said to have sourced the low-density ultra-lightweight alloy for this car from the British Magnesium Elektron Limited rather than purchase it from the Germans just across the border. Ettore had in fact been experimenting with magnesium alloy for more than ten years, not least in his alloy wheel castings and engine components, notably its engine blocks. However, building an entire car body out of the new alloy was pushing the boundaries of knowledge and expense, so it was perfect for Bugatti to try!

TYPE 59S 'ELEKTRON'

If the limited production run of the Type 59 as a racing car was not mythical enough, then the on-off creation by Jean of an Elektron-bodied Type 59 takes us further into legend. The car was first seen at the 1935 (some say it was 1936) Paris Salon and the highly unusual body seems to have divided opinion. It has been suggested that Jean Bugatti envisaged each of the front wing housing(s) or 'spats' turning with the wheel(s), but this feature did not make it to the one-off 'show' car, although magnesium alloy construction did.

Possibly envisaged as a Le Mans entry car, it never competed. After its exhibition at the Paris Salon, the car rather surprisingly remained unsold and was returned to Molsheim,

Long, low and decidedly 'Le Mans' in appearance, the Type 59S 'Elektron' was, rather surprisingly, unsold after its exhibition at the 1936 Paris Salon and was returned to Molsheim, where Jean Bugatti drove it regularly. Yet it seems the factory may have disposed of the body around 1939.

where it was regularly driven by Jean Bugatti. It was truly *superleggera* (lightweight) and consequently very fast, especially as it had an uprated supercharger. But what happened to the car? Bugatti was said by some to have destroyed the body before 1939, or it was destroyed at the factory during the war by occupying forces. If so, how come the engine, chassis and components were saved and kept together? Unless of course, those German forces realised the rarity and value of the magnesium body and shipped it off to Heinkel, Junkers or some other major aviation company for use and left the other parts behind. Did the Nazi rocket programme utilise the stolen magnesium alloy body after it had been melted down?

Myths abound about the car's body. As for the unique chassis and the engine, these were said to have been stored at the Bugatti factory until it was closed down in 1961, when a factory employee purchased the parts and sat on them for years.

As with so much of Bugatti, it becomes hard to 'prove' things, not least because of the shenanigans that took place over how the numbers on the chassis and components at Molsheim were stamped, over-stamped or remained un-stamped.

Decades later, when Jim and Tonya Hull brought their unique Type 59S Elektron Torpedo 'recreation' all the way from California to traverse British and Irish roads, all but the hardened Bugatti puritans were touched. This was no copycat modern reinterpretation, but a car with an accurately constructed new body over authentic Bugatti parts of, shall we say, interesting provenance.

Hull's car is not a 'copy', a 'fake' or a 'continuation', not least because it is built upon an 'original' Bugatti chassis, or parts thereof, that came from Uwe Hucke, who had sourced it and many parts direct from the Bugatti factory stores manager François Seyfried. We rely on Seyfried's insistence that the chassis' provenance was the original Elektron torpedo's, even if Bugatti did not (as reputed) number his 'gondola' chassis. So whilst proof is in the eye of the beholder, this is a 'Bugatti' in generic terminology.

The parts that came with the engine included a unique oversized Bugatti Type 50 supercharger (as per 1935–6 specification), which may have added over 50hp to the base engine's rating. According to Hull, in conversation with the author, the car can run on a methanol additive that might take the engine towards a rather heady 300hp.

Seeing and hearing the car in action is certainly an occasion and there is no denying its torque, speed, handling and incredible sound. It also seems to handle extremely well.

Hull's car uses many original Bugatti parts, and the body is a direct, toolroom-exact recreation of the original body that Bugatti may have scrapped, and was built using the correct traditional methodology. Based on 1935 components, the car in its 1930s form as an original 'competition' model was shown at the Paris Salon alongside the even more remarkable Aérolithe, precursor of the Atlantic coupés. The Hull car has been painstakingly recreated over the relevant 'gondola' or tapered Bugatti chassis, and was hand-formed and riveted without recourse to welding the panels, and as such

There are clearly elements of the Type 59 and Atlantic in the rear-end styling of the magnesium body, replete with its 'spine'.

'Unoriginal but original' might be a way to describe the accurate re-creation of the Type 59S's dashboard.

was built just as the original body had been – after all, welding Elektron tends to make it catch fire.

It was Jerry Weeks who built the body for Hull and the difficulties of working with the alloy meant that it took several years to complete. The brittle and easily corroded magnesium alloy was nickel-coated to improve its lifespan. The car was assembled by P. Reilly and Company and then sent to British Bugatti specialist Tom Dark for further work.[4]

First revealed in 2013 at the Monterey Motorsports Reunion, the car has made more than one overseas foray and the sight of it careering through the British countryside in the rain was something very special indeed. Whilst it might not be the original Type 59 'holy grail' of the ex-King Leopold Type 59 in *that* car's original patina and character, surely only the hardest-hearted purist would dismiss Hull's car. In the author's view, and those of others more qualified to comment, it is *not* a 'fake'; it might not be purer than pure, but it is an exact recreation of a Bugatti body built in the correct factory manner in the exact alloy as originally used, and then mounted upon many original Bugatti parts. Let's hear no carping and salute Mr Hull for his resolution and financial commitment. You are, of course, entitled to a different opinion.

This design detail is authentic provenance.

External suspension and boat-tailed stern make for classic stuff.

The Elektron's visit to Prescott was a rare and very special event.

Hustling away with a burble of Bugatti power and the scything of a magnesium body that is identical with the original. A lovely Bugatti moment.

TYPE 251: THE SUPERCAR THAT NEVER WAS

With World War II over and history being written by the victors – nations who had no qualms about 'liberating' thousands of tons of advanced pre-war German science, as well as that associated with the Nazis (which was an entirely separate field), to take it back to their own research institutes – what was to stop Bugatti framing its own future?

There followed the last attempt to revive the fortunes of Bugatti and with it Jean's legacy. Ettore's wife Barbara had died in 1944 and two years later he married his mistress, Geneviève Delcuze, by whom he already had two children. In 1947, however, Ettore too died. The new head of the firm was the 25-year-old and untested Roland Bugatti and there were still disputes with the French government over the ownership of Bugatti's factory and lands. The company's trustees took the decision to try and start all over again. A principal figure in this was the new general manager, Pierre Marco, whose career with Bugatti went back to the 1920s. Work began on rebuilding the Bugatti factory from 1947. Former Bugatti technical director Noël Domboy's influence on the affair was not invisible either. The new car's engineering design, however, was principally by Gioacchino Colombo.

Ettore's widow remarried in 1951. Her new husband was the millionaire who owned the Rizla cigarette paper empire and he was prepared to help fund a revived Bugatti, although there would need to an arrangement between Geneviève and the surviving children from Ettore's first marriage.

Between 1948 and 1951 the ideas for new Bugattis came and went. A new car to be known as the Type 73 was publicly announced, but only a prototype was built. There was also a revival of the 1939 design project that was to be the ill-fated 'new' Type 101, which draped a rather Graber-esque roadster body style, actually designed by Gangloff, over rewarmed Type 57 elements, including the 3.3-litre engine. A Guilloré-styled four-door saloon variant was also one of the rare Type 101 iterations, as was a Van Antem coupé-bodied variant. Seven Type 101s were reputedly built plus an un-bodied chassis. Rather curiously, as late as 1965, the famed American car designer Virgil Exner would clothe the last Type 101 chassis in a contemporary American-themed Bugatti styling 'update'.

With the world of 1950s motor racing regaining strength after wartime, a new 2.5-litre Grand Prix formula was announced. Was there a chance that not just a new Bugatti racing car but a new Bugatti racing team might be created? In 1953 plans gained pace at Molsheim ready for the 1954 racing season.

Going back to its roots, the newly funded Bugatti company created a pure racing car – in fact a Formula One grand prix challenger that evoked all the legends of Bugatti's illustrious past cars and drivers. In *theory* here was the car to resurrect Bugatti via the podiums of motor racing as arguably its greatest mid-century era was unfolding.

The ingredients were very pure: the Gioacchino Colombo-designed transversely positioned straight-8 of 2500cc with 4 cylinders in a two-part cylinder (magnesium alloy) block bolted together at the head and a two-part crankshaft with a central drivetrain for the camshaft gear, upon which ten main bearings relied – amid 8-cylinders in true Ettore style. The gearbox was fitted *in situ* and a transmission directed drive to the rear wheels (not all four wheels). There were gear-driven Marelli magnetos, four twin-choke Weber carburettors, vented-disc hydraulic brakes of Bugatti design, a dry multi-plate clutch and, rather dangerously, large petrol tanks mounted amidships on each external side of the chassis rails.

The chassis itself was a structural space frame of welded steel tube, with all the efficiencies and dangers that entailed, but this was not a chassis designed for impact safety: it was a chassis created for racing efficiency.

A typically solid Bugatti front axle might have jarred, but it did have coil springs and multi-link locating arms. The coil spring-to-damper mechanisms were unusually configured, diagonally across the chassis. The famous Bugatti square-headed bolts were used in construction, as were Type 57 parts (such as the live rear axle, but with added de Dion link) and many drilled items. That rear axle was 'live' yet slid on a centre trunnion abetted by twin-links and had vertical push-rod bell-crank mountings at each wheel hub. Diagonal, chassis-braced dampers were also fitted. The front and rear suspension were thus effectively similar. Yet the front axle was rigid and, of course, hollow – evoking old pre-war Bugatti technology that should have been dispensed with.[5]

As usual, no expense had been spared – it was a Bugatti after all. The bodyshell featured advanced aerodynamics, with fairings or shrouds ahead of the front wheels and a fluted tailpiece to try to control the airflow off the back. This was later modified into a cleaner, more curved, yet perhaps less aerodynamically efficient (due to potential induced lift) panel in the second Type 251 prototype.

In the Type 251 was presented a low, very wide, ellipsoid single-seat racing car that clearly had massive potential both on the track and for a likely road-car derivative. Here all the elements of Bugatti design were coming together, although the gearbox seemed to owe a nod to Porsche design. A Type 252 sports car was also envisioned, and design and engineering work started on a 1.5-litre Michelotti-styled roadster. This single prototype was to be the sole example of the new Bugatti. A further new design, drafted as the Type 451, was to be last true design from Bugatti. It was a larger sports car intended as some form of de facto Ferrari competitor, but it got no further than the drawing board.

Prior to those last gasps, there had been a second prototype Type 251 with longer wheelbase, modified suspension, and nose and tail body design changes. Extensive public testing took place, yet despite its clever design the Type 251, with its wide chord body, short wheelbase and live axles, was somewhat twitchy in the handling department. Somehow it was too clever, too big, the opposite of the lightweight racing car philosophy that would soon emerge.

Maurice Trintignant, Louis's younger brother, was the racing driver honoured with testing the Type 251 and taking the revised second prototype to 18th position in the 1956 French Grand Prix, during which the Bugatti finally expired. The car had been a handful and its handling somewhat difficult, which was definitely not Bugatti's aim.

Orders from other racing teams were not forthcoming: overnight Bugatti was a company with no future, no car and a somewhat tarnished short-term legacy. The money dried up just as Bugatti was spending huge sums on the Type 251's debut.

All of this happened despite the Type 251 being a technical tour de force and well ahead of its time. Sadly, some commentators describe it as a 'tank' by another name. Perhaps not surprisingly, the fact that the Type 251 and Type 101 combined ideas and requirements from more than one mind resulted in a car that never really was.

It would be 2020 before an evocation of such a Bugatti design exercise would reappear in a Chiron-based form as the unofficial, one-off 251 Evo concept car, designed by Alessio Minchella, who had trained with Pininfarina, and modelled into three-dimensional reality by Luigi Memola.

Without Jean, Bugatti had lost its direction. After Ettore's death in 1947 the company entered various stages of legal status and disputes. Attempts to reincarnate the brand with the Type 61 and Type 73 did not achieve series production. A planned new factory in Paris remained unbuilt. Bugatti's last motor show stand was seen at the 1952 Paris Salon. Bugatti gained a series of military supply contracts with the French government for non-car production, turning out military hardware at Molsheim, but in a stroke of bad luck this lifeline was lost in 1954 following the end of France's involvement in Indo-China. Roland Bugatti still attempted to build on the legend of his family brand, but the Type 251 racing car project, limited to two prototypes, was terminated in 1956 and the derivative Type 252 sports car concept was

From Type 251 came Type 252, the new Bugatti roadster for the 1950s, but sadly it was not to be. Note the departure from the earlier Bugatti grille/radiator design motif. In theory this car should have been Bugatti's supercar saviour for the 1960s boom years of the sports car.

stillborn. As the 1960s dawned, Bugatti was financially bereft and effectively dead as a trading enterprise.

In the post-war period Bugatti built fewer than ten cars up to its true demise. The Type 101 was a Type 57 reincarnated using warmed-over components and a Schlatter-designed Gangloff body designed for Bugatti. We can only really imagine what the Type 64 and Type 68 might have been. The decline of the once revered brand was strangely poignant. Anyone interested in this fascinating period of success and failure, of magic and myth laid low, can do no better than read John Barton's wonderful book *Bugatti: The Twilight Years, 1943–1963*, in which this experienced Bugattiste and restorer tells the story in a manner fitting to the characters and exploits involved in Bugatti's last hurrah.[6]

In 1963 the Hispano-Suiza Company took over the remaining Bugatti engineering interests. Meanwhile Hans and Fritz Schlumpf began to buy up Bugatti cars in ever larger numbers for their unique collection. Bugatti as it was originally known had gone, its supercars, stunning design and engineering skills seemingly consigned to collector's corner. No amount of money could bring Bugatti back from the brink. The ultimate cruel irony was that this coincided with the great 1960s boom in cars and motoring. Jaguar's E-Type, various Maseratis, Ferraris, Alfa Romeos, Lancias, Aston Martins, Mercedes-Benzes and Porsches scooped up buyers with sports cars that combined engineering excellence with performance, style and 'design'. Bugatti could have triumphed but, in all but name, it was dead and buried.

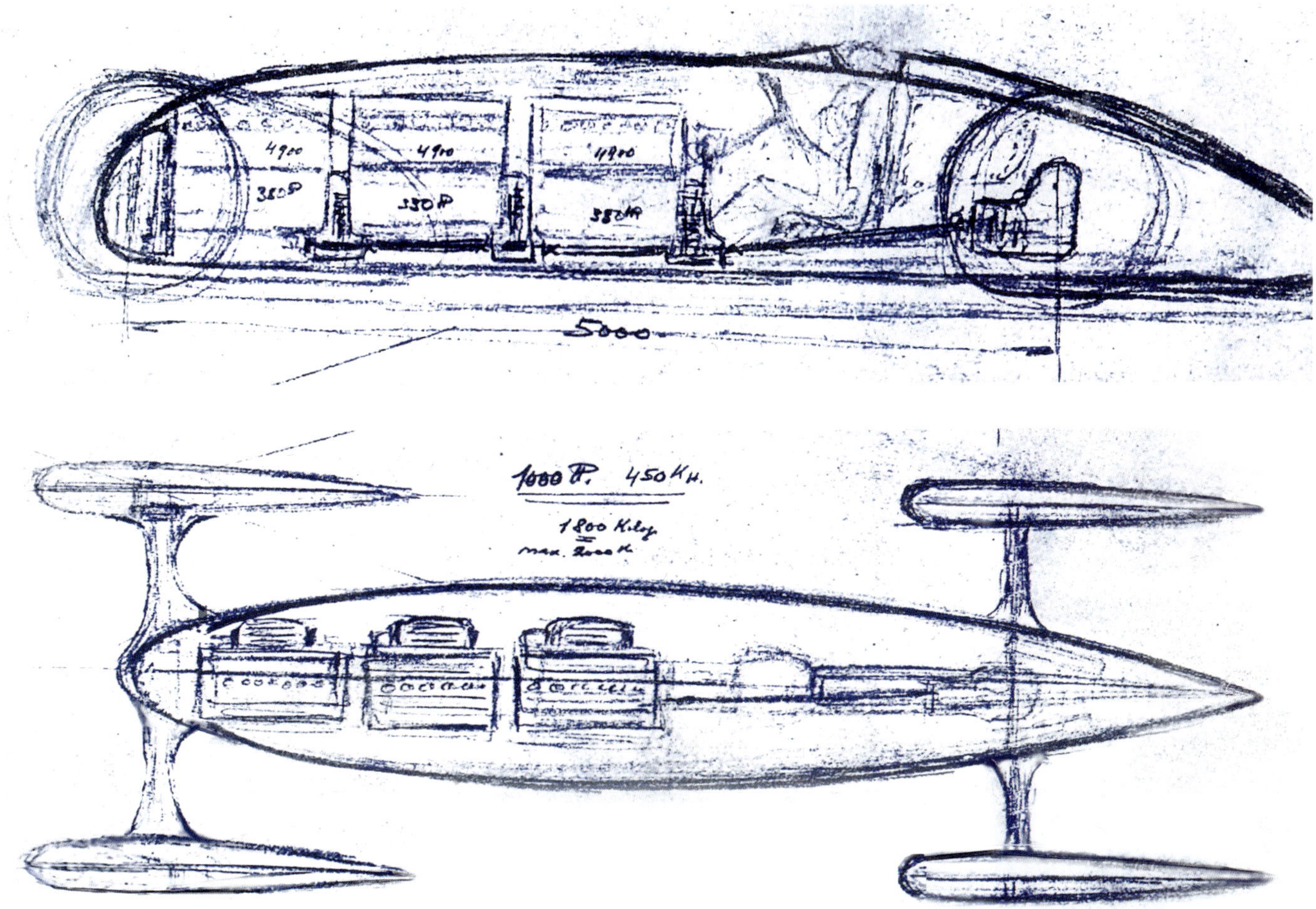

The Bugatti supercar that never was: the little-known Jean Bugatti design sketch of 1937 for a world land speed record car that may have been aimed at Auto Union's dominance and likely to have been subject to official French government sponsorship. Of note are the three shaft-linked supercharged Type 50B 4.9-litre engines. The aerodynamically faired front wheels were designed to turn through 18 degrees but were not connected to the suspension. A proposed 5-metre wheelbase aided stability. Power of 1,000bhp and an average run speed of 450km/h were Jean's target with this stunning alloy-bodied streamliner that sadly never was and which might have been Bugatti's first true hypercar. (Unfortunately part of the right-hand edge of the original sketch is now lost.)

KEY BUGATTI SUPERCARS, 1919–39

Type 13 Brescia

1919–26 as the (16-valve) variant from the earlier Type 13 series post-1911. Won at Le Mans 1920 and at Brescia 1921. Achieved 160km/h (100mph) lap at Montlhéry.

Type 35 Grand Prix

1924 onwards: Supercharged B variant in 1927–30. Roller bearing crankshaft, three-valves per cylinder Won over 1,500 races worldwide with 69 major class event victories. The car that defined grand prix car design of an era.

Type 40 and Type 43 Grand Sport

1926–30: Two defining new Bugatti ranges offering the Type 40 'entry-level' and the sporting variant as the Type 43. The Type 43 Grand Sport offers the Type 35B engine in a more comfortable touring road car with performance. The Type 43GS was the first true production sports car with reliable 160km/h (100mph) road-going performance. Can carry four people if necessary.

Type 41 Royale

1927 onwards: The Bugatti supercar-into-hypercar of 13-litres, incredible build and appearance. A massive, grand scale car destined for stardom yet ultimate commercial failure as an indulgent use of the Bugatti design and engineering talents. Six examples built.

Type 44 Tourer

1927–30: Employed the new 3-litre straight-8 engine with overhead camshaft driven from crankshaft centre. Had wide sales and owner appeal: 1,075 made in varying specifications.

Type 46S

1931–6: A large and powerful car notably attractive as a saloon of 'mini-Royale' character and appearance, but effectively at two-thirds scale. Used a transaxle type gearbox. 400 cars built, of which 20 were supercharged.

Type 50

Large-engined grand Bugatti that was the base for Le Mans entry cars and various coachwork and specification variants.

Type 51 Grand Prix

1931: Another attempt at a pure racing car following the Type 35. Used the twin-cam Miller-influenced Bugatti engine, supercharger, one-piece alloy wheels, twin fuel fillers and revised dynamics. Driven by Chiron, Varzi and Dreyfus to several grand prix successes.

A never-seen-before shot of Ettore with his beloved horses in his courtyard. Photographed by George, 5th Marquess of Cholmondeley in the late 1920s.

Type 55 Super Sport Roadster and Fixed Head

1932: A Jean Bugatti design that mated the Type 51 Grand Prix engine to a closed coupé, or a convertible low-line, two-seat body of exquisite beauty. Huge performance allied to style, with a top speed of 177km/h (110mph). Most Molsheim-bodied and all with racing-type alloy wheels. Today one of the rarest and most desirable Bugattis.

Type 57

1934–40: The new supercar with a range of bodies and specifications. 3.3-litre 8-cylinder engines similar to the Type 59, some with supercharged developments and varying design improvements. Ventoux, Stelvio and Atalante Type 57s, with T, S, C and SC variants available. This become the most famous of the range.

Type 57 Atlantic

A different type of Type 57 development with a different chassis of *surbaisse* (lowered) type with a unique two-seat coupé 'aero' body design. The ultimate Bugatti of the late 1930s, it achieved international fame then (and now) as arguably the greatest example of Bugatti supercar design and engineering of its era. Only four built.

Type 59

1934–6: The final hurrah of the Bugatti Grand Prix racing car as a 3.3-litre supercharged engine, yet with outdated brakes and suspension that were behind its rivals' new technology. Notable for its wheel design technology and engine-chassis combination: a potent and dynamic racing car of 241km/h (150mph) capability yet ultimately a failure. Only six were made (plus between one and three others being cited as later builds).

The 'supercar' that never was. The rare, original Bugatti-signed design sketch of Jean's idea for a post war 'economy' car development – in effect a smaller supercar.

EB110 SS seen head-on in all its glory.

CHAPTER 8

EB110: REINCARNATION REVISITED

When we started to manufacture Bugatti cars, we certainly asked ourselves what would Ettore Bugatti do if he were still alive. Therefore we set up everything … to make a real Bugatti.

Romano Artioli, Automobili Bugatti SpA

Was it sacrilege to even begin to suggest that Bugatti could be revived? Was it naive to try and evoke, or capture, or indeed to mimic the design legend of Bugatti – father and son? And was it just exploitation of a heritage? The answer was that it was not, because the car that resulted, the EB110, was the apogee of the hypercar then and for years afterwards. Let's recall that the Lamborghini Diablo VT four-wheel drive came out after the EB110, and that sadly the Jaguar XJ220 was not delivered as designed or promised, but the EB110 was. The only thing that comes close to an EB110 is a Veyron, or a Chiron – but no, actually it's a Centodieci, another Bugatti.

The EB110, in both its GT and Super Sport models, raised the bar and in some respects still has not been equalled. Those of us who love the EB110 are not blind to its minor faults, but the fact is that it was one of the greatest cars of the century of the car. Was it perfect? No – but nearly. Was Romano Artioli perfect? All we know is that the machine and the man made history, although there are many reasons why the project was laid low. Artioli has his detractors, but the author aligns himself with those who feel that he was the hero of the EB110 'moment' and that we owe him and his legacy a great deal. Such a vision of the future was a rare, brave and risky process for one man.

Some mistakenly thought the EB110 was a marketing-led exercise, but the car, events and time have proved them wrong. Despite some hiccups along the way, the EB110 did evoke something of the spirit of the original marque, which was not just captured, but turned into production reality. Surely only the hardest-hearted cynic would refute such a claim today.

Romano Artioli was the brains, the energy and the visionary behind the EB110. For him the EB110 was no hyped marketing communications machine and certainly not a vehicle for corporate ego in the mould of, allegedly, the De Lorean.

Others were essential to the plot, but it is to the perfectionist Artioli that we look for achieving the outcome some thought would never happen. No one is suggesting he got it all right, but the point is he made it happen. Three decades later the EB110 reigns supreme as what Giampaolo Benedini called the world's first hypercar.

As a businessman Artioli needed to turn a profit, but the EB110 encapsulated so much more. Beyond business, Artioli was and remains a man with a passion for cars. All but his detractors who have their own agendas can see that what he did with the EB110 was an act of bravery and heroism, a blend of head and heart. The global economic recession and fuel crisis are what slowed the EB110's progress, not any issue with the car or its design. Someone might suggest that the new Bugatti company went a bit over the top with its wonderful 'new age' factory and its enormous cost to build, but that is an argument for elsewhere.

Artioli was a powerful entrepreneur, but above all he was a car man, a heart and soul enthusiast who had his own collection of old Bugattis. Like so many Bugattistes then and now, he seems to have been addicted, and who could blame him. With encouragement from contemporaries including Ferrucio Lamborghini and Paolo Stanzini, the ex-Lamborghini engineer, Artioli inevitably attempted a revival of the legend, the mythical Bugatti. In fact all three men were part of the founding and structure of the new, revived Bugatti brand of the 1990s. Artioli was experienced and wealthy, and he understood the special ingredient without which no amount of money would re-create the Bugatti legend in a car.

They acquired the rights to the brand name from SNECMA, which had absorbed both Hispano-Suiza and Messier-Bugatti. Things started moving in 1987, but it took years for the group to persuade the French authorities to release the rights to brand Bugatti. A holding company, Bugatti International, was founded in Luxembourg by Professor Jean-Marc Borel, who was a key part of the revival project, with Jan K. Breitfeld as President. Then a new evolved company, Bugatti Automobili SpA, was registered in 1988 via Bugatti International. Interestingly, Michael Bugatti, Ettore's youngest son, was on the Board. A one-third shareholding was held by a company named Tecnostile, an independent Italian engineering outfit with Lamborghini links. Three Tecnostile men would be key to the plot (*see* below).

A new Bugatti factory at Campogalliano in the heart of Modena's 'car valley' was built at great expense and opened in 1990. The factory was the most advanced, most technically efficient architectural delight filled with light, windows, peace and serenity, a 'classic' in its own right, and came to be referred to as the 'blue factory' (*Fabbrica Blu*). The sheer scale and success of what Bugatti achieved under Artioli cannot be denied.

Romano Artioli's wife, Renata Kettmeir Artioli, played a significant role in re-establishing the Bugatti brand and the design of 'EB' accessory offerings of the highest quality. She also had a background in architecture and design. Significantly, she oversaw a new Ettore Bugatti 'EB' themed cultural design and exhibition facility at Ora (known in German as Auer), near Bolzano, which featured the trademark Bugatti 'arched' structures, studios and gardens, and played a role in the realisation of the EB110. It was at the Ora centre that the original works of Carlo, Rembrandt, Ettore and Jean were collated and exhibited to inspire a new generation (just as they now are at The Bugatti Trust).

Renata Artioli was clear about the collection's importance to the new Bugatti Automobili and its designers: 'The Bugatti historical archives constitute an inexhaustible source of inspiration. They stimulate and favour continuous discoveries that provoke great euphoria among our stylists who are always on the lookout for new elements and angles to draw into their design work.'

Today, as Bugatti pays homage to the EB110 through its recent Centodieci design, we should look back at what Artioli and his team achieved, with respect and more, for this was a risky and monumental task. True, Artioli 'bet the farm', as was said of Boeing when creating the 747 airliner, its dedicated new factory and the massive design and construction costs.

Romano Artioli, the hero behind the EB110, captured at his desk in an official Bugatti image.

Ultimately, Ferrucio Lamborghini stepped back a little at Bugatti Automobili, leaving Artioli behind the wheel.

The EB110 was so advanced that it was not overtaken in terms of its technology, engineering or design fashion for a very long time. This car was the first large composite-constructed and moulded monocoque-chassis 'tub' of the supercar or hypercar era. An initial honeycomb aluminium-alloy 'sandwich' construction bodyshell was ruled out, not least as over time such construction can be subject to stresses and compression and tension forces that can lead to a loss of torsional rigidity or even a rapid unscheduled disassembly, to use American phraseology.

Artioli was an early promotor of passive, structural safety and the EB110 was subjected to the then unlegislated 'offset-frontal' or 'overlap' front crash test, long before the European New Car Assessment Programme (Euro NCAP) and American legislation made such impact testing fashionable and essential. The EB110 did far better in those offset crash tests than other cars of the era, be they saloons or supercars. In fact it showed minimal internal floor deformation and minor A-pillar intrusion. Side-impact and roll-over tests were also met (the EB110 had big side members for this reason). The tests were carried out by TNO, the respected technical testing body of the Netherlands. In comparison to a Lamborghini, Ferrari or other contemporary, the EB110 crash-tested well in terms of its cabin structure with only scuttle and dashboard movement noted: it was probably the 'safest' supercar of its era (with Porsche's 928 also being notable for its structural safety).

In the context of its day, the EB110 had to be better than the four-wheel-drive Porsche 959, the 928, Ferrari F40 and the Jaguar XJ220, and beyond that it had to be 'better' and be a true Bugatti. Otherwise what was the point?

Indeed, the Jaguar XJ220 was twice the price of an EB110, did not come with the engine that was marketed with it ready installed, and its world-record-breaking speed was a test-track affair. The Ferrari F40, however magical, was not a daily driver – but the EB110 was!

Contemporary with the EB110 was Bugatti Automobili's time at the helm of Lotus in the 1990s. Something very pure that reflects the early Bugatti ethos may perhaps be seen in the later Lotus Elise. That would be no surprise given Bugatti's involvement with Lotus for a few short years. It may be significant that the Elise concept seemingly had some small degree of reverse-engineered links to the Bugatti-Suzuki 'Expresso' small sportster car project (see below).

The initial focus in the development of the new EB110 began with the engine, which was entrusted to three of the staff at Tecnostile, Tiziano Benedetti, Oliviero Pedrazzi and Achille Bevini, who together had previously developed the legendary Lamborghini Miura and were vital to the plot. At this stage it was Stanzani's engineering expertise that was the key to realising the EB110 engine, but 'events' would later lead to him leaving the project.

The EB110 in blue makes its timeless design statement.

The EB110 was mid-engined magic and undoubtedly captured the true spirit of the Bugatti epoch that had preceded it so many decades before. The EB110 was far more than the sum of its parts.

QUAD-CAM, QUAD-TURBO V12

The longitudinally mounted, mid-body configured, 60-valve, 3.5-litre, 60-degree V12 engine had five valves per cylinder and four small, in-sequence, easier to spool-up turbochargers.

With a bore and stroke of 81 × 56.1mm, the engine was 'over-square' in the Bugatti tradition. The short stroke gives it its high-power, high-revving and high-torque character. Only 200rpm separated maximum power from the maximum revs engine limit of 8,200rpm. The engine would in fact approach 10,000rpm, perhaps suggesting what could be achieved with a later Honda production supercar engine.

The EB110's engine was a wet-liner design (old-fashioned French-style), but unusually it had alloy liners (impregnated with silicone), not steel. Three inlets and two exhausts per cylinder made this a true multi-valve engine at the forefront of design practice.

There were no cam belts or principal chains, for the valves were gear operated – exquisite stuff. The engine was a 'twin-plenum' type in its air breathing via 36 inlet valves and forced induction. Each of the four IHI-brand intercooled turbochargers pressurised the feed to three cylinders. Boost pressure was higher from 3,500rpm (4,000rpm in the S-model) and the boost pressure was differentially tuned to create a sequential twin-boost effect as they were sequenced (or de facto geared) to come into use by pairs, two tuned for low-speed pick up and two tuned for high-speed boost (above 5,000rpm), operating at pressures of 1.05 bar and 1.2 bar, respectively.

The car had four catalytic converters as well as petrol and oil vapour collectors – another rarely specified item long before environmentalism ruled the legislation.

The later EB110 GT variant produced just over 552bhp at a rather heady 8,250rpm, but if we take the 'standard' engine at a slightly lower rpm, the output was in the high 400bhp region, which was matched by or just exceeded by the 451lb ft of torque at 3,750rpm. When an engine's torque figure matches or exceeds its horsepower or PS figure, then you know it is a very well-designed and highly efficient power unit. The later EB110 Super Sport (Sport Stradale) of 1994 was tuned up to 602bhp at 8,250rpm, which would be at full velocity on a racing straight, of course.

These engine power, torque and performance output figures were on a par with a state-of-art Formula One class engine of the era, but in a road car that was also docile enough to go shopping in.

The engine required a special new oil to cope with its demands, which was developed by one of the new Bugatti's backers, Essence Lubricants France (ELF).

Through the gears performance was astounding with 0–60mph being recorded at 3.7 seconds and a top speed of 341km/h (212.6mph). The Super Sport was even faster, almost hitting the 3 seconds mark for 0–60mph. The vital overtaking sector of 48–112km/h (30–70mph) was also lightning quick: an EB110 Super Sport could top 354km/h (220mph) – even a Veyron would have to breathe deeply to do that today.

A six-speed manual transmission was designed to drive all four wheels, mounted within the engine block to minimise transfer losses. The sixth 'top' speed gear was set to a gear ratio of 0.949:1.

The power vectoring was changed from a 40:60 ratio biased towards the rear, to a rather forceful 28:72 ratio towards the rear – somewhat reducing the handling benefits of the four-wheel-drive system yet without compromise as the car was never intended to be an Audi Quattro or a rally car.

Loris Bicocchi was the first test driver on the EB110, as he later was for the Veyron. Jean-Philippe Vittecoq, another Bugatti factory test driver, broke the Jaguar XJ220's brief hold on a speed record (secured at the Nardò Ring track), with an EB110 world production car record maximum velocity of 341km/h (212.6mph) at Nardò. According to Bicocchi and Vittecoq, the EB110's revised ratio reduced the front-end understeer that they had noticed due to too much torque at the front axle: supercars ought not to be understeerers.

The EB110S would make the standing kilometre speed test in 19.61 seconds at an exit speed of 276.5km/h (171.81mph) – a record and the first production car ever to do so in under 20 seconds.

Double wishbone suspension and accurate location of the wheels and axle ensured true handling consistency. The rear axle/wheel unit was a multi-link, double shock absorber and damper design with a forwards-cranked link arm that gave an effective wishbone location effect. An 'active' air suspension system was under development. The tyres were specially commissioned Michelin MXX3 325/30s at the rear and 245/50s at the front. Special emphasis was put on their construction, tread pattern and sidewall hysteresis to cope with the speeds and loads. In later years another tyre make was sometimes fitted by private owners.

The two-piece wheels were cast-alloy, finned and magnesium-rich in design and metal. They were as clever as any of Ettore and Jean's wheels and echoed those of the late 1920s Royale model in their design and function. Anti-lock brakes (ABS) were standard and naturally the calipers were from Brembo. Big, ventilated brake discs were needed to retard the car from its high speeds.

The EB110's significant cooling demands were solved by aerodynamically drawing air over, under and into the car through ducts and funnels: the main radiator was front mounted and piped to the mid-mounted engine. Ducts in the bonnet carefully allowed airflow ingress. The later Veyron would need similar work on its own cooling requirements. Turbos get very hot indeed and heat-soak can affect much more than the local sheet metal and can be deleterious to composites, as can humidity and the ingress of moisture.

THE EB110 AND THE ARCHITECTURE OF THE AUTOMOBILE

Calls for the new Bugatti car body design had car designers scurrying to their drawing board. Paolo Martin, a key figure at Pininfarina, presented his idea coded PM110 PM1, which was vital, characterful and radical – yet despite these attributes it was deemed too radical, maybe too brutal to reflect the Bugatti legacy and DNA. On reflection, we can see Ferrari F40 overtones and other abstract references in Martin's superb design study.

Only the original interior of the EB110 seemed a bit tame, but it was still a very exclusive place to be.

Intriguingly, although Giorgetto Giugiaro's ID90 design proposal for the new Bugatti was rejected, aspects of its frontal design and cabin turret shapes seem familiar. Like many Giugiaro concepts, elements of the ID90 were evoked in his later projects.

Bertone had a go too, with designer Marc Deschamps creating a design proposal that was rejected, but in which, curiously, elements in newer American and Japanese supercar designs can clearly be seen. Many years later a Deschamps design would sit on a left-over EB110 composite chassis tub design and be known as the B Engineering Edonis, which is generically described as sharing an EB110 composite chassis yet having a redesigned body and interior.

Given Marcello Gandini's links to the Italian automotive industry and to Lamborghini itself, it was hardly a surprise that his design found favour, but it did so upon its own merits even if it arguably displayed some overt Lamborghini design language. Gandini and Artioli were reported to have failed to resolve certain styling disagreements and Gandini, who had been in on the EB110 project from the start, saw his original design finalised for production by others.

But had Gandini, so often credited with the EB110 concept, in fact produced a car that allegedly was more like a Lamborghini than a suggested 'new' Bugatti? And what of the body design of the slightly similar Maserati Chubasco concept car design of 1990? Was any of that 'one-off' inherent within the themes of Gandini's Bugatti proposal or the actual EB110 as finally resolved by Giampaolo Benedini? If so, or if not, did it matter?

The original Gandini rolling prototype was known as the DMD80. Gandini had drawn up the original EB110 design/styling proposal, but that was far from the production vehicle itself: his design had a flat, trapezoidal windscreen of minimal curvature in the trademark Lamborghini Countach style, and the body panel shapes were somewhat angular.

The design proposal was deemed to need work and Artioli appointed Giampaolo Benedini to oversee the process of taking the design through to production. Benedini's role was hugely significant in converting a styling exercise into a production Bugatti (*see* below).

Meanwhile, Stanzani also remove himself from the on-going design project in 1990. This might suggest that Artioli was assuming a 'Le Patron' type role, driving through his own ideas to their outcome. Whatever criticism some might wish to propose, the facts are that the EB110 needed someone of vision and singular, focused drive and tenacity to achieve its realisation, and that man was Romano Artioli. That the cards fell differently to the plan is another matter: the car was the point and the team that made it were all dedicated car enthusiasts.

As part of the realisation of the EB110, Nicola Materazzi, an experienced engineer and racing car constructor who had worked on cars like the Ferrari 288 GTO, Lancia Fulvia and the stunning and radical Lancia Stratos, was appointed Technical Director

LEAD EB110 PROJECT ENGINEERS AND DEVELOPERS

A small team of subject experts were gathered to take EB110 from concept to car and on to testing, records and competition. Amongst them were:

Ing. Gianpaolo Simonini (head of vehicle testing)

Ing. Federico Trombi (head of research and design/homologation)

Ing. Tommaso Caletti (head of motor sports/competition programme)

Ing. Luca Giacomoni (data engineer)

Ing. Claudio Galletti (engine electronics leader)

Further team members included electrical, mechanical, bodywork and chassis specialists: Alberto Mazzini, Andrea Stenico, Stefano Bruni, Francesco Sassoli, Alessandro Benedetti, Giuseppe Montorsi. Gianni Sighinolfi was head of the production development workshop.

Engineer Pavel Rajmis, an ex-Audi Quattro/Sport drivetrain engineer, worked on the Bugatti four-wheel-drive system and its development.

Ing. Fernando Gabellini, the chief electrical man at Bugatti, was also a leading figure in the subsequent EB112 project.[1]

(Please note that any omissions are accidental.)

Key to the command structure in engineering terms was Mauro Forghieri, formerly of the Ferrari Formula One team and who had led it to a record eight constructor's titles and four driver's titles. More recently he had worked at Lamborghini. Forghieri was an old friend and business associate of Artioli's and his appointment as Technical Director at Bugatti Automobili had a massive impact on making things happen correctly, as he said at the time: 'Campogalliano was not created simply as a factory, but as the concrete result of great entrepreneurial opportunity.' Forghieri pointed out that the EB110 cars were individually built to each customer's specification, like an original pre-1939 Bugatti. Robotisation of the build process was not applied as the panacea being introduced across the car industry at that time. The EB110 was a hand-built jewel and manufactured in a manner that was not dissimilar to the original Bugattis.

Not all was plain sailing. Originally it was intended that the EB110 would have the world's first fully composite monocoque-chassis tub moulding, but this became an issue in the light of costs and design production. New specialist constructors for this carbon fibre design were commissioned in France (Aérospatiale and Composites Aquitaine). The French, of course, had learned much about composite construction via Airbus, Concorde and certain racing cars. External aluminium cladding added to the 'composite' mix of the car's skeletal tub, but Glare, a glass reinforced composite now seen in modern airliners, had not been fully realised for car production at that time. Ultimately the inner composite tub structure was produced, but with alloy skin panels. Of interest, the inner front wings were part-alloy too.

Five pre-production prototypes (A1 to A5) were built incorporating construction and styling developments as the design evolved. These prototypes had an aluminium/sandwich-built chassis of Gandini design, Cars C6 to C14 had a carbon composite chassis to the developing Benedini design: production car C12 was launched at the Paris show in 1992 as the EB110GT, while crash testing destroyed car C14. Car P1 was the first production status model.

The composite bodyshell was significantly more rigid than any metal or alloyed monocoque, yet weighed less

The early EB110 had this lovely rear 'flying buttress' type roof pillar and ellipsoid side window, both of which were removed in the EB110 SS update. The early car also had an 'active' movable rear spoiler, which was replaced by a static version in the update.

Overhead view of the EB110's 60-valve, 3.5-litre, V12 engine.

A factory line-up headed by the very rare dark red metallic paint option.

than anyone thought possible. The roof A-pillars carried strong steel inset rods and connected into a roll-hoop at the B-pillar. The upwards opening, cranked doors had been seen before, of course, on the Lamborghini Countach.

Giampaolo Benedini (Vice-President of Bugatti and head of Style) was the new lead EB110 designer who not only designed the final car, he also designed the new factory in Modena where it was built – not in Molsheim. Benedini trained as an architect (he is also Artioli's cousin) and, contrary to some views, many famous car designers have had an architectural training, notably the esteemed Robert Opron, father of the Citroën SM and much more.

Resolving the Gandini prototype saw Benedini reshape not just the front windscreen design form, but actually extend it and add clever curvature to each side of the windscreen glass. This created a radical new look and much better aerodynamics down the side of the car.

Reshaping the body side panels and panel-to-panel joins, and a new frontal design with distinctive headlamp motifs, all added to the re-design. The detailing at the rear was a stunning example of 'design language' in action.

Was there a touch of the Bauhaus to the EB110? Achim Anscheidt, who retired in 2023 after nineteen years as Design Director at Bugatti, thinks so: Benedini was a follower of the

Bauhaus tradition and an architect, so some lineage is hard to deny, especially in the vented or slotted rear valance panel, which was decidedly 'industrial' in its simple effect. But there was more to the EB110's scaling and sculpture than the Bauhaus alone.

In its hull shape can be seen the application of aerodynamics and hydrodynamics, grand scaling, surfaces that caught and 'worked' the light, and an elemental construction that was grand yet harmonious. In terms of its radicalism, think of the effect of Jørn Utzon's design for the Sydney Opera House, or the impact of a building by Le Corbusier, and how such innovation can somehow be amalgamated into a car shape. There were also elements of the earlier French 'Aerodyne' movement and of Cayla, Gerin, Voisin and Flaminio Bertoni.

The French auto and industrial designer Steeve Bernaud-Heyd worked on the EB110 as a young designer in his twenties and told the author that 'Benedini never changed the car's dimensions or wheelbase, but he smoothed all the edges. Then the effect was improved. Benedini is an architect and he did things on the EB110 that a car designer would never have done: the flat side and the repetition of small openings.'[2]

Bernaud-Heyd worked on EB110 design details (see below) and also collaborated with another French designer named Eric Serafini, notably on the rear bumper/valance design of the car.

Of significant interest to the car design enthusiast, the EB110 was initially seen with the most amazing pair of full-scale rear wheel spats, which were of the most stunningly original design. Sadly they did not make it to later production.

The EB110 clay-model design study also showed two massive exhaust pipes poking out of the rear like some Spielberg-esque film car. They too were deleted – shame!

It becomes clear that the EB110 truly was automotive architecture and original (even if we must cite Gandini and Benedini's dual, yet separate, contributions), not a retro-pastiche or a derivative. Many see this car's body design as a very rare, unique and significant moment in car design. Indeed, we might observe that the later EB112 concept car design from Giugiaro was more obviously a curved, Jean Bugatti-inspired device and one that was certainly more traditional; but it is the EB110 design that has lasted better.

In the flesh, and curiously colour dependent for its effect, the EB110 has so many elements to its shape. The sail-like tautness of certain flat panels and the buttress effect to the rear of the cabin turret side pillar were Benedini's brilliant ideas. The windscreen with its smooth and highly curved edges, which eased around to define the shape of the cabin, and the chamfered panels together created a stunning effect of true industrial design. The EB110's 'cab-forward' styling and a low front were true innovations, not just following a fashion. Many of the supercars that followed it simply aped these elements and proportions.

You might argue that adding a 'horseshoe' front grille motif was an add-on, but Benedini did far more to resolve the EB110 into the reality of a car that has aged very well indeed.

It was rumoured that the esteemed industrial designer and car stylist Tom Tjaarda (based in Italy and the son of 1930s car designer Johan Tjaarda van Starkenburg, designer of the 1937 Lincoln Zephyr streamliner) was asked to

COLOURS

Initially launched in the expected Bugatti blue (albeit the later darker hue, not the lighter 1920s racing hue), the EB110 was finally available in a distinct range of very modern colours: Monaco White, Bugatti Blue, Bugatti Yellow and Deep Black. Then came the metallic (*metallizzato*) Dark Blue, Light Grey, Medium Grey, Dark Green and Dark Red. Interiors were available in contrasting grey, champagne beige, black, blue, and a blisteringly bright red. Giampaolo Benedini said of the colours:

> We have maintained the blue colour as ... above all to reinforce our image united in the renaissance of the marque ... today, however the needs of the consumer in terms of personalisation of the vehicle and the factory finds itself having to confront new and vaster markets. It was therefore inevitable to expand the range of colours dedicated to the EB110. The Super Sport version was presented abandoning the blue in favour of a classic metallic grey livery.[3]

That new silvery grey was highly reflective and revealed more of the subtle sculpting and swage lines as highlights to the body. EB110 fanatics will forever argue as to which colour best suits the car, but perhaps Benedini's choice of silver grey may be the correct outcome.

DESIGNER DETAIL: STEEVE BERNAUD-HEYD

In the 1930s a very young and talented designer named Lucien Schlatter made major contributions to Bugatti design via Gangloff's work with the Molsheim design studio. Fast forward and another young French designer, Steeve Bernaud-Heyd, was brought in by Artioli in June 1992, just three months short of his twentieth birthday to work on the details and realisation of the EB110's design. What an opportunity for a design hopeful, however junior the role.

Bernaud-Heyd worked with Eric Serafini on the design and production realisation for the EB110's rear bumper and valance, and then on design revisions for the US version. These included the car's added 'impact' bumpers, which uniquely in the history of modern car design actually added to the car's looks. Bernaud-Heyd confirmed to the author that much design work went on at the EB110's rear end, not least to solve the engine cooling requirements by improving the airflow over the panels. He also confirmed an attempt to incorporate some Type 35 tail design elements to the EB110. Bernaud-Heyd would go on to work on Artioli's next project, the EB112.

Despite Bugatti's short tenure of Lotus, Bernaud-Heyd reputedly had an effect on at least the conceptual origin of the later Lotus Elise, the little-known story of Artioli, Suzuki, Bernaud-Heyd and 'Project Espresso'.

Inside Bugatti, Artioli was always thinking of new design projects and new ways to monetise what he did. This was not a philanthropist's ego trip, it was a company with employees that needed to turn a profit. Artioli owned the rights to Suzuki in Italy and loved the buzzy little 3-cylinder engine used in the Japanese small Kei-class Suzuki Cappuccino. That car, however, was not engineered to pass new European safety regulations at that time. Ever safety conscious, Artioli dreamed up the idea of producing a small, cheap but safe, 'modular' and lightweight two-seater roadster with youth appeal and great sales potential. The car would have a punt chassis with thick side members, a mid-engine configuration and minimal frontal area, allied to a targa-type roof as well as superb handling dynamics. The little Suzuki engine was ideal for its powerplant. Suzuki backed the project: effectively Bugatti was designing a car for Suzuki.

Inside Bugatti's wonderful light-filled factory at Campogalliano, it was Steeve Bernaud-Heyd who designed for the project a lovely little two-seat car that had shades of the EB110 in certain of its styling elements, notably around the windscreen and side panels. This was the car known as 'Project Espresso' (born out of the Suzuki Cappuccino), but sadly it never saw production. Bernaud-Heyd, Artioli and his team, which included Bugatti's Lotus production manager Steve Wood, had created and drawn up much of what was required to create a car. It weighed less than 725kg.

However, although not a Suzuki out of Bugatti, the car did have an effect because the subsequent Lotus Elise was similar in concept and format. It is obvious that we can in some small degree cite Bernaud-Heyd's Espresso car design as a possible inspiration for the Elise, but not for the actual car as that was wonderfully designed and engineered by Julian Thomson and Richard Rackham, respectively. Car designers often reach similar solutions to the same challenges.

Yet it is obvious to the viewer that the Elise and the consequent Exige might somehow, shall we say, 'owe' just a little something to Artioli's Project Espresso via a young Bernaud-Heyd's pen. The curved, flying buttress type rear 'arch' of the Series 2 Elise and Exige rear roof and rear pillars, for example, seems to hint at Bernaud-Heyd's earlier sketches for the Espresso project.

Call it coincidence or prescience, but perhaps Bernaud-Heyd might be owed a nod in the credits, though he makes it clear that he has no claim to the Elise's origins. On his behalf, however, the author makes the point for debate and consideration.

That subsequent Series 2 Elise was principally the design work of Steve Crijns under Russell Carr's overall design lead. It had an arched, rear buttress 'hoop' as the cabin roof and rear styling that was clearly not dissimilar to that of the earlier Espresso. Crijns joined Lotus in 1994, just as the Bugatti-Lotus story was taking another step towards its outcome. Crijns was the designer behind the style of the superbly cohesive and characterful Lotus Evora, something for which he deserves great credit. He went on to a senior design role at McLaren. We should remember that Bugatti owned Lotus, that the Elise is named after Artioli's granddaughter and that, despite its short tenure, Bugatti helped Lotus on its way via Artioli's global contacts and business links.

So without detracting from the design credits of the Series 1 and 2 Elise, as cited above, we might add to the story a touch of those original sketches made by the Bugatti design team for the Suzuki Project Espresso at a time of direct contact between Bugatti and Lotus before the Elise appeared, just a couple of years later.

Steeve Bernaud-Heyd spent three years with Bugatti. He later rose to lead design at Carrozzeria Touring Superleggera, designed more than 40 automotive projects with leading brands and helped create the T-Rex multi-purpose vehicle. In later years he worked on Uwe Hucke's Type 68 projected recreation/reinterpretation of Roland Bugatti's small gull-winged, Jean-Bugatti-inspired coupé – the 'shrunken' or 'mini'-Type 57 Atlantic idea, following Angela Hucke's move to take up the project after her father's death and to display the car at Retromobile with Tim Dutton's assistance.

Steeve Bernaud-Heyd remains one of the lesser-known original members of team EB110 and its stunning realisation. He was only a small player in the design story, but it took him on to greater things. And like many, he might recognise that it was Giampaolo Benedini's design and realisation of the EB110 from concept to actual car that was the prime mover behind the EB110 body design story.[4]

Steeve's father Henri Bernaud is a respected classic car restorer who runs a stunning 1932 Bugatti Type 51 and he used to own a Type 37. In his youth Henri knew Michel Bugatti, Ettore's son with Geneviève Delcuze. Henri also owns an Austin Healey 3000 and an earlier Mini Cooper S. He has driven every type of Bugatti and passed his love of the marque down to his sons: Daniel is a professional restorer of classic carrosserie. Steeve continues to work as a consultant for Bugatti all these years after his youthful EB110 contribution.

further refine the next version of the car's body design, but time was against that plan.

The revised EB110 shape by Benedini 'worked' and had presence and massive graphical impact.

It was at the rear end of the EB110 where the conflicts of style, cooling and aerodynamics presented several problems for the small design team to solve.

Aerodynamics testing was carried out in the Pininfarina Centro Stile wind tunnel at Grugliasco and some body-shape tuning was required to tune out unwanted lift and localised airflow effects. Whilst a low drag coefficient (C_d) is desirable, it is not the sole arbiter of good road vehicle aerodynamic performance: the EB110 is cited as having a wind-tunnel test C_d of 0.30, rising to 0.32 C_d in production form. Adding spoilers, wings, wheel arch extensions and so on could only add to that figure. The EB110 was designed and tuned to offer good side or crosswind performance, low lift, tuned rear-deck wake vortex separation, and also had a lower frontal area and cross-sectional drag coefficient than its contemporaries. The expensively curved edges to the windscreen were vital aerodynamic elements that most people failed to spot, being more subtle than the outrageous arc of the Lancia Stratos windscreen.

Adding a rear 'wing' tamed any unwanted induced lift over the rear end at very high speeds, but the standard car was entirely safe in that respect on normal roads.

LAUNCH OF THE EB110

The EB110GT was officially launched to coincide with what would have been Ettore's 110th birthday, 15 September 1991. The actor Alain Delon posed in a bright blue EB110 in front of Paris's latest wonder, the Grande Arche de la Défense, and

The famed EB110 Le Mans racer entered by Michel Hommell and driven by Alain Cudini, Éric Hélary and Jean-Christophe Boullion. It is now resident at the wonderful Musée Le Manoir de l'Automobile at Lohéac, Brittany.

The revised EB110 Super Sport (Sport Stradale) was tuned up to 602bhp at 8,250rpm. Note the revised aerodynamic design to the front valance.

was then escorted by police and a pack of photographers down the Avenue des Champs-Elysées. That evening there was an enormous reception in the Orangery at Versailles.

The British launch in February 1993 was superbly framed and executed by PR Angela Hucke, who had been immersed in Bugatti since childhood, with parades of EB110s and older 'vintage' Bugattis in London, a trip through Hyde Park and events at the Grosvenor House Hotel on Park Lane. Press coverage was huge and the response was positive: people believed in this car. The official UK Bugatti Automobili dealer in London was H.R. Owen.[5]

The Japanese launch of the Bugatti Automobili brand was similarly well-funded and made a big mark on Japanese car enthusiasts.

The planned American market launch was, of course, essentially to become a failure, even if certain exemptions had been granted to the EB110 'America' specification type on technical grounds by the US authorities. The EB110 was approved under construction and use regulations in the USA for 1994 and all the parts of the vital US sales operation were set up. Eight sales outlets for the EB110 were appointed across the USA, of which the official West Coast retail outlet was Bugatti of Beverly Hills, which sounded rather swish. The advertising strapline for EB110 in America was: 'The New Legend … EB110'.

Rather like Ettore, Artioli wanted control over who bought his Bugattis and it is said that prospective EB110 purchasers were 'interviewed' for their suitability.

ALTERNATIVE FUEL AND PERFORMANCE

Performance was key to the EB110 and Artioli continued to prove that when, on 3 July 1994 at the Nardò circuit, a production-specification EB110GT using the Ecogas 2000 injection system developed by Bugatti Electronics achieved 344.7km/h (214.2mph), breaking the world speed record for production cars (road use).

Present was Arturo Barbanti, the inventor of the special liquefied methane gas injection system (not the butane, propane, propylene mix normally cited as LPG) and his son Giovanni Barbanti as president of the Bugatti Electronics division. Just as Brazilian cars had previously run for years on the cleaner sugar cane fuel derivative, the new methane gas injection and combustion monitoring system meant lower emissions than pure petroleum fuel. Barbanti's methane fuel injection system meant that even something as rare and exquisitely engineered as the EB110's V12 could be run on a gas-based fuel through the use of the adjusting sensors. The gas tank to supply the car was rather riskily mounted on the passenger seat. Methane was different from the 'usual' liquefied petroleum gas choice and had much lower emissions.

Key engineers in the 'gas' EB110 included the electronics expert Loris Dall'Aglio, engineer Federico Trombi, engineer Luca Giacomoni, and two expert mechanics Antonio Monti and Claudi Bettuzzi. Loris Bicocchi was the test driver.

The car's performance was superb and no internal modifications were required to the mighty quad-cam V12 in order to run on gas, such was its robust design. This experimental episode provided further proof of what Artioli planned for the EB110 and Bugatti. Had LPG gas taken off as an alternative fuel, rather than the brief years when it was in fashion, Barbanti's system and Bugatti's assistance in putting it into production would have meant millions in income for Bugatti.[6]

GT TO SS TO COMPETIZIONE

The EB110 Super Sport (SS) was announced for 1992–3 with numerous engine and design/aerodynamic modifications: this was the *Modifié*. New cast-alloy spoked wheels, a revised interior and aerodynamic changes to the body very effectively modernised the car. The front bumper shape was altered and various edges and triggers of aerodynamic effect were added.

Changes to the GT's rear side windows and flanks for the revised SS also saw the very individual hole or 'scalloped' panels added for the revised version. The change lost the sculptural and architectural ellipsoid arc to the sweeping rear side pillar and window curve, yet provided a very strong new graphical motif. Steeve Bernaud-Heyd confirmed to the author that he and his colleague Eric Serafini worked on this new rear side panel design and that 'originally we had seven small tubes [holes]. Then we changed to five bigger ones. We tested it in the wind tunnel and its effect was not so bad.'[7] The key benefit was getting more cooling air through the body.

A weight reduction of 150kg (330lb) was also achieved for the car by removing alloy panels and using carbon/Kevlar parts. A speed-sensitive, lifting rear wing was also available.

A revised engine control unit, larger injectors and a flowed exhaust allowed better induction and exhalation to the engine. The maximum ratings for the Super Sport were 605bhp (450kW/612Ps) at 8,250rpm. Michael Schumacher bought a yellow one in early 1994.

The Super Sport achieved 0–60mph in a stunning 3.2 seconds and topped out at nearly 355km/h (221mph).

The EB110 SS had revised rear aerodynamics and five-holed vents on each rear flank to direct more cooling air.

Romano Artioli's own EB110 Super Sport had uprated turbochargers taking the maximum power rating to 650bhp. It also featured his favourite blue paint, having originally been factory-silver and used as the US demo and press car.

Approximately 86 examples of the EB110GT were built for sale, together with a further 32 of the EB110 Super Sports, the last creeping out of the factory in 1995 just before bankruptcy was fact. Several EB110s were later 'Federalized' for private sale in the USA. In 2022 an EB110 Super Sport sold for $3.16 million dollars, such was the lure of the brand and the car.

Intriguingly, in 1994 the tuner Rinspeed turned its hand to modifying the EB110 with podded headlamps, a rear 'bridge' spoiler and various other changes that somewhat detracted from the car's design purity.

The EB110 Super Sport's engine could send it from 0–60mph in 3.2 seconds.

BUGATTI BACK AT LE MANS

Visit the wonderful Musée Le Manoir de l'Automobile at Lohéac in southern Brittany and not only will you be visiting one of the finest car museums in Europe, if not the world, you will also see a Bugatti EB110 with a competition history. This car is the 1994 EB110 SS entered by Michel Hommell with three drivers: Alain Cudini, Éric Hélary and Jean-Christophe Boullion. Sadly, a turbocharger issue and then a small Le Mans 'moment' stopped the car finishing the race.

The car in the Lohéac museum was one of two 'LM' specification EB110s built in 1994. But what of the second car of similar specification known as the Competizione car?

In March 1995 Gildo Pallanca Pastor of the Monaco Racing Team, who had become fascinated by the EB110 and the brand, set a speed record of 296.6km/h (184.3mph) on an ice track in Finland in a production-based EB110 Super Sport. But he was actually more interested in entering official races, so he ordered a race car from Bugatti at the end of 1994 to participate in the International Motor Sports Association (IMSA) series in the USA and in other endurance races from 1995.

The EB110 Sport Competizione (SC) was developed within the course of six months: weight-reduced, reconceptualised and incredibly fast. There were plans to produce three vehicles, but by June 1995 only one had been made due to financial difficulties and supplier issues.

It was this vehicle that Gildo Pallanca Pastor, who was later closely associated with the wonderful Venturi sports car, entered for IMSA races and participated in the BPR Global GT Series. The EB110 SC performed well, but spare parts became rarer and rarer as it was the time when the market for super sports cars collapsed amid the global economic problems.

Gildo Pallanca Pastor succeeded in extracting the EB110 SC from the Bugatti assets after the company's failure. The car had been left in the factory.

Pallanca Pastor managed to put together a three-driver EB110 entry for the 24 Hours of Daytona race in January 1996, and then began to prepare for the 24 Hours of Le Mans. This included races in Dijon, France, in early June. The car achieved fourth place during practice, and in the first race Pallanca Pastor's car managed to move into third place. He was satisfied with the performance of his driver, Patrick Tambay, and was already looking forward to the next race. But during the second lap the car collided with another entrant and the race was over: the EB110 failed to make it to the finishing line.

The lack of available spare EB110 parts meant the mechanics were unable to repair the race car in time, so the EB110 Sport Competizione also missed out on competing in the 1996 24 Hours of Le Mans. This brought a close to the short motor sport career of the last factory race car built by Bugatti in that era.

It takes even big companies with billions in the bank at least four years to create a new car to replace an existing one. So the fact that Bugatti created and put into production not just a new design but a new engine, a new factory and a revived brand in four years speaks volumes for the commitment of the people that made it happen.

If the Veyron, the Chiron and the other later Bugattis are the apogees of engineering and design in the context of supercars or hypercar, then we can claim that these cars would not be such without their spiritual forebear, the EB110.

EB110 SS on the fly at Prescott – a rather unusual sight.

EB110 ACHIEVEMENTS

- The first true production supercar as a hypercar, with advances and innovations across all areas of design and construction
- The fastest such car in the world
- The first supercar to achieve the standing kilometre speed test in under 20 seconds
- The first car to use composite carbon fibre and alloy modular monocoque/unit construction, pre-dating the McLaren F1 and others
- The safest and strongest car of its type at the time
- The most aerodynamically efficient and stable car of its type
- The best-driving and the best-handling supercar and with four-wheel drive
- The most advanced and dynamically efficient quad-cam, V12, quad-turbo, multi-valve engine designed to that date
- The first 'reinterpretation' car design to accurately and authentically evoke the true Bugatti design and engineering ethos, yet in an original style all its own

Yet by 23 September 1995 the new Bugatti Company was suffering the effects of a global economic storm, arguably made worse by a touch of over-reach through its involvement with Lotus. Certain other Italian companies are also alleged to have made things difficult on the supplier front. Artioli became a victim of his own company's fate. After manufacturing just 139 examples of the EB110 in all its guises, the company went into receivership. So died the first hypercar of the modern era, but was it the last Bugatti?

Today the EB110 is revered by many. Even some dyed-in-the-wool 'vintage' Bugatti enthusiasts concede that it properly evoked the Bugatti ethos – the 'Bugattism' of engineering and design style. Witness the words of Sir John Venables-Llewelyn, a serial 'vintage' Bugatti owner and former chair of the Bugatti Owners' Club, who told the author: 'Of all the later or new Bugattis I really do like the EB110, it does capture the Bugatti feel.'[8]

We should recall that the EB110 really was a significant event in automotive engineering and design, not just a brilliant piece of branding. The EB110 was not a retro-pastiche: it was new, yet somehow reflected the Bugatti brand foundations with integrity. Sadly the EB112 saloon, which was planned next, did not get to the market.

EB112

The next chapter in Artioli's grand vision was for a four-door Bugatti super saloon with the EB110's engine. At Ital Design, Giorgetto Giugiaro designed the prototype and built one example of this four-door device with a rear 'spine' and curvaceous styling motifs that echoed Jean Bugatti's 1930s highlights. Artioli is said to have even challenged Giugiaro's initial design sketches and allegedly told him to make it more 'Bugatti', an act that an American might describe as 'awesome'.

The resultant design was striking but few could agree with *Automobile* magazine that it was then 'the most beautiful car in the world'. And did the overall shape, shall we say, 'inspire' the original Porsche Panamera fastback saloon of the early 2020s? And was the EB112's styling dangerously bordering on 'retro', let alone 'pastiche'? Opinions differ, but the author believes it was not as 'original' as the EB110.

The original EB112 development test driver was Valentino Balboni, the legendary Lamborghini development engineer/driver. The EB112 chassis #39001 was used as the photography car and sole factory demonstrator. Somewhat surprisingly, it had a manual transmission. With its V12 engine with 6 litres and 60 valves, and four seats, was this the ultimate land yacht of a *grand routière*?

After Bugatti Automobili SpA was declared bankrupt, two unfinished EB112s were secured from the assets by EB110 racer Gildo Pallanca Pastor, who then had his company finish building the EB112s. The EB112 chassis #39001 was completed as late as 2000. Could the EB112 have been a success? Seen through the design context of its time, the answer has to be a yes.

Back with the EB110, its integrity and effect remain authentic and real some three decades later. What a shame that this, one of the greatest cars ever conceived and realised, should be stifled by geopolitical events and not become the global icon it should have been. Yet with hindsight, the EB110 has proved its creator's point.

Therein lies the proof that it was indeed one of the great cars of the century of the car, and a great Bugatti.

The delightful Giugiaro-designed EB112 grand saloon that Artioli had planned may have been thought a touch 'retro'.

After the company's bankruptcy, the remains of EB110 production were not wasted. Seventeen or eighteen unfinished carbon composite chassis/body tub monocoques remained and also a large supply of spare parts and engine components. Most of these were acquired by Dauer Sportwagen GmbH and B Engineering, an Italian company with two of the EB110's original backers on its management team. Gildo Pallanca Pastor also acquired some relevant EB110 components to go with his two EB112s. As late as 2018 plans were still afoot to build EB110-originated cars with further investment via an American company.

DAUER EB110

Ex-racing driver Jochen Dauer of Dauer Racing GmbH, who had acquired not just components and the parts-bin but the rights to the name EB110, undertook small-scale production of a total of five revised EB110s, all reflecting the EB110 Super Sport specification.

Having completed the remaining factory 'continuation' EB110s, Dauer then decided to create new-build EB110s to a modified design and specification as the Dauer EB110S. Several more, perhaps seven, were later built. Significant changes to the use of carbon fibre in the hull, replacing the metal outer skin, made the new body easier and cheaper to build. Dauer also made alterations to the turbochargers and reputedly got the engine to over 700bhp.

With its minor body changes, a newly trimmed interior and a generally modernised feel, the Dauer EB110S was no 'kit' car, but sadly the project was over by 2008.

RIDING THE EB110 ROCKET

Stunned by the shock of the inspired exterior design, there was a mild touch of disappointment when I stepped down into the ruched and leathered cabin. Yes, there was a sense of occasion and the experience was special, but the facia/dashboard design and moulding did not seem to match the innovation of the car's exterior design and its others details.

The great mass of the one-piece moulded front facia panel, reaching in a swathe of apparently 'leatherised', moulded-type grey plasticised material looked more like something lifted from a General Motors (GM) Opel interior – or maybe something American from the GM stable of interior mouldings. Although not offensive, it lacked the shock of 'design' and looked a bit too luxurious. Space, however, is not at a premium. Even so, the EB110's interior was tamer than expected.

Such present-day criticisms, of course, are outside the context of when the car was designed and presented. In the case of the EB110 Super Sport, however, these issues were addressed by introducing new expensive leather trim, revised mouldings and colours, details and a new steering wheel, all of which transformed the interior into something 'edgier'.

Looking beyond the great acreage of facia grey, it was time to fire up the Bugatti from the fantastic seat. Would there be a jet-type rumble or a Ferrari 280GTO or F40 style roar and bellow? The answer lay with neither. Instead, there was an induction whine, a throatier, deeper breath and then a smooth rumble from behind one's head. Warmed up it all settled down and I was reminded of the smoothness of a Wankel-cycle engine. Strange.

I sat low, with a touch of 'long-arm' Italian design syndrome but nothing too awkward. Engaging gears that would sweeten with warm oil, the capsule taxied forwards on a smooth clutch and no issues of any kind. Direct steering, although a touch ponderous at a slower pace, soon became beautifully weighted turning onto the main road and then going up through the gears. Also revealed was a two-stage power application courtesy of those sequenced turbochargers.

But what was very interesting was just how smooth this big V12 'lump' was behind me. It was not a lump, of course, but a beautifully wrought piece of incredible mechanical delight and utterly smooth mechanism. Even the exhaust was muted until you pushed hard. What druidic magic had touched this engine? How smooth were the special metals lining the cylinder heads? A Ferrari V12 would quite rightly bellow and roar, yet this V12 seemed to do that in a different tone. It was a different symphony.

Flying forwards, with the road coming up fast though the landscape aperture of that big windscreen, the noise did increase to a rumble and a touch of a howl, but the car felt secure and stable. Scything into descending, then ascending, switchback bends at pace revealed sublime steering telepathy, super damping and rebound rates, with not a hint of a jiggle from the suspension and levels of grip that defied the driver's talents or lack thereof. Snicking down a gear and squeezing the accelerator made the EB110 pick itself up and launch, but with utter finesse and no sense of a lurking threat to life. Pushed too hard, a touch of front-wheel scrabble was lightly evoked in a bend. That four-wheel-drive bias ratio was evident as the more driven back end had a sort of rear-steer power effect upon the front. The development test drivers had done a superlative job.

Then it was a long straight and the sheer force of induction, turbocharging (a slight pause as the upper pair of sequential turbos lagged, spooled and forced their effect) and the intergalactic nature of warp-speed travel by the EB110 was obvious. Here it became a hypercar and flew like a fighter, yet an utterly stable one. The engine's soundtrack had reminded me of the two-stage spool up of four Rolls-Royce RB211 524 G/H series jets on the wing of a Boeing 747 as take-off power was first palmed in and then, at quarter revs, rammed up with a resultant bang, howl and a haunting wail of mechanical process and combustive effort.

Winding down, with a touch of heat soak felt and relief I had not bent the thing, I realised that the drive had been almost telepathic. Having to change gear manually was authentic and yet the only thing that dated the drive in terms of today's digital and electromechanical devices – no double clutch dork plunger device for the EB110 – just a proper gearbox with a real *levier de changement de vitesse*; how nice.

What a car, what an achievement and, as for the styling, what a piece of sculpture. I cannot help but think that Ettore, Jean and even Rembrandt Bugatti would all have liked it. But the final words about the EB110 and Romano Artioli should go to Achim Anscheidt:

> *We at Bugatti today have much to thank Romano for. He is such a warm-hearted man with a great passion for our brand. Out of his generosity in reviving Bugatti in the 1980s and defining a vision for it in the modern day, he laid the foundations for the creation of Veyron and the character of Bugatti today.*

Pure design language was never more evident than on the rump of the EB110. Note the new rear wing and revised tail ridge.

The Veyron Grand Sport in orange and black with the open roof on display – an iron fist in a velvet glove. This was the fastest roadster in the world at the time.

CHAPTER 9

NEW JOURNEY: VEYRON TO CHIRON

The allegedly mercurial Ferdinand K. Piëch applied his high IQ engineer's brain and Porsche family DNA to Bugatti during his time as chairman of the Volkswagen Group executive board, and he deserves our thanks for ensuring that, through the Veyron, the modern Bugatti really is more than a badge trading on a brand. Piëch was a 'Le Patron' figure in his own right and we might opine that the Veyron did indeed reflect his personality as well as some of Ettore Bugatti's own thinking and achievements.

Piëch, a grandson of Ferdinand Porsche, had power, money, breeding, hierarchy, willpower and ability; defeat, not least at Le Mans, was never an option. As such he might even have exceeded Ettore Bugatti in the 'family' corporate power stakes. And the Veyron would indeed reflect his personality: dominant, intelligent and powerful. Proof of this assertion comes in the words of Stephan Winkelmann, then the President of Bugatti,

> *The ideas of the outstanding engineer Ferdinand Piëch in 1997 were a testament to a brilliant mind. As well as his incredible concept of a powerful engine, he was also the driving force behind the resurrection of the Bugatti brand at its original site, the French city of Molsheim.*

If the early Bugattis reflected and encompassed the personalities of Ettore and Jean Bugatti, can we make the case that the Veyron and its ingredients reflected the personality and power of its instigator and guider, Ferdinand Piëch?

One of the important legacies of Romano Artioli was how he managed to get the Bugatti brand into the financially secure hands of Volkswagen, which after 1997 would eventually lead to the Veyron. So once again Artioli had a hand in Bugatti's renaissance. The brand was reborn in 1998 as a VW subsidiary, Bugatti Automobiles S.A.S. (Société par actions simplifiée), a French legal entity that did not have a board but was allowed partnerships under the 'Bugatti' brand and would soon get its hands on Ettore's old home near Molsheim to use as its base.

Legend has it that in 1997 a sketch was drawn on the Shinkansen express train between Tokyo and Nagoya that would change much. Following discussions with the then Head of Powertrain Development at VW, Karl-Heinz Neumann, Piëch had dreamed up the engine that was the spirit of the Bugatti Veyron 16.4 and which embodied the first hypercar of the 21st century. The Veyron coupé would become the first series production car to produce more than around 1,000hp (or just over 1,000PS) and to drive faster than 408km/h (254mph). The Veyron was an engineering masterpiece; years of concentration and a vast amount of money went into creating the 'new' Bugatti.

Piëch originally designed an 18-cylinder engine by joining together three of his ultra-smooth VW Golf engine VR6 cylinder banks, offset to each other by 60 degrees. The naturally aspirated engine delivered 555 PS from a displacement of 6.25 litres, also providing exceptional running smoothness.

The truth is that the engine was not designed for a 'Bugatti'. It was designed by Piëch for a supercar that not only did not then exist, neither was it intended for any brand in particular.

In his position at VW Piëch had been on the look-out to purchase or reinterpret a major historical and exclusive brand with a rich history. During his Easter vacation on Majorca in 1998 Piëch heard that BMW was about to buy the name rights to Bugatti. As it happened, Piëch's son Gregor asked him to buy him a model car version of a Bugatti Type 57SC Atlantic. In his book *Auto.Biographie* Piëch described this as 'an amusing stroke of fate'. He bought a second Bugatti model car and presented it to Jens Neumann, then a Member of the VW Executive Board and in charge of strategy. Piëch asked the Board to check the rights to the French brand and purchase them if possible.[1]

Mirror-finish was a popular option for the Veyron. This car is part of the Singh Collection of Bugattis.

VW secured the brand rights after negotiations in 1998 and Bugatti was reborn as a registered brand in 2000. By this time its defining engine had already been thought of, even if it was not designed with a Bugatti in mind. Given that decades earlier Ettore Bugatti was focused on engine design, it seems appropriate that Piëch should also have put the engine first.

THE PROCESS

Three initial design concept prototypes were commissioned by VW for the Bugatti brand and its new car. These stemmed from VW discussions about realising the form of the new car, with the proviso that the form was to be dictated by its engine and engineering, not some Bugatti-esque retro-pastiche.

The first 18-cylinder concept car was the EB118, then came a four-door version that followed the early scoping of the design study as the EB218. Bugatti then switched from a luxury saloon to a super sports car design proposal for the first time with the EB 18/3, known as the 'Chiron' – but this was not the Chiron of 2015. This original Chiron was to be a sports car without equal.

The third concept came from Italdesign, in cooperation with the then head of Volkswagen design, Hartmut Warkuss. It broke with tradition and developed a radical new design idea. The concept car was presented for the first time at the International Motor Show Germany at Frankfurt in 1999. Bugatti made it clear that this was a true super sports car. The name Chiron was somewhat of a misnomer then because the car became the Veyron, a different name but still a memory of an old Bugatti grand prix-era *pilote*.

The process evolved via the normal route of drawings and models of increasing scale. The fourth and definitive design was presented to the world at the 1999 Tokyo Motor Show, this time under the direction of Warkuss and the young Slovakian designer Jozef Kabaň (sometimes cited as Kaba), who essentially had shaped the new car as a pebble, the bolide, the pure 'aero-weapon' that was to become a car named after Pierre Veyron, one of Ettore's original grand prix car drivers. Wolfgang Schreiber is credited as the lead chief technical officer in the Veyron's development. Kabaň would go on to work for BMW and then Rolls-Royce, before returning to the VW fold.

A key name in the development of the Veyron, the Chiron and later composite-equipped new Bugattis was that of VW technology specialist Frank Götzke, who has a record of innovation in the field of carbon fibre. He was Bugatti's chassis development lead up to 2006 at the behest of Ferdinand Piëch, who surrounded himself with the right people, reputedly at no expense spared. Of note, it was Götzke who devised the use of carbon fibre composite brakes for the Veyron.

The Veyron probably wasn't a beauty, but neither was it ugly. In fact the Veyron was a product of its time and design era. Chamfered like a pebble, powered by an 'earthquake' of an engine and sadly too often driven by celebrities, the Veyron redefined the image and ability of Bugatti.

The Bugatti EB 16.4 Veyron was introduced in Paris in September 2000, but now, instead of using an 18-cylinder engine based on the VR6, the engineers decided on a 'W' configured 16-cylinder engine. This was more compact than a classic V-engine and therefore lighter. Two VR8 engines were arranged at an angle of 90 degrees to each other, and the cylinder banks of each V8 unit were separated by an angle of 15 degrees. The final capacity would be 7993cc.

This arrangement created a space-saving W-configuration in which the piston strokes of all four cylinder banks act on a single central crankshaft, hence the W16 name. Ettore would have loved this solution, say the experts.

This permitted a displacement of more than 7 litres for the engine and the use of four turbochargers, as with the EB110. Four-wheel drive was involved too. Again, this was a de facto continuation of Artioli's EB110 concept from two decades earlier.

In 2001 Bugatti announced that series production of the Veyron in a limited production run had now finally been decided. A 16-cylinder engine of nearly 8 litres capacity would provide the hyper sports car with 987bhp/1,001 PS (736kW) and a torque of 1,250Nm. Aiming for 1,500bhp was not to be sniffed at and the World Record (WR) Veyron Super Sport would later achieve 431km/h (267.8mph) in 2010. The need for a seven-speed gearbox (an electromechanical, dual-clutch computerised automatic) was obvious and it was engineered by the long-established company of Ricardo in England. If Ettore Bugatti had favoured the French Cotal electromechanical automatic gearbox in the 1930s, it was refreshing that Piëch preferred a British-designed gearbox.

The name and the basic layout of the drivetrain were now fixed, and the engineers started working on creating an appropriate design for this tremendously powerful engine. Apart from the immense power output, the specifications demanded acceleration from 0 to 100km/h in 2.5 seconds as well as a top speed of more than 406km/h (252km/h). But why this top speed in particular? During his time at Porsche Ferdinand Piëch had developed the legendary Porsche 917 in the 1960s, as well as a 16-cylinder engine for the Porsche 917 PA in the 1970s. This, however, was never used in a race after tests in the Porsche Development Centre at Weissach. With a V12 engine, the 917 had won the 24 Hours of Le Mans for the first time for Porsche in almost 50 years – with a top speed of 406km/h on the Hunaudières or Mulsanne straight. It was clear that the Veyron had to be faster.

Only the limitations of tyre construction technology then current would stop the Veyron Super Sport going even faster. This was the black car seen with orange fine detailing and sill-edge wrapping around the lower valances of the body. *Top Gear* presenter James May took a Veyron Super Sport (not the WR version) to 417.6km/h (259.4mph) at the VW Ehra-Lessien test track. The same day the official Veyron test driver Pierre-Henri Raphanel got the car to 431.01km/h (267.8mph) for a recognised and officially witnessed record.

The Veyron was cited as a 'car of the decade' and that somehow seems enough, but not simply because this effect started a power war and a design riot. Stephan Winkelmann paid tribute to the spirit of Bugatti: 'The Veyron catapulted Bugatti into an unprecedented new dimension. The

Several Bugatti design proposals were made before the Veyron. This one evokes the curves of Jean Bugatti's earlier cars, but it was perhaps too contemporary and not one that looked to the future.

A four-door large grand touring cruiser was another design proposal on the way to the Veyron and Chiron. Again, it was a lovely design, but not exactly radical in its effect.

hyper sports car enabled the resurrection of the brand in the spirit of Ettore Bugatti. He elevated engineering to an art form. He was always striving for ultimate perfection in everything he did.'[2]

Among the key issues for the Veyron were cooling and aerodynamics, which were not unrelated. The car had a sleek profile and a large rear deck area that was clearly a natural generator of unwanted aerodynamic lift. With many hours spent in the wind tunnel, the airflow over the roof, the critical separation point (CSP), the boundary layer airflow, the wake and the vortices were all designed to lessen lift, add sidewind stability and not compromise on drag coefficient reduction. For really high speeds, however, the Veyron had a rear 'wing' that looked more like the spoiler or a thrust damper of a Boeing 747. It goes up to a 55-degree 'lift-dump' spoiler position, just as in an aircraft wing application, and can also act as a braking device. Curiously, this device had to be manually set and activated (using a special key) before any high-speed motoring as it was not a 'live' adaptive device. The rear wing panel or 'sail' added much downforce, but increased drag in a carefully calculated trade-off.

At varying speeds, the Veyron reacted with varying modes so that the aerodynamic downforce was 'active' at all times. The tyre pressure 'footprint' on the road was generated by an adaptive aerodynamic system perfected by Bugatti engineers, headed by Dr Schreiber. The variable control system comprises two diffuser flaps in front of the front wheels and another aerodynamic unit at the rear, consisting of a wing and a spoiler. Depending on the car's road speed, they produce an additional downforce of several hundred kilograms and balance lift, downforce and pressure over the car. Porsche, of course, knew all about this sort of advanced art from its own racing cars and road cars and the knowledge transfer was invaluable.

The low frontal area of just over 2 metres squared defined the snout of the Veyron as highly aerodynamically efficient with a C_dA of 0.74m^2 (8.0sq ft); so too was the transition of airflow over and into the car. Force-feeding the plethora of ten radiators was key to keeping the engine and turbochargers cool and not overcooked. Three radiators cooled the engine, but three more cooled the vital intercoolers. Further radiators cooled the oil, the air conditioning and more.

All these requirements meant that the Veyron initially had a surprisingly high drag figure of C_d 0.41, which was borderline acceptable for a supercar. Happily, revisions saw that fall to below C_d 0.39. Of note the suspension settings significantly altered the C_d. At standard ride height, around C_d 0.38–0.39 was cited; lowering the car for a maximum velocity run brought the C_d down to a credible 0.36. However, putting the rear wing up for downforce took the Veyron C_d to a high-drag state of C_d 0.59 – almost C_d 0.60.

This very rare paint treatment changed the Veyron's looks. It is seen alongside an earlier Bugatti type in Ettore's favourite yellow over black livery.

The Veyron, however, was less about low ultimate drag and more about stability, cooling, handling and a low frontal area. The car's aero package was an engineer's classic compromise.

The Veyron's four-wheel-drive system was deployed with the Swedish Haldex type of traction regulating system and the tyres were vital. Specially built Michelin PAX tyres were key to the safety of the car at very high speed. These aviation-quality tyres were so crucial to the Haldex sensing and four-wheel-drive system that they all had to be replaced if even one was punctured, simply because the difference in tread wear could upset the system. This may seem expensive, but in truth it applied to many cheaper cars with electronically sensed four-wheel-drive systems. The brakes were carbon fibre and carbide material: this type of design stemmed from original design and testing using such brakes 40 years earlier on the BAC/Aérospatiale Concorde. AP-type alloy brake calipers are fitted, as are titanium brake pistons. ABS is standard and apparently is also fitted within the handbrake function!

Between 2005 and 2015 the Veyron and the Bugatti concern thrived at VW as CEOs such as Franz-Josef Paefgen and Wolfgang Dürheimer guided the company and the car's evolution. It soon became clear that the Veyron was a new beginning and the new hypercar.

The Veyron came in numerous guises and was torsionally stiff enough to have its roof removed, although it remained stiffer with the B-pillar 'hoop' left *in situ* as the targa-top seen in the later variants. The Grand Sport Vitesse model (2012–15) defined the targa-topped Veyron and looked great in its 'Bugatti blu' edged, dark-bodied variant.

The 199bhp increase of the Vitesse over the 'standard' Grand Sport was achieved by using four larger turbochargers with new intercoolers. Bugatti has extensively reinforced all drivetrain components in order to transfer the immense forces safely. The gearing of the seven-speed dual-clutch direct shift gearbox (DSG) in particular was adapted to the new torque levels. In this context, as on the Super Sport, Bugatti also modified the air ducting in the area of the drivetrain. As a consequence of the larger turbochargers and the overall reduced back pressure, it was even possible to reduce the fuel consumption slightly despite the increased output. The fuel system, with a four fuel-pump-equipped tank was also used in the Super Sport model.

Revised damper settings and new parameters to the electronic stability programme (ESP) meant that the Grand Sport Vitesse could be driven faster at higher lateral g loadings and powered out of a bend faster. A new front spoiler design that had been designed in a similar way to the splitters used in motor racing aided stability at high speed. For the very rare roadster version, special shielding reduced turbulence in the open cockpit.

The Veyron special edition 'Le Ciel Californien' (Californian sky) captured the historical blue and white hue of Bugatti as well as the hot colours of California (or maybe even Provence). The targa-topped Grand Sport Vitesse and the same car as a 'La Finale' version were rare specification cars up to early 2015.

VEYRON VARIATIONS

16.4	2005–11	253 built
Grand Sport	2009–15	58 built
Super Sport	2010–11	48 built
Grand Sport Vitesse	2012–15	92 built

Low numbers of special-built specifications were available through the Bugatti Veyron 'Configurator' package.

Altering the paint scheme and highlighting the lower panels created significant visual changes to the Veyron Super Sport, of which 48 were manufactured. Top speed was 431km/h (267.8mph).

The Veyron Super Sport seen at speed with the maximum downforce setting on the deployable rear wing. Note the NACA ducts on the roof as highlighted in orange.

It is fitting that a Veyron Pur Sang should be seen at Prescott. BUG III is a famous registration plate

The Veyron Pur Sang powering out of Ettore's Bend at Prescott. The sound reverberated around the track.

The Pur Sang, Hermès, Sang Noir, Bleu Centenaire, Le Ciel Californien and Hermann zu Leiningen were all Veyron special editions. An Ettore Bugatti edition Veyron was also built among a series of 'Legends' editions celebrating early Bugatti racing drivers: Wimille, Varzi, Campbell and Costantini; three examples were built for each driver name. Further special Veyrons were the Rembrandt, Black Bess and Jean, individual editions with minor specification changes and notable paint and interior schemes.

Private-build special editions by tuners and modifiers have also been created for the Veyron, including the Veyron Linea Vincero built by Mansory of Germany, which featured what was essentially an upmarket body-kit as a customised car. A gold (*d'Oro*) version was offered with a V-shaped grille badge and gold edge all the way around the car, including the wheels. Mansory also offered a white two-tone Veyron trim known as Linea Vivere. A 'marblised' paintwork edition known as the Linea Vivere Diamond had various trim and lighting design changes.

By 2014 just over 400 Veyrons had been built (407), of which 405 were released to paying customers, but a No. 450 was cited as the last numbered car sold in mid-2014. So the Veyron unit numbers actually made, but not all used for sale, totals 450 chassis. The last Grand Sport Finale car was built in late 2014 and shown at the 2015 Geneva Motor Show.

DRIVING THE VEYRON

The experience of driving a Veyron was exactly as a good Bugatti should be, beyond compare. Not even a McLaren F1 could begin to enter the stratospheric arena that was a

The stunning interior looks classy in this colour, but some prefer a darker-hued cabin. There is a true sense of occasion when you climb aboard the Veyron. The sound system was by Burmester Audiosysteme.

The Veyron Super Sport Vagues de Lumière edition featured a special finish that did indeed capture the light.

The Veyron Grand Sport Vitesse reached 408.8km/h (254.0mph) on test in 2013.

The 1,001bhp Veyron Grand Sport 16.4, here seen in white, was released in 2008. It shared its name with the famous grand tourer types of the 1920s and 1930s and somehow evoked a similar sense of rarity.

Veyron drive. A Veyron was beyond a jet fighter, beyond a 'Concorde' moment, for driving or even just travelling in a Veyron was akin to what we might imagine space travel in some great ship of the galaxy to be like. The Veyron was smooth thunder, not a Lamborghini or Ferrari 'beast' of a V12 or some such. The power delivery was combustive yet linear, the ride as if magnetically levitated, the handling and the performance so stunning you might wonder if your brain synapses and your senses could keep up. What *was* this experience? How many owners ever left the atmosphere of road-going normality and ventured into the outer reaches of Veyron's consciousness? Probably very few.

Thundering down the autobahn south of Munich faster than Concorde's take-off speed, with the airflow carving itself over the cabin, was one of the few places where the Veyron dream became reality, short of a test track. We cannot help but wonder what Ettore and Jean might have thought of the Bugatti as a spaceship, a bomber or some wheeled Zeppelin, yet one with the handling of a racing car. Ferdinand Piëch must have been laughing all the way to the bank, not least as we can now see that Veyron was the last hurrah of the internal combustion engine at its height. Eleven miles per gallon (25.7ltr/100km) seems a bit strange now, but it is all a matter of context and nuance, for when did you last complain about how much fuel your Boeing 787 Dreamliner or Airbus A350 consumed at full take-off thrust when you were making use of them as a transportation vehicle?

In the Veyron lay true reincarnation in a modern context without a hint of 'retro'. It may have been 'genetically modified', yet it remained a Bugatti nonetheless, even if it was using an engine that was designed without its creator having the name Bugatti in mind. It is a strange paradox, yet this is a car with a past that has become a landmark guiding the way to the future.

CHIRON

If the Veyron was a bomber of a bolide, the Chiron was something as powerful and more so yet a touch more elegant – less of a boxer's punch and more of an iron hand in a velvet glove, but certainly not a ballerina's kick.

According to the Chiron's chief designer its major features were born of technical necessity and reflect the enormous increase in power over its predecessor. This focused approach distils the sculpture of a Chiron to an authentic design statement, apparently, yet in terms of engine and substructure, some might describe the Chiron as a 'variant' of the Veyron.

The Chiron was a clever reworking of the Veyron with more elegance and more power, cleverly hiding the Veyron structure underneath a new body skin.

What is for sure is that the Chiron has had a massive impact and redefined not just Bugatti in a new era but also how we classify a hypercar. The top speed is limited to 420km/h (261mph), but it is the 1,479bhp and 1180lb ft of torque that are what we might call defining, even if this is essentially a Veyron engine re-purposed.

Before the Chiron there came the 16C Galibier, which sadly was completely lost on those involved in corporate machinations at VW in the face of realpolitik and financial reality. So died a traditional coupé with a long bonnet and rear 'haunches', and in came a reinterpretation of the Veyron's cab-forward styling. The Galibier was elegant yet somewhat 'static' in its design philosophy and language: the Chiron would be new, the 'shock of the new', to coin a phrase.

The precursors to the Chiron were interesting in that the final concept was different but also related to the production car that emerged. In 2015 VW, as the owners of the Bugatti brand, presented the elegant and suitably long-nosed and front-engined Atlantic prototype as a design concept car touted as a new Bugatti. This was a further concept design developed from the previous modern take on the Galibier of 2009 and from Veyron themes. The new Atlantic had a V8 engine and was of GT proportions as opposed to the more recent short-nosed fashion seen across McLaren, Ferrari, Lamborghini and Bugatti. Finished in black as an homage

ACHIM ANSCHEIDT

Achim Anscheidt famously drives a Porsche 911, but he has spent years restoring a Bugatti Type 35 with original components. He was to prove the true inheritor and commander of the great Bugatti design legacy created by multiple contributors and the occasional contradiction, but never, ever subject to the dreaded 'retro'.

He is the son of Hans Georg Anscheidt, a works racing Suzuki rider and three times motorcycle world champion in the 1960s. Achim retired in 2023 after nearly two decades at the helm of Bugatti design, but he will remain a consultant to the new major Bugatti shareholder Rimac.

Anscheidt studied at Pforzheim University and then went to the ArtCenter College of Design in Pasadena on a Porsche scholarship assisted by Harm Lagaay, then Porsche's design chief. After graduating in 1993 he secured a junior role at the Porsche Weissach studio before rising in the ranks and then moving into the wider range of VW group design. He became design director at Bugatti in 2004.

Anscheidt confirms the parallels between Ettore Bugatti's philosophy and that of Ferdinand Porsche Snr, stating: 'Ettore Bugatti and Ferdinand Porsche were technical perfectionists. They were pioneers in seeking superior power-to-weight ratios and in finding the sophisticated solutions to match.'[3]

to the original *La Voiture Noire* back story of the Type 57 Atlantic, the car's stunningly evocative and exotic body was principally designed by Bugatti's then lead designer Achim Anscheidt, a man steeped in a passion for petrol-powered devices and who also owns a Type 35.

This would have been a cheaper Bugatti, something more akin to a Maserati, Ferrari or Jaguar, and as such it was not enough because a Bugatti needed to beyond compare.

Sadly the new Atlantic never made it to reality. Although the later, very composed Chiron can hardly be argued with as a design achievement, some Bugatti fans think the 'long-nosed' style of the Atlantic was a clearer link to Bugatti styling of the past.

The car's tan and black 'sculptural' interior with milled alloy effects to the cabin also evoked a design DNA link to the past without being too retro.

An interesting precursor was the one-off Atlantic design proposal, which was stunning and well received, yet probably not the 'future-vision' solution that the Chiron became.

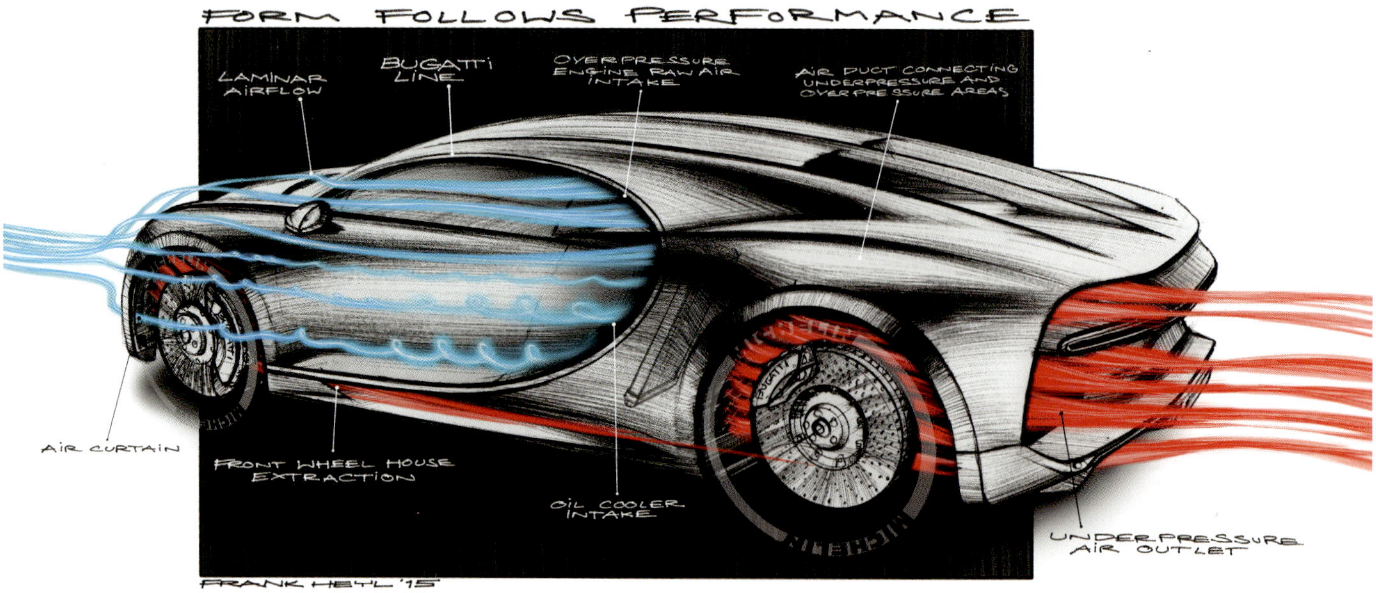

The Chiron's advanced aerodynamics package, as explained by a Bugatti design bureau drawing.

A Chiron letting loose from the start line at Prescott. Bugatti blue side panels offer a glimpse of past colours on curves.

The Atlantic, however, did feature a large, chrome-edged 'hockey stick' styling swage running from the front wings along the flanks and then curving up around the door and window line into the roof. The same styling feature also made it on to the Chiron, which emerged at the same time. The Atlantic had a beautiful coupé fastback rear end, employing the elegant and timeless proportions of the swept-tailed, long-nosed classic GT type of design seen so often from the 1950s to the 1990s. Perhaps only the somewhat swollen nature of the 'horseshoe' grille jarred in terms of taste. The design of the front end clearly took inspiration from the 2008 Veyron Barchetta design proposal, which was also stillborn. Somehow this design blended brutalism with sheer elegance in the same manner as Jean Bugatti's own designs.

Under the bonnet of the Atlantic was a 500bhp twin-turbo V8 of Bentley legacy, something that might have turned a few hairs grey at Molsheim, although Bentley was also part of the VW empire. Thought was also given in the design to a roadster version and even an electric powerplant consideration with four asynchronous electric motors within the chassis.

Planned for a launch on the lawn at Pebble Beach and then an official 2016 sales launch as the next big moment in Bugatti's future, the geopolitical circumstances and branding politics surrounding Volkswagen, the parent group, meant that the car was cancelled. Rather like Jaguar's planned new F-Type of two decades earlier, it was a loss. Here was a nimble, narrower, more drivable 'entry level' long-nosed, more accessible new Bugatti supercar, yet the resources to make it, the Chiron and more were curtailed at the time for many reasons.

Concept cars and design studies come and go, but the author, and others, really do feel that this Atlantic design study represents a lost opportunity for Bugatti because its design was more obviously of Bugatti styling heritage and yet in no sense was it a retro-pastiche or branding 'con'. The car would have been cheaper to purchase than a Chiron too. If it were launched today with a hybrid engine system, surely this might be *the* Bugatti of the decade? Such is just an opinion and one not presented as a fact, but sometimes facts are not impartial and this 'lost' Bugatti may represent just such a defining design moment.

Curiously, the proportions of the new Atlantic re-emerged in the subsequent Bugatti Rembrandt design concept, which would in theory have sat above the Chiron in the model hierarchy. The Chiron that eventually evolved from the Veyron brought about a new, true Bugatti design language. Whatever you might think, at least there was and remains not a hint of retro.

A key name behind the engine and engineering of the Chiron was Willi Netuschil, who was chief of technical development as the Veyron evolved into the Chiron.

The Chiron spent more than 300 hours in a wind tunnel and was later modified into a 'long-tail' version that created less lift and less drag. This rare combination was made possible without sticking a 'fence' wing disrupter crudely on the back. The retractable rear spoiler offers four positions and is engineered to work across several requirements.

The Chiron's most noteworthy design feature has to be the large, curved razor-edge arc of the bodyline that runs back from the front wing along the sills and then dramatically curves up into the roof. It is a stylistic sculpture, of course, but it also has the aerodynamic purpose of cleanly separating and also guiding the airflow over the car or into the engine bay. With careful detailing, a roof 'edge' to control air over the rump, and expert attention to the transition of airflow over, under and across its body, the Chiron combined aerodynamics with a radical style that made a huge statement.

The Chiron Super Sport had the longer tail, which improved the aerodynamics off the Chiron's rear end with less drag and less lift combined. This is a 1,578bhp car that sold new for £3.5 million. A 'Golden Era' edition for 2024 traded off visions of Bugattis past, yet with exquisite finish.

Inside the Chiron Profilée edition, which was then the most expensive Bugatti ever and the last of the W16-engined Bugatti specials. Inspired by the Type 46 Superprofilée of the late 1920s, this new car was a true one-off car that sold for nearly 10 million euros.

CHIRON SUPER SPORT 300+

The first production car to explore a new dimension of straight-line performance was Bugatti's record-breaking sensation, the Chiron Super Sport 300+. This was a modified long-tailed Chiron with exposed carbon and no less than 1,578bhp under the hood.

When the Chiron Super Sport 300+ first made headlines in 2019, Bugatti established an entirely new standard of performance by blasting through the seemingly unbreakable 300mph barrier and setting a new world record at a speed of 490.4km/h (304.7mph). Shortly after, to mark the 110th anniversary of the French luxury marque, it was announced that 30 units of the Chiron Super Sport 300+ would be built at Bugatti's factory in Molsheim.

Boosting performance to ever greater heights, Bugatti engineers developed a new thermal management system for the hypercar's engine and gearbox, ensuring that all components remain cool even when travelling at top speed. Software refinements to the engine, gearbox, powertrain and turbochargers were all necessary additions to the Chiron Super Sport 300+, contributing towards the car's overall performance.

Visually and technically distinct from the Chiron, the Chiron Super Sport 300+'s capacity for speed is defined by its aerodynamically optimised body, enabling it to pass through

Another Chiron rarity was the 'Sky View' with a glass roof of two portals either side of the main roof centre line. The glass was four layers thick and treated with reflective chemicals. The roof also added a touch of extra headroom, echoing certain 1930s Bugatti modifications to achieve just that.

The Chiron, here seen in green, was also available in a range of carbon-fibre effect finishes. Such treatments altered the car's character compared to the launch models' colour schemes.

This drawing clearly illustrates the aerodynamic work done by Bugatti to improve the Chiron's airflow by using the long-tail effect. The drag wake envelope is smaller as a result.

The Chiron was beyond comparison and therefore a true Bugatti.

the air with complete stability beyond 420km/h (261mph). Most notably, the hyper sports car's long-tailed rear end, extending the body by 25cm, allows the aerodynamic (laminar) flow to pass over the body for a longer period of time, therefore significantly reducing the aerodynamic 'stall' and separation by more than 40 per cent.

Air curtains adorning the hyper sports car's front corners disperse excess air pressure towards the car's sides. Simultaneously, air outlets at the wheel arches and behind the front wheels guide excess pressure away from each wheel arch, therefore reducing drag by also producing a small amount of negative lift.

The Chiron Super Sport 300+'s streamlined bodywork is crafted using exposed jet-black carbon fibre, complemented by a Jet Orange racing stripe running through the centre of the car. Carbon continues to flow through into the car's

Out of the Chiron came the Divo, launched at the 2019 Geneva Motor Show – faster, more sporting, more 'active' aerodynamics and 35kg (77lb) lighter than a Chiron. With a starting price of $5.8 million, only 40 were built.

Much work went into the 'aero' package and quad exhausts at the rear of the Divo.

engine cover and even the windscreen wiper. It was the fastest hyper sports car Bugatti has ever made and is a true testament to the engineering passion.

The limited edition of just 30 Chiron Super Sport 300+ cars, each starting at a net price of 3.5 million euros, sold out. Deliveries continued at the time of writing.

DIVO – AERO WEAPON

The Chiron, for want of a better word, morphed into the Bugatti Divo in 2018 and became another interesting model named after a famous racing driver of the first Bugatti epoch of the 1920s. The Divo, however, was not simply trading on a name. It was a design in its own right and a study in aerodynamics, which was its forte. The design was credited to Frank Heyl and Nils Sajonz, once again in a team led by Achim Anscheidt.

Deploying advanced aerodynamics and changes to materials to reduce weight, as well as engine modifications, the Divo was both hard core and niche. Only 40 were being built and all were snapped up. With the W16 engine under the centre body pumping out its usual near 1,500bhp (1,500PS), this car could get to 99.8km/h (62mph) in 2.4 seconds. True, the Koenigsegg Jesko Absolut has more raw power, but the Divo used advanced and 'active' aerodynamic devices to pursue its goal.

The Divo's longer tail with reshaped flanks improved the inherited Chiron aerodynamics. A new exhaust diffuser and tail valance also assist the airflow under, over and off the rear of the car. A large fixed rear wing and a NACA duct on the roof, allied to re-profiled lower side skirts, and an under-the-nose splitter, all contributed to better aerodynamics at high speed than the base Chiron. Extensive wind-tunnel testing with advanced measuring sensors led to the Divo's final 'chamfered' and ducted form and its good aerodynamic performance.

An example of how niche or nerdy Bugatti can go lies in the windscreen wipers, which are carbon fibre. The Divo is nearly 80kg lighter than the Chiron and was a full 8.0 seconds faster around the set distance track at Nardò. The ultimate terminal velocity, however, was reduced due to the drag from the downforce-inducing fixed rear wing: a case of a classic engineering compromise.

The last Divo of a sold-out run left the factory in July 2021.

Bugatti brothers – then and now: Type 57 Atlantic seen behind the one-off long-tailed Type 57 Chiron Super Sport variant designed for a customer through the Bugatti customer design scheme headed by Jascha Straub.

The Centodieci is its own car. It clearly alludes to the wonderful EB110 yet is neither a copy nor a retro-pastiche. As such it is a stunning piece of car design.

CHAPTER 10

CENTODIECI AND MORE

Retro design is a stylistic dead end. If a modern day product wants to create a link to a mesmerizing icon of the past, it needs to reflect a new interpretation of the essence that made it remarkable in its days.

Achim Anscheidt

If the Mistral, *La Voiture Noire* and the Centodieci somehow say it all, the point is proven about 'real' design. Although some find the Centodieci's slightly angular styling does challenge their views, the car is what it set out to be as a new hypercar and as a true reflection of the design cues of the EB110, but seen in a modern context. True, it does not employ the old design language, but then why bother with that: a new design language was what was required and in the Centodieci it arrived. Creating a copy or a pastiche would surely have been an expensive dead end. One thing is for sure, the Centodieci is authentic: it is no retro-pastiche. As such it is a real design and not a reinterpreted one, as is often seen hailing from a long way east of Central Europe.

Leading up to the Centodieci, there were some great new 'moments' of design from Bugatti and Bugatti Rimac, and all became supercar or hypercar hits. In the process Bugatti became a new company with new partners and a new future. But the commitment to the ethos of Bugatti surely remains.

BUGATTI RIMAC (BR)

Enter Bugatti Rimac as the new corporate structure and ownership. Through Porsche, VW has created a new venture alongside a hugely successful tech start-up that remains little known to the public: Rimac of Croatia, headed by Mate Rimac. This company, founded in 2009, is now a respected world leader in hybrid, electric and other technologies and has built an enviable reputation within the automotive technology world in a very short time. Electric sports car, drivetrains, batteries and systems are its core business and the company consults across the global automotive industry, often in secret. Rimac's Concept One was at the time of its introduction the world's fastest production electric vehicle. In 2018 Rimac launched the Rimac Nevera sports coupé, designed by Adriano Mudri, as its second vehicle. The first car was sold to former Formula One World Champion Nico Rosberg. The Nevera is built on the same production line as the Pininfarina Battista EV sports car.

On 2 November 2021 the Bugatti Rimac joint company project got underway. With it, Bugatti, Rimac and Porsche marked the beginning of a new chapter in automotive history. The Rimac Group has 55 per cent of the shares, while Porsche holds 45 per cent. Mate Rimac, founder and CEO of Rimac Automobili, is now CEO of Bugatti Rimac, with its headquarters in Sveta Nedelja, Croatia. Oliver Blume, chairman of Porsche AG, and Lutz Meschke, deputy chairman and CFO, are members of the supervisory board.[1]

Fittingly for twelve years the French designer Etienne Salomé was head of interior design at Bugatti. In 2023 long-standing design boss Achim Anscheidt retired, although he is still a consultant to Bugatti. He was replaced as the Bugatti Rimac (BR) head of design by his former deputy, Frank Heyl, whose team includes BR chief designer (Exterior) Jan Schmid and BR Chief Designer (Interior) Ignacio Martinez. Bugatti has two remote studios or ateliers, one in Berlin and one in Zagreb.

Before Bugatti Rimac became real, Bugatti turned up the wick and poured out some very special cars. It continues to do so as Bugatti Rimac. The Centodieci is, in the eyes of many, the stunning marker, the pathfinder flare to a new era of Bugatti resurgence in a contemporary context.

LA VOITURE NOIRE: TAKE TWO 2019

One of the most expensive cars ever when sold as new, and also a breathtaking work of sculpture, perfect in form and entirely finished in black, the one-off *La Voiture Noire* was created exclusively for a Bugatti enthusiast within the space of two years. In homage to Jean Bugatti's skills, this new piece of automotive couture, finished in a moody black hue, was delivered following extensive development work and testing.

Black paint is not favoured by car designers as it masks form and scale, and tends to minimise sculpted features. Yet if you keep it clean and put it under the right light, black bodywork looks exquisite. Somehow, in this car, the paradox of black paint, shape, scale and sculpture amid light falling on metal somehow worked. Stephan Winkelmann, then President of Bugatti, described this effect:

> *With the completed La Voiture Noire, we are demonstrating once again that we develop the world's most sophisticated hyper sports cars. With its use of visible carbon fibre in jet black, the coupé's breathtaking sculpture looks especially elegant. It's a veritable grand tourer that went from being a vision to a reality – a unique project which stands for Bugatti's full creativity and artistry.*

The name *La Voiture Noire* has a particular ring in the automotive world: Jean Bugatti developed and drove one of just four Type 57SC Atlantics produced, a vehicle that was the most perfect and the fastest car of its time. Jean named his model *La Voiture Noire* (the black car). The vehicle disappeared without a trace shortly before World War II. It is now considered to be one of the greatest mysteries of the automotive world and as a vehicle of indescribable value, perhaps more than 100 milion euros.

The idea for this homage came to Achim Anscheidt more than 20 years ago, but years passed until it became possible to realise this unusual project, as he explained:

> *We were rather in awe of the idea of developing La Voiture Noire. No other vehicle in the long history of Bugatti has acquired the same legendary status as the Type 57SC Atlantic and has become so synonymous with the brand. We had a great deal of respect for this historical responsibility as well as for the customer.*

The fascinating, sculptural and commanding appearance of this black automobile that disappeared is forever unique. Jean Bugatti had a real flair for shapes and developed saloons and coupés of dramatic beauty. With the Atlantic, he created a masterpiece. For the reinterpretation, the designers had to cast their minds back and seek to understand the automobile, and then update this work to the 21st century.

The design brief for *La Voiture Noire* was for a minimalist coupé much like the Atlantic back then, achieved by reducing the essentials and lines, and the absence of a large and dominant rear wing. The designers reinterpreted the spirit of the historical vehicle and developed a specific shape stylistically and technically speaking. This included the dorsal seam down the centreline, the extended front section, the clear lines and the romanticism of the rear. With great attention to detail, the design team created a bodywork with a unique surface finish, comprising visible carbon fibre with a clear coat known as 'Black Carbon Glossy'.

This effect generates virtually no reflections, but plenty of tension and drama. The bumpers were integrated gently into the bodywork while the windscreen appeared to merge with the side windows like a helmet visor. The lack of disruptive lines meant the surface appears to have been cast in one piece with nothing interrupting the visual flow. This transformed the vehicle's attitude from a hyper sports car to a grand tourer. A unique sense of drama was generated.

In addition, the car boasts some extraordinary details. There are more than 25 individually milled light elements per side in the headlamps – an immense amount of work, even for a one-off. The rear was dominated by an elegant

Chiron-based, the hand-built one-off *La Voiture Noire* evokes a mythical past Bugatti in a modern version. Announced in 2019, yet not completed until sometime later, this tribute to the missing Type 57 Atlantic sold for more than $15 million.

rear light, which for the first time featured a single-piece surround without any joints. Six individual tailpipes served as a nod to the vehicle's well-known template, the Type 57 Atlantic. A newly developed parametric design at the front and rear means the body parts appear to be sealed, but they are actually air-permeable. This gives *La Voiture Noire* its incomparable coupé shape.

Bugatti fitted the interior entirely with grain leather in Havana Brown, basing its choice on the historical Type 57 model's classic interior. This natural material contrasts with specially polished and turned aluminium inlays in various locations on the centre console, the centre spine and the doors. The driving modes can be changed by means of a sophisticated rosewood switch.

'*La Voiture Noire* is the ultimate dream car for long distances such as a drive from Molsheim to Milan. The combination of perfect beauty and powerful drive culminates in this one-off as a declaration of love for the automobile', explained Achim Anscheidt.

Underneath, *La Voiture Noire* is in effect a re-purposed and modified Chiron in terms of chassis, substructure and engine. Pierre Rommelfanger, Head of Coachbuilding Projects at Bugatti, was closely involved in the building of the modified car, which has a longer wheelbase and longer overhangs than the Chiron upon which it is based.

The extended wheelbase and the newly developed bodywork resulted in new aerodynamics and new handling worthy of a grand tourer. The car is powerful, fast and exceptionally comfortable. This one-of-a-kind Bugatti has already been sold to a Bugatti enthusiast for over $15 million.[2]

BOLIDE

It may perhaps have been a simplification to say that the Bolide was not a normal road car, but a fantasy Bugatti tailored for very rich people to enjoy a track day, yet it was undeniably niche, very niche. Stemming from the VW Wolfsburg workshop in 2020, the car uses the W16 engine mid-mounted in a lightweight composite body to achieve a very low power-to-weight ratio. In fact this was the last Bugatti but one to use the W16 engine. It seemed fitting that the Bolide debuted at Le Mans, as Christophe Piochon, President of Bugatti Automobiles, explained: 'There can be no better way than to celebrate 100 years of Le Mans by debuting a Bugatti tour de force that is simply unlike anything we have ever done before.'

The Bolide as a concept stemmed in key areas from the ideas of Bugatti's carbon fibre composites expert and all-round brilliant in-house 'guru' Frank Götzke, whose main design team consisted of Nils Sajonz, Florian Westermann, Artur Hindalong, Jan Schmid and Max Lask. Alongside the enlarged W16 rated at 1,579bhp (1,600PS), the car used the existing seven-speed dual-clutch gearbox and was put on public sale in early 2023 for use as a track-only car. Larger, more efficient blades inside the turbochargers manage to force in more 'charge' and this is where the power boost comes from. Yet it is in the 'aero' package that Bolide achieves so much.

Christian Willmann, Chief Engineer for the Bolide, explains the true nature of Bolide's advances: 'This extensive aerodynamic work usually only takes place in the top level of motor sport, but has allowed us to meticulously develop the Bolide for ultimate performance and drivability.'

The Bolide's sophisticated aerodynamics package can create up to 2,630kg (5,800lb) of downforce, at the expense of a degree of drag, of course. However, laminar-flowed 'dimple' surfaced technology applied to the body, specifically at the air scoop, and an aerospace-inspired 'area-ruled' and flowed body shape make significant drag reductions at higher speeds. The 'dimple' or golf ball aerodynamic skin and boundary/laminar flow effect it creates is a counter-intuitive yet positive benefit of localised flow turbulence that was researched and taken further as part of his academic thesis by a young Bugatti engineer, Nils Ballerstein.[3]

Coming into effect at higher speeds, this is an early application of 'morphable' or adaptive 'skin' surface technology on a car at high speed, something that will become 'normal' in years to come. Ballerstein's scoop reduced lift by nearly 20 per cent and drag by 10 per cent in just one area of body application. More than 60 such 'dimples' were applied to the Bolide to achieve the effect.

A number of other technical innovations are also integral to the Bolide's performance. Specially designed air 'curtains' in front of the front wheels help the air flow perfectly around the car, reducing overall drag. Winglets on the outer edges of the front splitter develop a spiral airflow, generating vortices that energise the airflow to the diffuser wing panel and helping to improve rear downforce. The narrow cab allows ideal airflow to the side intercoolers, where large inlets and deep shafts help to ensure an optimum operating temperature for the engine. Even the wing mirrors have been precisely designed to exact specifications to divert air towards the intercoolers, increasing their efficiency.

The Bolide had a composite body and used titanium for many of the chassis and component pressings. It looked like the international LMP1 racing car class vehicles but, like them, it was designed to certain needs and parameters and the results are not dissimilar whoever makes the car. The car weighs 1,240kg or under 2,750lb.

The Bugatti Bolide is a track-focused niche product and the last series car produced with the W16 engine. Mid-engined and fitted with all-wheel drive, this is a pure racer.

The Bolide seen from the rear with all the 'aero' work evident. A mix of carbon fibre, alloys and titanium, this is an LMP1 racer class-evolved design. 40 Bolides were cited for build into and beyond 2024.

The revised W16 engine has a torque figure of 1,600Nm (1,180lb ft), allied to a power output of 1,177kW (1,578hp) at a low 2,500rpm. Experiments with 100+ octane fuel increased these outputs, but the production version needs to run on standard high grade (98 Octane) fuel for reliability reasons. Somewhat incredibly, Bugatti quote a 0–501km/h (311mph) speed time of 33.6 seconds. Is this a car or a fighter jet?

The engine is not quite air-cooled, but it does not use a traditional air-to-water cooling function, instead using cooled air via an intercooler, and also pre-cooled water from twin-cooler radiators for high-speed temperatures. The system exceeds even the latest Formula 1 design trend for cooling.

As for stopping the thing, experts at Brembo, the Italian-based world leader in the field of automotive brake technology, have created a highly advanced and tailored braking system for the Bolide with 390mm brake discs and unique calipers (eight pistons on the front axle and six pistons on the rear axle), ensuring the car's stopping power can master its dynamic capabilities.

When Nils Sajonz, now Head of Special Projects at Bugatti, said that designing the Bolide was a 'phenomenal experience', he might not have been underestimating the achievement. Certainly this was a no-compromises car, yet Sajonz was just 27 when he designed the Bolide as part of a young team.

The Bugatti Bolide, first revealed in 2020 as the most extreme Bugatti ever created by the French luxury marque, has been named the world's most beautiful hypercar. During the 36th Festival Automobile International in Paris, an expert jury of design professionals awarded the experimental vehicle from Molsheim the victory in the 'Hypercars' category by a substantial margin, among a total of four finalists.

Delivery of the first Bolides is due for 2024 at a price per car of around 4 million euros each.

Andy Wallace, a Le Mans winner in 1988, took the wheel for the Bolide's first public outing, suitably enough at Le Mans:

> *The Bolide looks and feels – in every respect – like a real racing car with genuine outstanding high-performance capabilities. The fact that it generates around twice its own weight in downforce at maximum speed, giving the car a very high level of grip and stability in high-speed corners, is in its own right incredibly impressive. But to then match that prowess with Bugatti's W16 engine, developing 1,600PS, takes the Bolide to an entirely new level. The car is breathtaking in every sense.*[4]

A track-day only car, but nevertheless a supercar into hypercar of the highest order: is this lightweight car the perfect embodiment of the spirit of Bugatti allied to the facts of the future, in a car of the here and now? Very probably. Its spirit will surely filter down to the next Bugatti road car.

CENTODIECI: 110 NOT OUT

Revealed in 2019, but beginning customer deliveries somewhat later, the Centodieci, whether you love or hate the styling, proves that brains are at work inside the 'new' Bugatti. It may be a homage to the EB110 in certain of its styling motifs, but it is not a copy or a retro-pastiche. It is a totally new design, a new hallmark, and for that it becomes a real car and real new Bugatti, even if some might identify some 'heritage' marketing motifs. The Centodieci is colour-sensitive, like the EB110. It probably looks best in grey-silver, or maybe blue, but in white it divides opinion. Light falling on metal and sculpture is often not granted many favours by white surfaces,

The Centodieci is lighter than the Chiron, yet looks larger and has nearly 1,600bhp on tap. It does, of course, drive sensationally in a real experience of hypercar motoring that, frankly, can only be had in a Bugatti.

Only ten have been built and all sold out at $8 million each. The design echoes past Bugatti themes, most notably the EB110 detailing, especially on the flanks and at the rear. But this new car has a stance and a scale all its own. True, it is perhaps more polarising of opinion than the Chiron, but it is that rare thing that is 'design', original design. The argument made by some critics that the Centodieci was a marketing exercise to make money, trading off history for a payday, does seem a little harsh if we look at the car's design and its driving quality. Admittedly it is another variation on the Chiron theme, yet who ever heard anyone complaining about Bach or Beethoven's variation of repeated and reinterpreted themes? Surely the Centodieci is different enough to be a symphony of its own?

Of particular development are the under-car aerodynamics, diffuser and cooling vents on the car body. At the front, the grille, vents, headlamps and lower valance all combine to blend styling with aerodynamics that work. At the rear, a glazed cover over the W16 engine lets admirers view the jewel. The LED-type bejewelled headlamps, however, might be rather expensive to replace.

Using the magic of digitalisation and virtual reality, the design was shaped and created in six months, instead of the

The Centodieci or '110' makes its own design statement whilst also reflecting a glorious Artioli era of the new Bugatti and evoking past Bugatti philosophies. Just ten examples have been built of the $10million dollar each car.

Seen from this angle, we can see that the Centodieci is a supreme design achievement that is new, innovative and yet also historical, but never 'retro'. Those vents on the flanks are, of course, EB110-inspired.

three years such shapes often require. The ten cars built for customer sale were the start of a delivery stream in 2022 that closed with final delivery just as 2023 dawned. As to the 380km/h (236mph) top speed, few are likely to even approach that limit.

With the W16, all-wheel drive and a radical new interior trim design, not to mention the 'space age' body design, the Centodieci was at once a collector's item. But it also signalled a change, since as the last of such derivations it also coincided with the new era of Bugatti Rimac and all that means for the illustrious brand's future.

MISTRAL, BLOWING IN THE BREEZE

Appropriately named after the French wind that traverses the Rhône valley to the south of France, the Bugatti Mistral two-seater roadster, first launched in August 2022, is about aerodynamics and style in a rare package without a roof. In the Mistral, the challenges of an open-cockpit car, and of feeding cooling air to the Bugatti W16 engine, are also conflicted by the requirements of road vehicle aerodynamics and structural issues in an open-topped car. This is the first

The evocative Mistral roadster signalled a new beginning for Bugatti design in 2022. Now under the Bugatti Rimac Company, Mistral is the talisman that keeps on giving, not least as the fastest roadster ever made.

'open' Bugatti since the 2012 Veyron roadster. It is also the fastest roadster in the world.

Only 99 examples of the W16 powered and carbon-clad Mistral will be built, priced at 5 million euros, with deliveries due to begin in 2024. The entire production run of the W16 Mistral is already sold out.

Emilio Scervo, Bugatti Rimac's Chief Technology Officer, said:

> *Managing both thermodynamics and aerodynamics effectively is key to achieving more than 420km/h in an open-top car, even with 1,600PS (1,578bhp) from perhaps the most advanced automotive engine ever created. We have to think very carefully about how we shape the W16 Mistral to guide air through the car and around the car to delicately balance both cooling and aerodynamics. But, of course, we must do all this with a sense of elegance befitting a Bugatti roadster. A car that is both designed for purpose, but simultaneously evokes a sense of timelessness.*[5]

At the front of the W16 Mistral a new wider, deeper and more three-dimensional version of the famous Bugatti horseshoe grille allows the high-temperature engine radiator to be fully fed purely from one intake, leaving the two side intakes to focus only on providing air to the intercoolers.

The airflow around the front corners is managed by two intakes: one by the wheel and one seamlessly integrated within a new three-dimensional headlamp design. The air is guided from an area of high pressure to a low pressure area in the wheel well, which would otherwise create turbulence and drag, affecting the Mistral's performance.

Achim Anscheidt, who together with Frank Heyl and Florian Westermann had a leading role in the Mistral's design, said:

> *The frontal appearance of the car is dominated by these large intakes, and while recognizably Bugatti, we take a number of cues from the few-off models; Divo, Centodieci and La Voiture Noire. The windscreen wraps around in an elegant visor motif and the front becomes more vertical to create a design that is both shaped for speed and beauty at the same time.*

One thing is clear: the Mistral is not, repeat not, a Chiron with the roof cut off. The Mistral is a new body and a new design.

With the new roadster profile, the team incorporated a reinvented Bugatti C-line, which traditionally marks the profile of the Chiron. The design line that wraps around the side air intake now connects into the top edge of the side windows and then three-dimensionally transforms across the top edge of the windscreen. Crucial to the visual identity of the Mistral, which appears to leap forwards, the creation of this new line was no simple task, as Anscheidt stated:

> *To get it right we needed to separate the air intake for the engine from the air intake for the oil cooler.*

Another interior beyond compare: the Mistral has no roof.

If we kept them together, the intake on each side of the car would have had to have been enlarged out of proportion. So, instead, we hark back to the Veyron 16.4 Vitesse and the Type 57 Roadster Grand Raid by incorporating engine air intakes behind the occupant headrests. This solution is both elegant, functional and safe; the svelte side intakes are proportionally perfect and feed air purely to the oil coolers, while the headrest engine intakes create a huge sense of aural drama, while also working to protect occupants in the event of a rollover.[6]

All air taken through the sides gets channelled across the two radiators, one on each side, over the rear wheels and then out through the Mistral's X-shaped tail lights, an elegant reinvention of the Bolide's iconic design. The vents

The recent design team who curate and create the amazing Bugatti design legacy (from left to right): Jay Schmid, Frank Heyl, Achim Anscheidt and Ignacio Martinez.

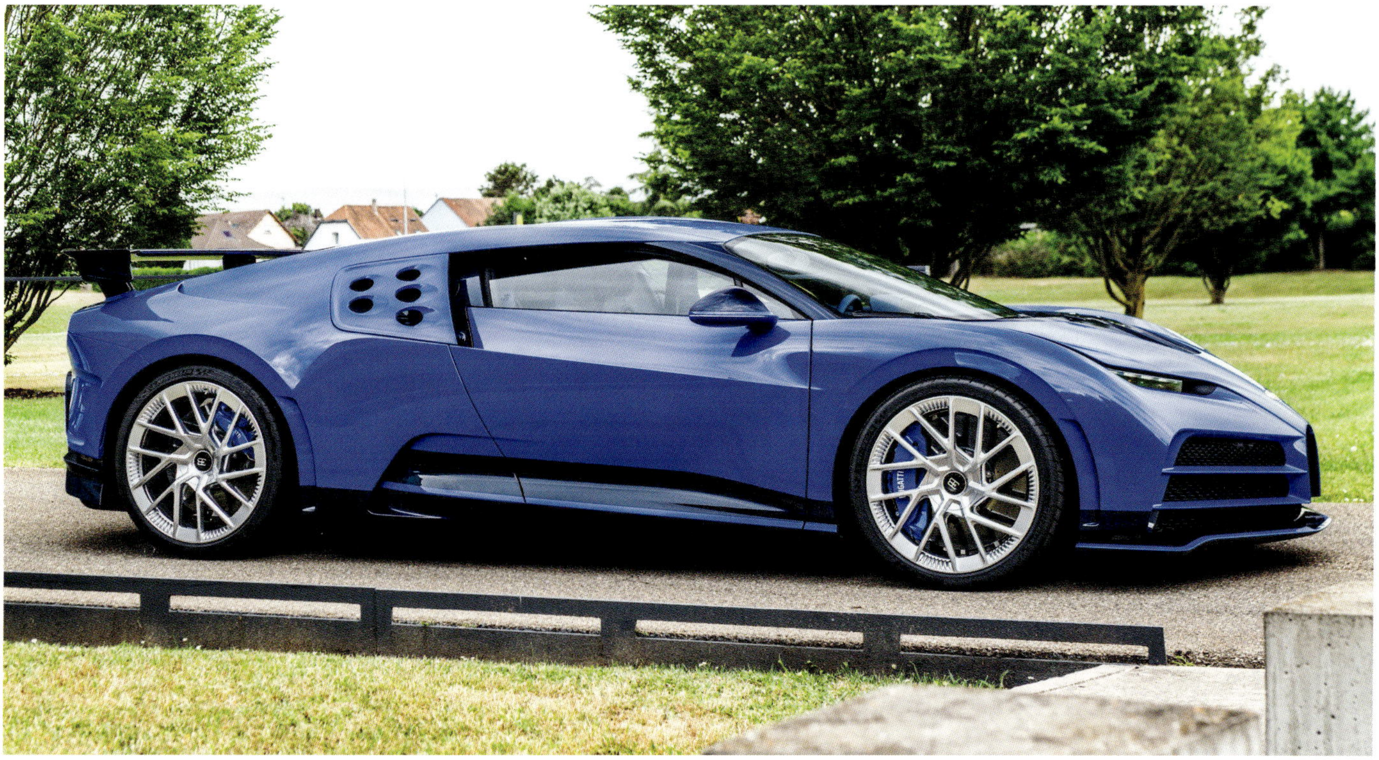

The Centodieci in Bugatti Blue looks very different to the car in silver or white.

Wind-tunnel work on the Centodieci to tune the airflow pattern and separation off the roof turret onto the rear wing.

A Mistral in gold truly captures the car's stunning design cohesion.

The traditional Bugatti radiator reinterpreted for the 2020s on the Mistral.

emerge in the triangular negative space in between the 'X' beams of the light, creating a pressure drop between the side intakes and the outlets at the back of the W16 Mistral, which helps to manage the temperature of the engine, even under high loads.

Such were the intricacies of designing and engineering the first true Bugatti roadster in years. Unlike the Veyron roadster of 2012, the Mistral was not a conversion through removing the roof: the Mistral started out as roadster and that had not happened at Bugatti since the early 1930s. With the W16, four-wheel drive and stunning design inside and out, this is a car that has been thought about far beyond any branding ethos.

The Mistral was the last blast of the W16 8-litre turbo-charged engine that began life under Ferdinand K. Piëch's watch twenty years previously. From here on it would seem obvious to use a hybridised powerplant. As Frank Heyl, the latest design chief of Bugatti, has said, the Mistral is a 'respectable' end to the end of the Chiron platform era.

From here on in, Bugatti Rimac will be taking its place on the rollercoaster that is the next chapter of the motor car in the age of digital design and electric power. We had better get used to it, or alternatively retreat to a glorious past that deserves all the respect and affection it is due, yet which is just that – the past.

Frank Heyl assures us that he strives to continue the Bugatti philosophy with the most technologically advanced, breathtakingly beautiful and authentic designs, saying, 'It is with great humility, respect, honour, pride, and joy that I take on this new responsibility to write the next chapter in this legendary brand's ethos with dignity.'[7]

TAILPIECE

Mate Rimac, the Bugatti Rimac CEO, recently said of the retiring Bugatti chief designer Achim Anscheidt:

> *Achim's understanding of the Bugatti identity, handed down from our founder Ettore and in the beautiful designs of his son Jean, is unrivalled, and his last commitment to Bugatti was to finalise the design of our next generation hyper sports car. Without saying too much, it's Achim's masterpiece and the most beautiful and authentic evolution of Bugatti I could have imagined. It's an honour to have Achim continue to develop the brand as our advisor, and with the stunning work that Frank Heyl has already undertaken, the future of Bugatti design is in the very best of hands.*[8]

Clearly, anyone who thinks the new Bugattis are not 'Bugattis' solely as they understand them to have *been*, needs to dig a bit deeper into what the people at Bugatti Automobili and now at Bugatti Rimac have done and are doing. From the EB110 to the Veyron, the Bolide and beyond, the 'new' Bugattis are cars of integrity, authenticity and a true philosophy that at the very least respect and reflect the original Bugattism that is so unique and vital in the history of the automobile and its design.

Bugatti supercars – framed by the afterwards and before, but always a philosophy and a place where, crucially in such matters, the car defines the brand, not the other way around. Let us hope it stays that way in the new era of the sensational supercars of Bugatti.

As the old guard say: 'Vive la Marque!'

Signature sign-off, the Mistral powers away leaving style in its wake and history in its design. The new Bugatti cars define the brand, not the other way around, which we must be thankful for.

Technical Specifications: The Classic Bugatti Supercars

	Brescia Type 13 and variants *Modifié*/Type 22/23 as applicable	**Type 35B**	**Type 41 'Royale'**	**Type 57 (S/SC variants as applicable)**
Chassis	Channel/rail and cross members	Aluminium sheet body of steel and alloy chassis rails, cross-braced	Pressed steel ladder type tail and channel frame chassis with max depth of up to 10in at centre	Pressed steel ladder channel and frame/brace, individual bodies offered ex-works and via coachbuilders. Later chassis revisions to improve rigidity*
Engine				
Type	4-cylinder	In-line, 8-cylinder ohc	Straight-8 monobloc with integral main bearings	8-cylinder, monobloc, twin ohc
Bore and stroke	69mm × 100mm	60 × 100mm	125 × 130mm**	72mm × 100mm
Cubic capacity/ displacement	1496cc (some earlier variants at 1453cc)	2622cc	13-litre (12763cc)	3257cc
Valves	16-valve ohc	3 valves per cylinder	3 valves per cylinder	2 valves per cylinder
Supercharger	n/a	Larger Roots-type at 10psi	None	No, except factory 57C (compressor) but with variations and retrofitting
Ignition	Magneto-driven electrical system, ×1, or ×2 (Racing/ Sports) as Bosch or SEV	Magneto-driven	Double ignition magneto and by coil with accumulator	Coil ignition on base 57, but magneto on S/SC variants
Carburettor	Operator-pumped pressure system with cam-driven mild pressure piston plunger pump for basic supply	Zenith carburettors and extra pump	Twin carburettors: Bugatti type/ Schebler system	Direct pump with x1 carburettor
Max power	Racing: 40hp Touring: 30hp	129bhp/95kW	BHP rating of 275bhp 205kW; up to 300bhp/220.8kW cited	135bhp (160bhp supercharged)
Petrol tank	50ltr	Rear-mounted, steel, 100ltr	190ltr	
Transmission	4-speed	4-speed manual gearbox	Rear-wheel drive 3-speed, including overdrive	4-speed with a central change mechanism
Suspension and Steering				
Suspension	Front leaf springs, rear quarter elliptics	Inverted leaf springs. ive axles front and rear	Front-semi-elliptics, rear-quarter elliptics with one pair behind axle	Front-half elliptic, rear-reversed quarter elliptic
Steering	Worm and worm	Worm and helical roller system		Worm and nut
Tyres	710 × 90 (varies)	711 × 120mm (28 × 4.75in)	Rapson type, 36in × 6.75/980 × 170mm	5.50 × 18, also 6.00 × 18 rear variation
Wheels	Wire	Cast alloys with integral cast brake drum housing; 8 spokes	Cast aluminium alloys (finned) with integral cast brake drum housing	Rudge-type wire
Brakes	Rear wheels via external hand lever; front wheel brakes fitted from 1926	Diameter: 330mm. Cable-operated with in-built tensioner and balancer mechanism	Bugatti cable system to all four wheels (drums)	1934–37: cable, 1938: hydraulic
Dimensions				
Length	Variable	3,685mm (145.1in)	Up to 4,600mm (21ft)	Varies by body type
Width	Variable	1,321 mm (52.0in)		Varies by body type
Track	1.15m (45.3in)	Front 1,143mm (45.0in), rear 1,194mm (47.0in)	1.6m (5ft 3in)	1,349mm (53in)
Wheelbase	Variable to type up to 2.55m	n/a	169.3in /4,300m,***	2.980/3,300mm
Weight	610kg and variations	n/a	Up to 7055lb (3,200kg)	2,090lb (950kg), 1,250kg
Performance				
Max. speed	75–91mph+ (approx.) specification-dependent	+/– 209km/h (130mph)	110mph (160km/h), 125mph (200km/h) cited	95mph (150km/h)–113.5mph (182.6km/h); variant dependent
Standing km	n/k	27s	n/a	Varies
Quarter mile	n/k	13s	n/a	VAries
0–60mph	135k	6.9s	n/a	10sec (varies with engine specification)

* Lowered chassis variations S 'Surbaisse' and S+C (compressor) have differing chassis design and minor variations as applicable. Grand Raid chassis alterations of note.

** Prototype often cited at 150mm stroke yet this now evidenced as erroneous by G. Morgan, Bugatti Trust lecture 2023

*** Prototype always cited at 4.600mm, but research by G. Morgan via The Bugatti Trust lecture 2023 evidences to the contrary

Technical Specifications: The Modern Bugatti Supercars

	EB110 GT/SS	Veyron (original) model	Chiron (original production type)
Chassis	Carbon fibre composite tub with steel and alloy additions/panels; GT has 'active' aerodynamic aids deployable	Carbon fibre with active aerodynamics aids and rear wing/spoiler mechanism; three-part chassis-body construction bolted together	Carbon fibre; active aerodynamics and cooling; long-tail version available latterly
Engine			
Type	Quad-turbocharged (sequential) V12	Quad-turbocharged four-cam, W16 configuration, longitudinally mounted	Quad-turbocharged (sequential) W16 configuration.
Bore and stroke	3.19 in x 2.23/81mm × 56.6mm	3.3in × 3.3in/ 86mm × 86mm	39in × 3.39in/86mm × 86mm
Cubic capacity	3500cc/213.5cu in, 3,498cm^3	8.0-litre (7993cc)	8.0-litre (7993cc)
Valves	60	64	64
Power	553bhp/412.3kW (560PS) at 8,000rpm. SS variant to 603bhp/ 449.6kW (612PS) at 8,250rpm. Quad-turbocharged (IHI) sequential boost settings (*see* text).	Standard type has 987bhp/736kW. Later types have 1,183bhp/882kW.	1,479bhp/1,103kW (later models 'Sport' etc, to Chiron Super Sport 300 to 1,578bhp/1,177kW)
Torque	469lb/ft (637.0Nm)	921ln/ft (1,250Nm)	1,180lb/ft (1,600Nm)
Petrol tank	Twin fuel tanks: 26.4 UK gallons (120ltr)	100ltr	100ltr
Transmission	6-speed manual, all-wheel drive, bias set drive asymmetry front-rear	7-speed twin-clutch DSG four-wheel drive system using dedicated transmission computer (ECU)	7-speed DSG dual-clutch automatic; Haldex all-wheel-drive system
Suspension and steering			
Suspension	Double-wishbone	Independent double-wishbone all round	Independent double-wishbone all round
Steering	Rack and pinion	Rack and pinion, speed sensitive electric assistance	Rack and pinion with electric assistance
Tyres	Front 245/40 R18, rear 325/30 R18	Michelin pilot Sport PAX run flat. Front 245/690, rear-365/710	Michelin Pilot Sport C2 285/30 front and 355/25 at rear
Wheels	Alloy (several designs)	Cast alloy of Oz type	Alloy
Brakes	Vented discs all-round	Carbon ceramic coated discs all round; racing-spec calipers	Ceramic discs all round; forged alloy calipers; titanium lightweight calipers developed later
Dimensions			
Length	173.23in (194cm)	175.7in (4,462mm)	178.9in (4,544mm). Longer tail version has extended length of 9.8in/25cm
Width	76.38in (194cm)	78.7in (1,998mm)	80.2in (2,038mm)
Wheelbase	100.4 in (2,550mm)	106.7in (2,710mm)	106.7in (2,711mm)
Weight	GT: 3,571lb (1,620kg) SS: 3,126lb (1,418kg)	4,052lb (1,838kg)	4,398lb (1,995kg)
Performance			
Max. speed	GT 0–60mph (97km/h) in 3.4 seconds; top speed of 212.5mph (342km/h)	253.8mph (408.4km/h)	261mph (420km/h), limited; 304mph (490km/h) possible unlimited

Note*

Sport Stradale (SS) version with modified aerodynamics and engineering.

Dauer EB110 Super Light Weight from 1999 saw cars of differing construction and performance to 645bhp/654PS, up to 705bhp. 715PS cited as variant. Also, there was a 507lbs (230kg) weight reduction.

B Engineering Edonis variations from 2000 with significant structural and mechanical differences, including 3760cc and up to 720bhp. Rear-wheel-drive-only transaxle cited.

Brabus-modified EB110 saw engine modifications on a single car.

APPENDIX II: THE BUGATTI TRUST

'The aim of The Bugatti Trust is to promote the works of Bugatti and to inspire the next generation of engineers and designers.'

From its museum, archive and study centre, the charitable trust that is The Bugatti Trust expands its mission to preserve and make available for study the works of Ettore Bugatti. Within the museum can be found the most outstanding collection of Bugatti items ranging from original drawings and parts, to cars, design, engineering and associated items and artefacts. Carlo Bugatti's furniture, Rembrandt Bugatti's sculptures and vital elements of Ettore and Jean's works are gathered in a unique world class collection and archive. Founded in 1987 by the late Hugh Conway Snr, officially opened by HRH The Prince Philip, Duke of Edinburgh, and run through a group of benefactors and trustees, the collection offers 27,000 technical drawings and more than 10,000 photographs as well as thousands of historic documents made available for academic, educational and enthusiast research.

An annual programme of exhibitions, displays, talks and education outreach programmes include relationships with Coventry University, Bath University, STEM activities, VEX Robotics, Formula Student, F1 in Schools, motor sport and automotive companies.

Contact details:
The Bugatti Trust
Prescott Hill
Gotherington
Cheltenham
Gloucestershire
GL52 9RD
UK

www.bugatti-trust.co.uk

Curator: Angela Hucke

BIBLIOGRAPHY AND REFERENCES

SELECT BIBLIOGRAPHY

Barton, John A.R., *Bugatti: The Twilight Years, 1943–1963* (Independent Publishing Network, 2020)

Borgeson, G., *Bugatti by Borgeson* (Osprey, 1981)

Conway, H.G., *Bugatti: 'Le pur-sang des automobiles'*, 4th edn (Foulis, 1987)

Conway, H.G., *Bugatti* (Octopus, 1984)

Eaglesfield, B., *Bugatti the Designer* (Brooklands Books, 2013)

Dreyfus, R., with B.R. Kimes, *My Two Lives: Race Driver to Restaurateur* (Aztex Corp., 1983)

Favre, E., *Automotrices Bugatti: Les 'Pursang' du rail* (2020)

Haslam, M., et al., *The Amazing Bugattis* (Design Council, 1979)

Hucke, U., and Kruta, J. (with Ulrich M.), *Bugatti from Milan to Molsheim* (Verlagshaus Monsenstein & Vannerdat, 2008)

Jenkinson, D. and Verstappen, P. *The Schlumpf Obsession: Inside a Legendary Treasure House* (Heron House/Hamlyn, 1977)

Kestler, P., *Bugatti: Evolution of a Style* (Edita, 1977)

King, R., *Bugattis in Australasia: A History of the Bugatti Car in Australia & New Zealand* (Turton & Armstrong, 1992)

Moncrieff, D.S., *Veteran and Edwardian Cars* (Batsford, 1955)

Price, B., *Bugatti Type 57: The Last French Bugatti* (Veloce, 1992)

Wood, J., *Bugatti: The Man and the Marque* (The Crowood Press, 1992)

Journals

The Bugatti Trust archives, *Newsletter* and journals, www.bugatti-trust.co.uk

The Bugatti Owners' Club, *Bugantics* and archives (editor John Staveley)

The Bugatti Aircraft Association (President Jaap Horst), www.bugattiaircraft.com

The *Bugatti Page* and newsletters, www.bugattipage.com

The Bugatti Revue, https://bugattirevue.com

Autocar

Motor

Car Magazine (1975–94)

EB Magazine (1992–93)

Articles, Letters & Communications

Bugatti Trust, *Newsletter*, 65 (Winter 2020) and 67 (Summer 2021), p.4 [M. Tomlinson]

Bugatti Trust, *Newsletter*, 68 (Winter 2021), pp.5–11 [Michael Firczuk]

Bugatti Trust, *Newsletter*, 68 (Winter 2021), pp.31–7 [Josef Pohl, citing Arnold Langen and Pierre Macoin]

Bugatti Trust, *Newsletter*, 69 (Spring 2022), pp.13–21 [conversations between Les Matthews and Robert Stoehr]

Bugatti Trust, *Newsletter*, 69 (Spring 2022), pp.31–2 [Horst Jaap]

Bugatti Trust, *Newsletter*, 70 (Summer 2022), pp.20–23

Bugatti Trust, *Newsletter*, 71 (Autumn 2022), pp.18–20

Bugatti Trust, *Newsletter*, 73 (Spring 2023) [Arnaud et al.]

Bugatti supplement, *Classic and Sportscar* (November 1987)

Conway, H.G., 'Another little bit of history', *Bugantics*, 45/4 (Winter 1982)

'A History of Australian Grand Prix, 1928–39', *Motor Sport* (July 1942)

King, R., *Bugantics*, 83/24 (Winter 2020), pp.4–13

Martin, C.E.C., *Bugantics* (6 January 1937)

Motor Sport (September 1944), p.186

Pinot, N., 'Lorsque Lucien Schlatter dessinait les plus belles Bugatti', *L'Alsace* (26 November 2019)

Plášil, M., 'The Bugatti Type 54 – 54201', *Bugatti Revue*, 28/1 (19 February 2023)

Venables-Llewelyn, Sir John, 'Why Bugatti's? Or an Addict's History', *Bugantics*, 83/1 (Spring 2020), pp.52–5

Walsh, M., 'Brescia Obsession', *Classic and Sportscar* (November 1987), Bugatti supplement, pp.22–5

Bugatti, Ettore, to Gabriel Espanet, letter, 11 April 1913, Bugatti Trust Archive

Bugatti, Ettore, letters, 20 September 1937, *Moteurs* 50. B.1 and 50. B.2, Bugatti Trust Archive

Bernaud-Heyd, Steeve, correspondence, 2023

Bugatti/Bugatti Rimac press releases, 2022–3, Archive and communications.

Personal communications: Angela Hucke, Charles Trevelyan, Piers Trevelyan, David Morys, Mark Morris, Barrie Price, Sir John Venables-Llewelyn Bt, The Hon. Sir Michael Kadoorie, Mike Marshall, Edmund Burgess, Stephen Gentry, Steeve Bernaud-Heyd, Paul Gibbons, Robert Hamilton

Author's industrial design archive and design studies, 1980 to date.

REFERENCES

Chapter 1

1 Eaglesfield, B., *Bugatti the Designer* (Brooklands Books, 2013).
2 Ibid.
3 Conway, H.G., 'Another little bit of history', *Bugantics*, 45/4 (Winter 1982). *See also* Bugatti Trust Archives.
4 Favre, E., *Automotrices Bugatti: Les 'Pursang' du rail* (2020)
5 Eaglesfield, *Bugatti the Designer*. Further information from The Bugatti Trust.
6 Bugatti Trust Archives, 2021.
7 Trevelyan, P., personal communications, Prescott, 2021.
8 Conway, H., personal communications, Prescott, 2019.
9 Wood, J., *Bugatti: The Man and the Marque* (The Crowood Press, 1992).
10 Bugatti Trust, *Newsletter*, 68 (Winter 2021), pp.31–7 [Josef Pohl, citing Arnold Langen and Pierre Macoin]

Chapter 2

1 Wood, *Bugatti: The Man and the Marque*.
2 Eckersley, J., personal communications, Prescott, 2019.
3 *Motor Sport* (September 1944), p.186.
4 King, R., *Bugattis in Australasia: A History of the Bugatti Car in Australia & New Zealand* (Turton & Armstrong, 1992).
5 Blanden, J., 'A History of Australian Grand Prix, 1928–1939', *Motor Sport* (July 1942).

Chapter 3

1 Stephen Gentry, Gentry Restorations, personal communications, Prescott, 2022. *See also* Dixon, M., 'Bugatti Type 35A: Driving a stunningly original prototype', *Octane*, 234 (December 2022). Also communications with Mark Morris, Bugatti Trust, March 2023.
2 King, *Bugattis in Australasia.*
3 Julia de Baldanza, personal communications, Prescott, 2019.
4 Angela Hucke, Curator, Bugatti Trust, personal communications, 2019.
5 Venables-Llewelyn, Sir John, 'Why Bugatti's? Or an Addict's History', *Bugantics*, 83/1 (Spring 2020), pp. 52–5. Also personal communications, Prescott, 2022.
6 Wood, *Bugatti: The Man and the Marque*.

Chapter 4

1 King, R., *Bugantics*, 83/24 (Winter 2020), pp.4–13. Also via The Bugatti Trust.
2 Wood, *Bugatti: The Man and the Marque*.
3 Bugatti Trust, *Newsletter*, 65 (Winter 2020) and 67 (Summer 2021), p. 4 [M. Tomlinson].
4 Julia de Baldanza, personal communications, Prescott, 2019. Also Conway, H.G., *Bugatti* (Octopus, 1984).
5 Conway, H.G., *Bugatti: 'Le pur-sang des automobiles'*, 4th edn (Foulis, 1987).
6 Ettore Bugatti to Gabriel Espanet, letter, 11 April 1913, Bugatti Trust.
7 Conway, *Bugatti: 'Le pur-sang des automobiles'.*
8 Mike Preston, personal communications, Prescott, 2023.
9 Plášil, M., 'The Bugatti Type 54 – 54201', *Bugatti Revue*, 28/1 (19 February 2023): further information from representatives of the Mullin Automotive Museum.
10 Wood, *Bugatti: The Man and the Marque*.
11 Corner, N., 'Three of a Kind', *Classic and Sportscar* (November 1987), Bugatti supplement, pp.8–15.

Chapter 5

1 Bugatti Trust, communications.
2 Price, B., *Bugatti Type 57: The Last French Bugatti* (Veloce, 1992).
3 Pinot, N., 'Lorsque Lucien Schlatter dessinait les plus belles Bugatti', *L'Alsace* (26 November 2019); Bugatti Trust archive, also via the *Bugatti Pages*.
4 Bugatti Trust, *Newsletter*, 71 (Autumn 2022), pp.18–20.

[5] Bugatti Trust, *Newsletter*, 65 (Winter 2020) and 67 (Summer 2021), p.4 [M. Tomlinson].
[6] Cholmondeley family, personal communications; also via The Bugatti Trust.

Chapter 6

[1] Bugatti Trust, *Newsletter*, 73 (Spring 2023) [Arnaud et al.].
[2] Bugatti Trust, *Newsletter*, 70 (Summer 2022), pp.20–23.
[3] Wood, *Bugatti: The Man and the Marque*.

Chapter 7

[1] Bugatti, Ettore, letters, 20 September 1937, *Moteurs* 50. B.1 and 50. B.2, Bugatti Trust Archive.
[2] Bugatti Trust, *Newsletter*, 68 (Winter 2021), pp.5–11 [Michael Firczuk], and 69 (Spring 2022), pp.31–2 [Horst Jaap]; also communications at The Bugatti Trust.
[3] 'Jean Bugatti and Jean-Pierre Wimille – Prescott 80 years ago', exhibition, Bugatti Trust Museum, 2019; and Angela Hucke, personal communications.
[4] Jim Hull, personal communications, Prescott.
[5] Wood, *Bugatti: The Man and the Marque*.
[6] Barton, John A. R., *Bugatti: The Twilight Years, 1943–1963* (Independent Publishing Network, 2020).

Chapter 8

[1] Bugatti EB110 Registry.
[2] Steeve Bernaud-Heyd, personal communications, UK and France, August 2023.
[3] *EB Magazine*, 7 (2 September 1994), pp.10–13.
[4] Steeve Bernaud-Heyd, personal communications; also via Angela Hucke at The Bugatti Trust.
[5] Angela Hucke, Curator, Bugatti Trust, personal communications, June–July 2023; also EB110 press launch materials.
[6] *EB Magazine*, 7 (2 September 1994), pp.5–8.
[7] Steeve Bernaud-Heyd, personal communications.
[8] Sir John Venables-Llewelyn Bt, personal communications, Bugatti Trust, July 2023.

Chapter 9

[1] Bugatti (SAS) press release.
[2] '15 Years of Bugatti Veyron: How It All Began', 15 April 2020, https://newsroom.bugatti.com.
[3] '911 in a car loft', 22 September 2016, https://newsroom.porsche.com.

Chapter 10

[1] Bugatti Rimac press release.
[2] Ibid.
[3] Ibid.; Ballerstein, N., with P. Horst, 'Manipulation of the aerodynamic behavior of the DrivAer model using dimple patterns', *Journal of Wind Engineering and Industrial Aerodynamics*, 233, February 2023, 105216.
[4] 'Bugatti Bolide Makes Spectacular Public Debut at 24 Hours of Le Mans Centenary', 12 June 2023, https://newsroom.bugatti.com.
[5] Bugatti Rimac press release.
[6] 'Bugatti W16 Mistral: Elegance at Extremes', 10 November 2022, https://newsroom.bugatti.com.
[7] 'Frank Heyl Begins New Chapter as Bugatti Director of Design', 1 August 2023, https://newsroom.bugatti.com.
[8] 'An Era Ends: Achim Anscheidt Passes the Baton at Bugatti', 20 July 2023, https://newsroom.bugatti.com.

PHOTO CREDITS

All photographs and artworks by the author except for the following:
Amalgam Collection: 114, 122–123; The Bugatti Trust: 22, 134, 135, 137; Bugatti Rimac: back cover, 4, 7, 10, 17, 22, 66, 68, 70, 72 lower, 78, 81, 87, 88 upper, 92, 94, 102–103, 112, 135, 138–150, 155–183; Remi Dargegen for Bugatti: 140; Bugatti Owners Club archive: 97; Bruce Phillips: 80 (both); Harry Pottle (harpofotografics): 13 lower, 159 (both); the Cholmondeley family: 136.

INDEX

First published in 2024 by
The Crowood Press Ltd
Ramsbury, Marlborough
Wiltshire SN8 2HR

enquiries@crowood.com
www.crowood.com

British Library Cataloguing-in-Publication Data
A catalogue record for this book is available from the British Library.

ISBN 978 0 7198 4372 3

Typeset by Envisage IT
Cover design by Sergey Tsvetkov
Printed and bound in India by Nutech Print Services

Dedication

In memory of the life and works of the film cinematographer Ralph Douglas Vladimir Slocombe OBE, BSC, ASC, GBCT (1913–2016).
Also for all those of forgotten name yet important deeds in the history of things wheeled and winged.

Acknowledgements

I owe much to The Bugatti Trust and the Bugatti Owners' Club for all the fun, friendship and learning that I have experienced as a trainee Bugattiste; I made some errors en route, but hopefully this book is closer to the apex. Specific thanks for kind help and advice must go to: Charles Trevelyan, Piers Trevelyan, Angela Trevelyan, Edmund Burgess, Angela Hucke, Sue Barnes, David Morys, Mark Morris, Paul Gibbons, Donald Peach, Barry Eaglesfield, Barrie Price, Hugh Price, Mike Marshall, Mike Preston, Julian Eckersley, Kraig Mycock, Nigel Upton, Tim Dutton, Stephen Gentry, Hugh Conway Jnr, the Rippon family and David, 7th Marquess of Cholmondeley.
I wish to acknowledge the work of the following authors whose books are listed in the Select Bibliography: Griffith Borgeson, Hugh Conway Snr, Barry Eaglesfield, Malcolm Haslam, Barrie Price and Jonathan Wood. Thanks also to Mike Read, Tim Read, Richard Wilding, Alan and Gill Ward, and Chris Charles. A specific mention goes to the actress and writer Emily Brewer – my daughter.

Also by the Author (non-fiction):
Boeing 747: The Original Jumbo Jet
British Leyland from Triumph to Tragedy: Petrol, Politics and Power
Bugatti Blue: Prescott and the Spirit of Bugatti
Bugatti Type 35 Grand Prix Car and its Variants
Citroën: The Complete Story
Citroën DS: French Design Classic
The Classic Car Adventure
Classic Car Gallery
Classic Car Museum Guide
Heavies: Big Jets in Action
Jaguar E-Type: British Motoring Masterpiece
The Jeep: Second World War
Long Haul: Global Airlines and their Aircraft
Porsche 911: Classic German Sports Car
Porsche: Model by Model
Porsche Passion: 911 Heaven and Beyond
Saab 92–96V4, the Original Saab: The Complete Story
Saab 99 and 900: The Complete Story
Saab Cars: The Complete Story
Saab Celebration: Swedish Style Remembered
Secret Wings of World War II: Nazi Technology and the Allied Arms Race
Secrets of the Spitfire
VC10, Icon of the Skies: BOAC, Boeing and a Jet Age Battle
Vickers VC10 & Super VC10
Allard: The Complete Story (with Alan Allard)

A donation from the proceeds of this book will be made to The Bugatti Trust.